Garfield
WiLL EaT FOR FOOD

BY JIM DAVIS

Ballantine Books • **New York**

A Ballantine Books Trade Paperback Original

Copyright © 2009 by PAWS, Inc. All rights reserved.
"GARFIELD" and the GARFIELD characters are trademarks of PAWS, Inc.

Published in the United States by Ballantine Books, an imprint of The Random House Publishing Group,
a division of Random House, Inc., New York.

BALLANTINE and colophon are registered trademarks of Random House, Inc.

ISBN 978-0-345-49176-3

Printed in the United States of America

www.ballantinebooks.com

9 8 7 6 5 4 3 2 1

ATTITUDE THIS!

It's rude, it's crude, it's Garfield's attitude!

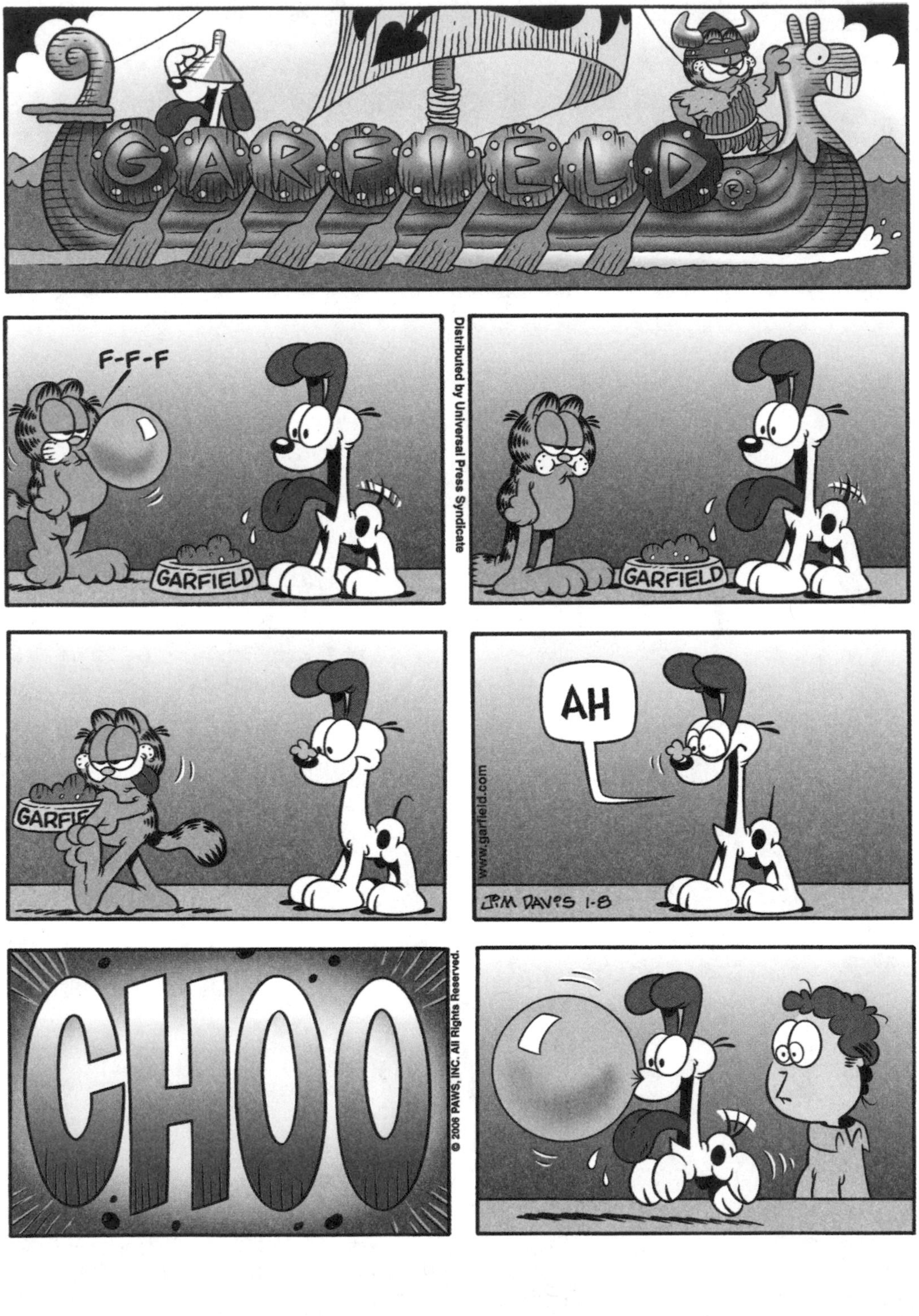
GARFIELD®
F-F-F
GARFIELD
Distributed by Universal Press Syndicate
GARFIELD
GARFIE
AH
www.garfield.com
JIM DAVIS 1-8
CHOO
© 2006 PAWS, INC. All Rights Reserved.

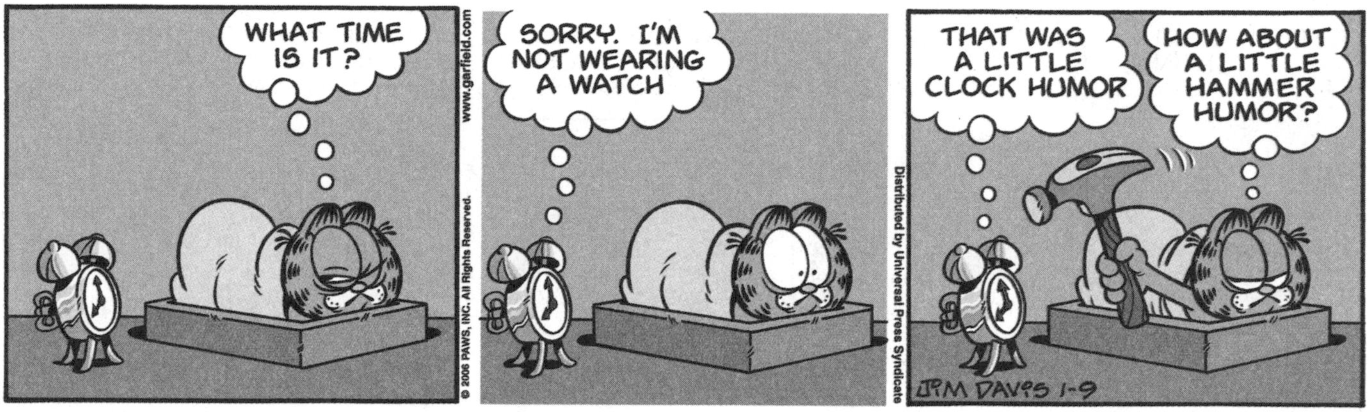
WHAT TIME IS IT?
SORRY. I'M NOT WEARING A WATCH
THAT WAS A LITTLE CLOCK HUMOR
HOW ABOUT A LITTLE HAMMER HUMOR?
© 2006 PAWS, INC. All Rights Reserved. www.garfield.com
Distributed by Universal Press Syndicate
JIM DAVIS 1-9

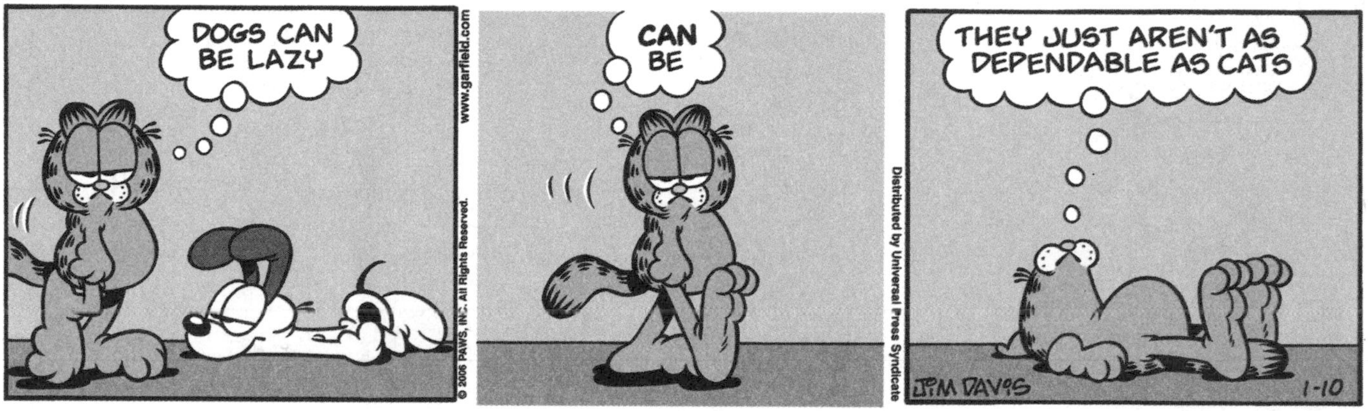
DOGS CAN BE LAZY
CAN BE
THEY JUST AREN'T AS DEPENDABLE AS CATS
© 2006 PAWS, INC. All Rights Reserved. www.garfield.com
Distributed by Universal Press Syndicate
JIM DAVIS 1-10

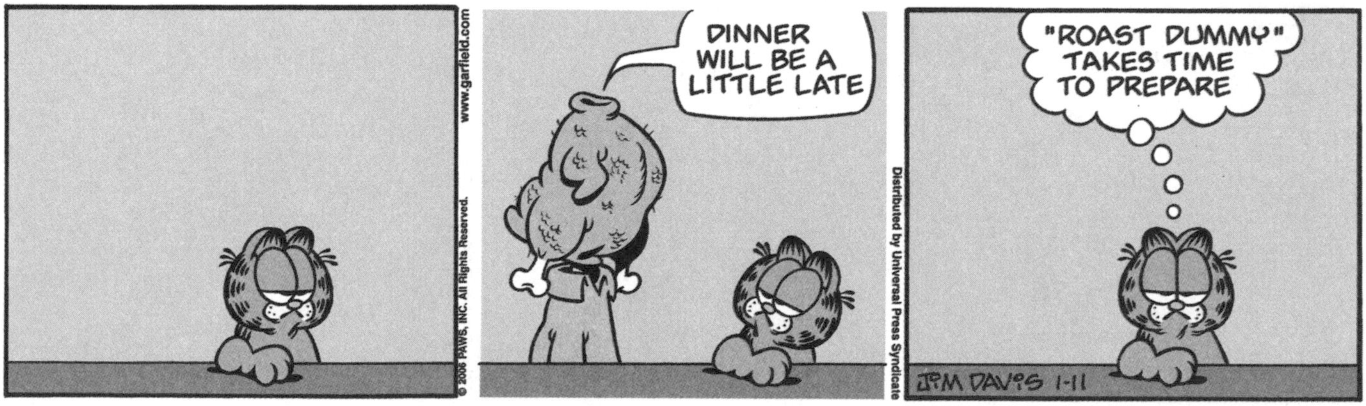
DINNER WILL BE A LITTLE LATE
"ROAST DUMMY" TAKES TIME TO PREPARE
© 2006 PAWS, INC. All Rights Reserved. www.garfield.com
Distributed by Universal Press Syndicate
JIM DAVIS 1-11

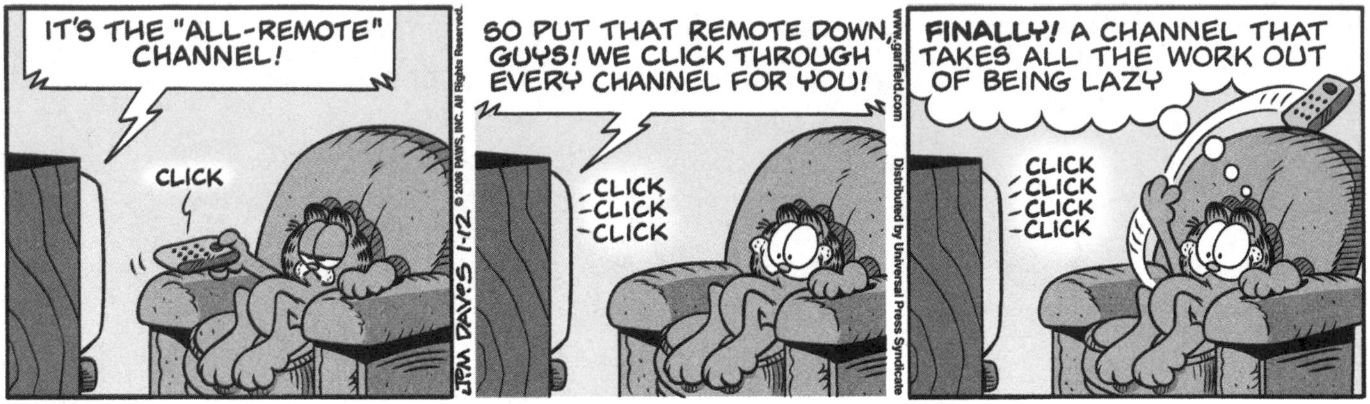
IT'S THE "ALL-REMOTE" CHANNEL!
CLICK
SO PUT THAT REMOTE DOWN, GUYS! WE CLICK THROUGH EVERY CHANNEL FOR YOU!
CLICK CLICK CLICK
FINALLY! A CHANNEL THAT TAKES ALL THE WORK OUT OF BEING LAZY
CLICK CLICK CLICK CLICK

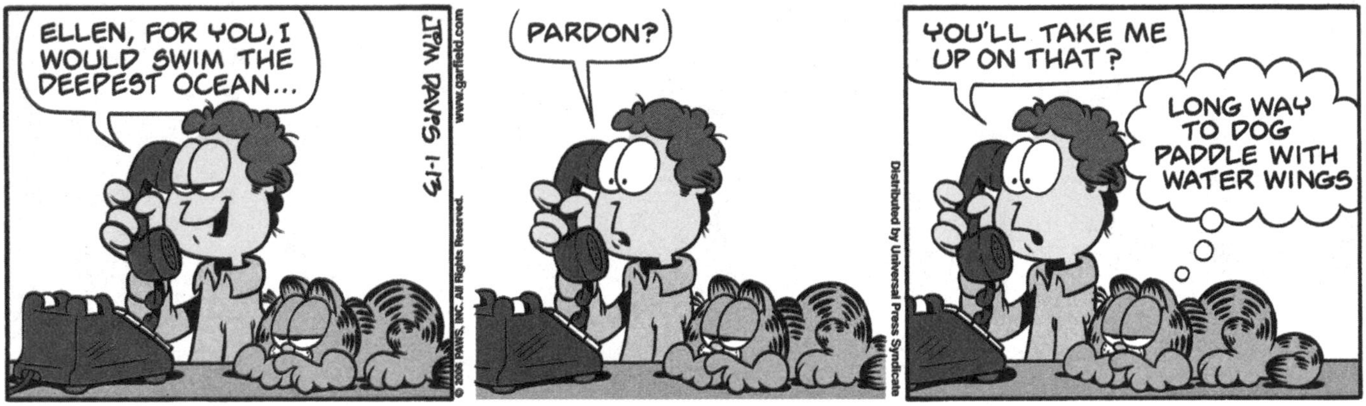
ELLEN, FOR YOU, I WOULD SWIM THE DEEPEST OCEAN...
PARDON?
YOU'LL TAKE ME UP ON THAT?
LONG WAY TO DOG PADDLE WITH WATER WINGS

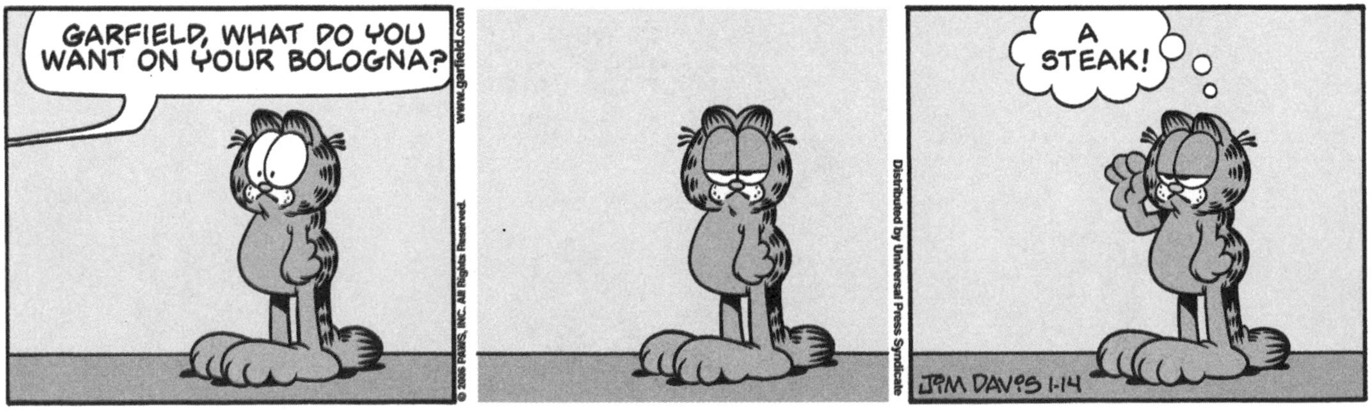
GARFIELD, WHAT DO YOU WANT ON YOUR BOLOGNA?
A STEAK!

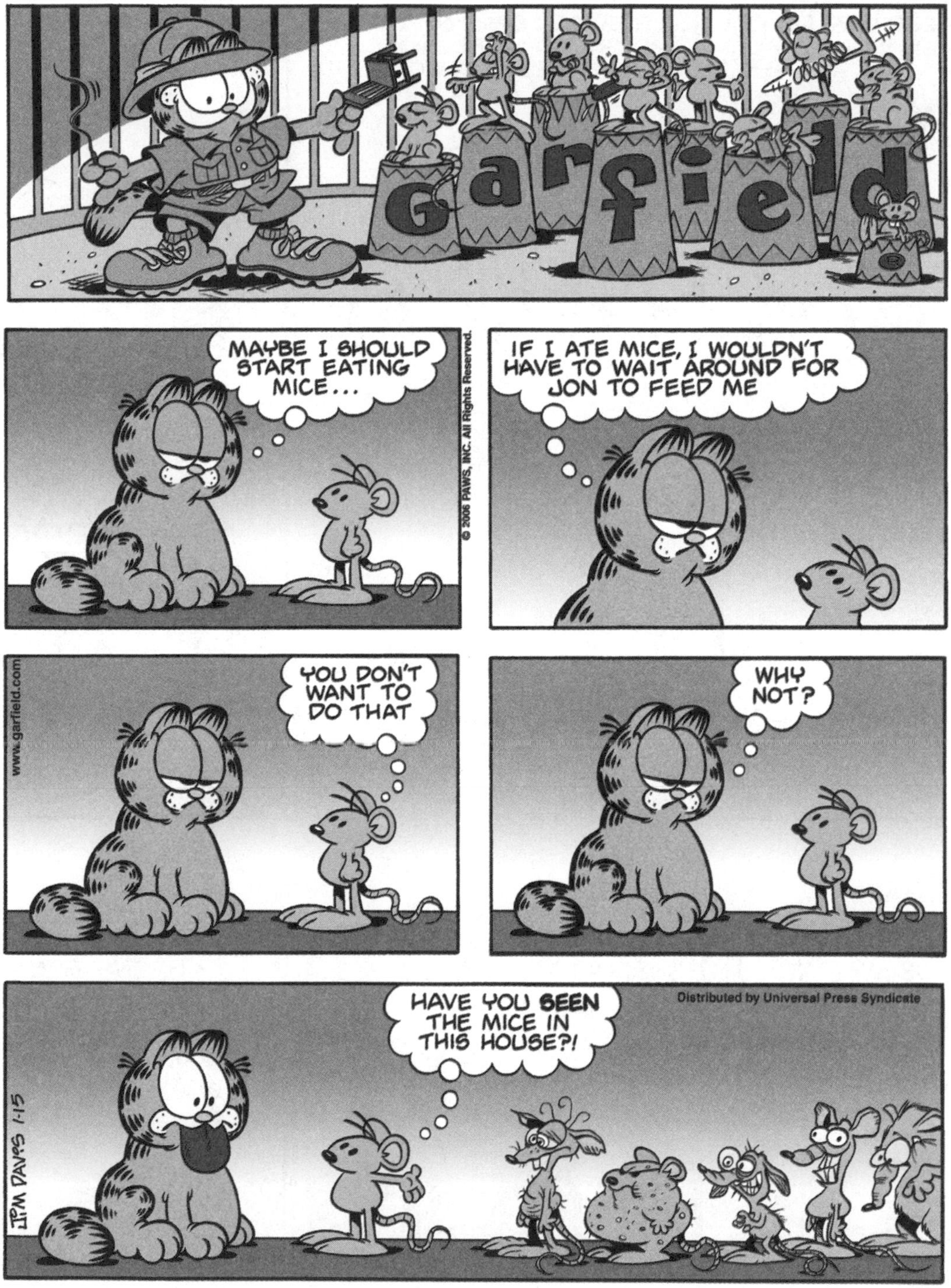
Garfield
MAYBE I SHOULD START EATING MICE...
© 2006 PAWS, INC. All Rights Reserved.
IF I ATE MICE, I WOULDN'T HAVE TO WAIT AROUND FOR JON TO FEED ME
www.garfield.com
YOU DON'T WANT TO DO THAT
WHY NOT?
Distributed by Universal Press Syndicate
HAVE YOU **SEEN** THE MICE IN THIS HOUSE?!
JPM DAVIS 1-15

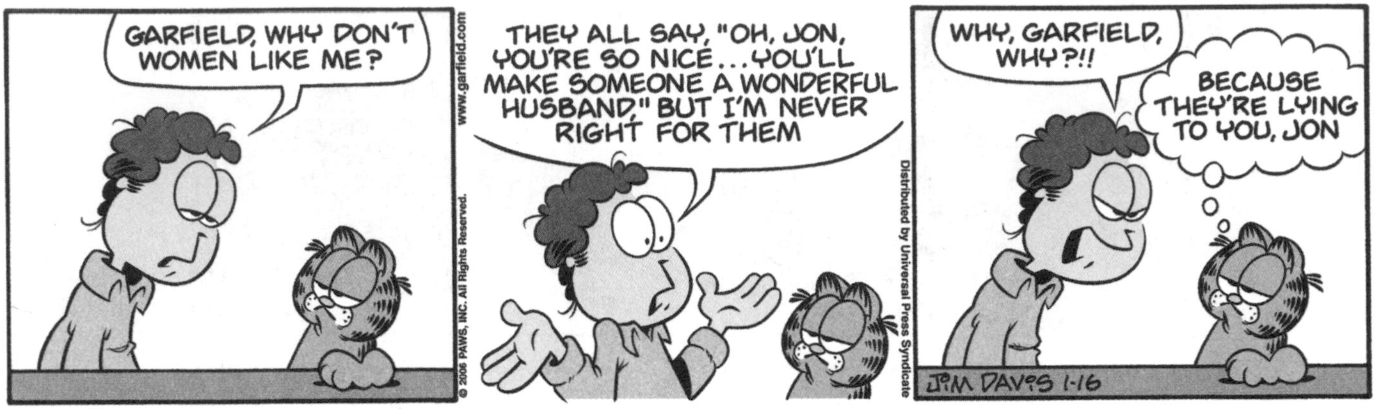
GARFIELD, WHY DON'T WOMEN LIKE ME?
THEY ALL SAY, "OH, JON, YOU'RE SO NICE...YOU'LL MAKE SOMEONE A WONDERFUL HUSBAND," BUT I'M NEVER RIGHT FOR THEM
WHY, GARFIELD, WHY?!!
BECAUSE THEY'RE LYING TO YOU, JON
JIM DAVIS 1-16
© 2006 PAWS, INC. All Rights Reserved. www.garfield.com
Distributed by Universal Press Syndicate

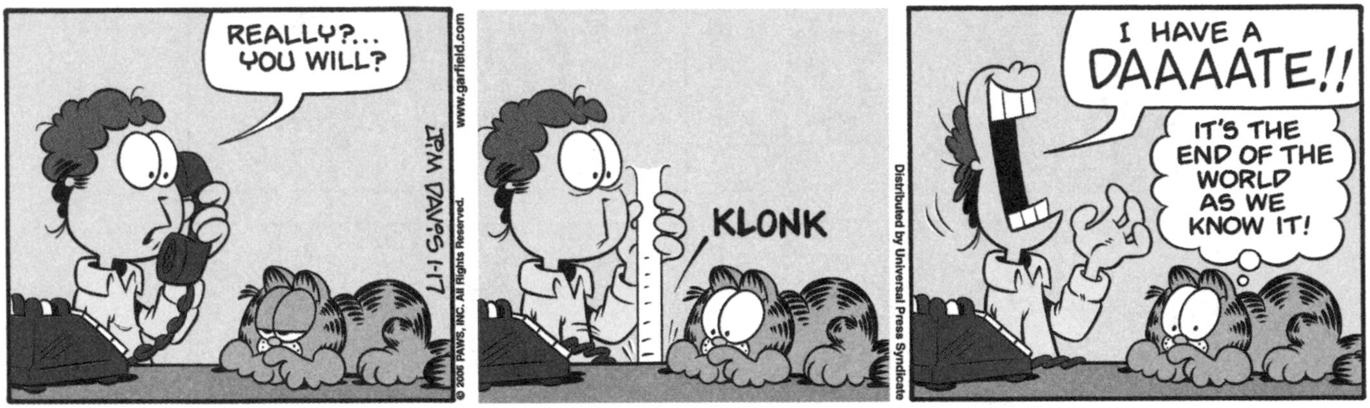
REALLY?... YOU WILL?
JIM DAVIS 1-17
KLONK
I HAVE A DAAAATE!!
IT'S THE END OF THE WORLD AS WE KNOW IT!
© 2006 PAWS, INC. All Rights Reserved. www.garfield.com
Distributed by Universal Press Syndicate

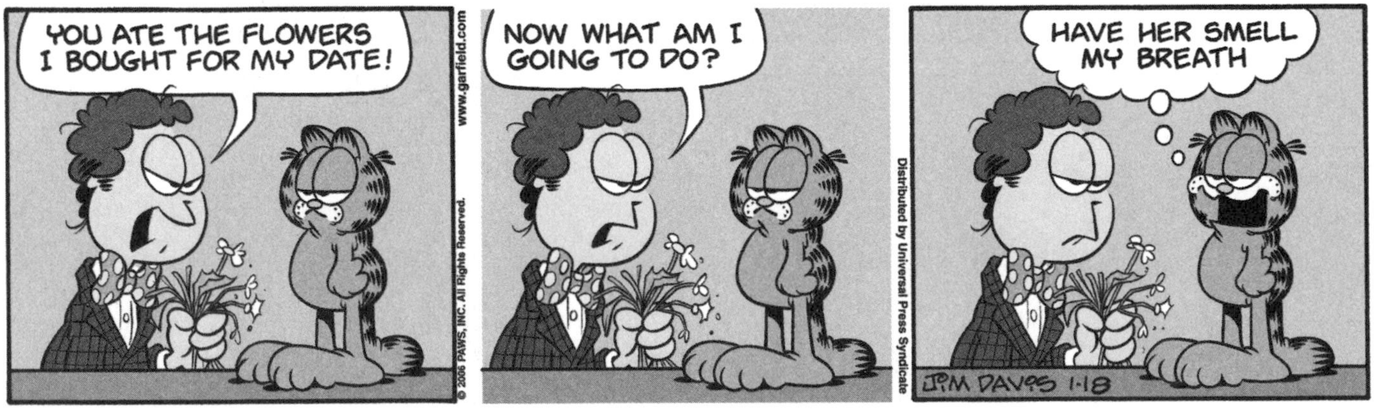
YOU ATE THE FLOWERS I BOUGHT FOR MY DATE!
NOW WHAT AM I GOING TO DO?
HAVE HER SMELL MY BREATH
JIM DAVIS 1-18
© 2006 PAWS, INC. All Rights Reserved. www.garfield.com
Distributed by Universal Press Syndicate

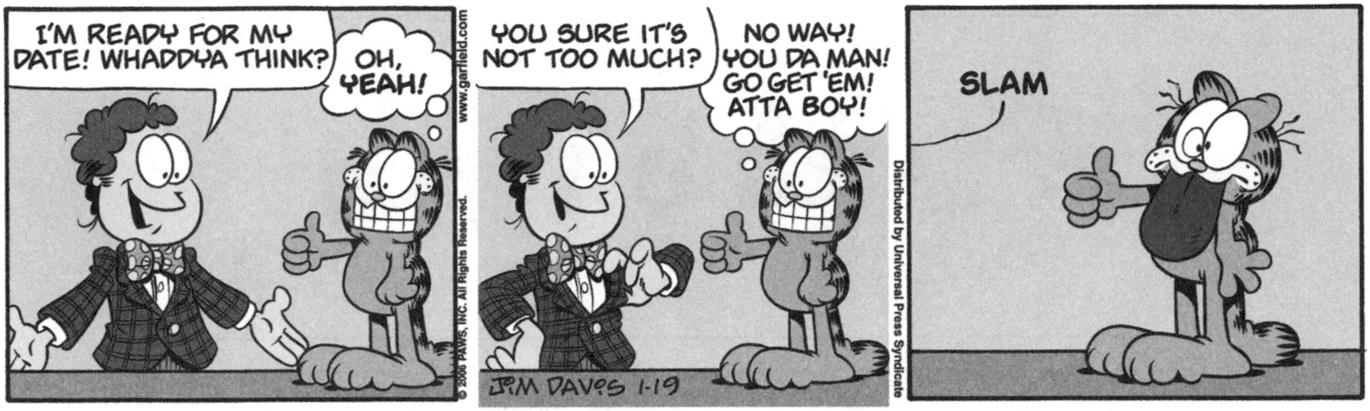
I'M READY FOR MY DATE! WHADDYA THINK?
OH, YEAH!
YOU SURE IT'S NOT TOO MUCH?
NO WAY! YOU DA MAN! GO GET 'EM! ATTA BOY!
SLAM
JIM DAVIS 1-19
© 2006 PAWS, INC. All Rights Reserved. www.garfield.com
Distributed by Universal Press Syndicate

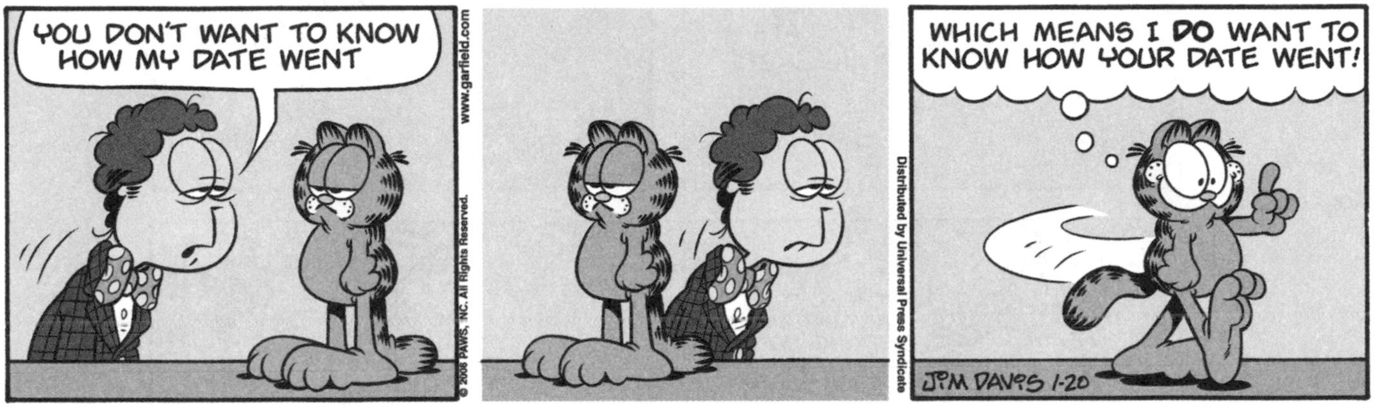
YOU DON'T WANT TO KNOW HOW MY DATE WENT
WHICH MEANS I **DO** WANT TO KNOW HOW YOUR DATE WENT!
JIM DAVIS 1-20
© 2006 PAWS, INC. All Rights Reserved. www.garfield.com
Distributed by Universal Press Syndicate

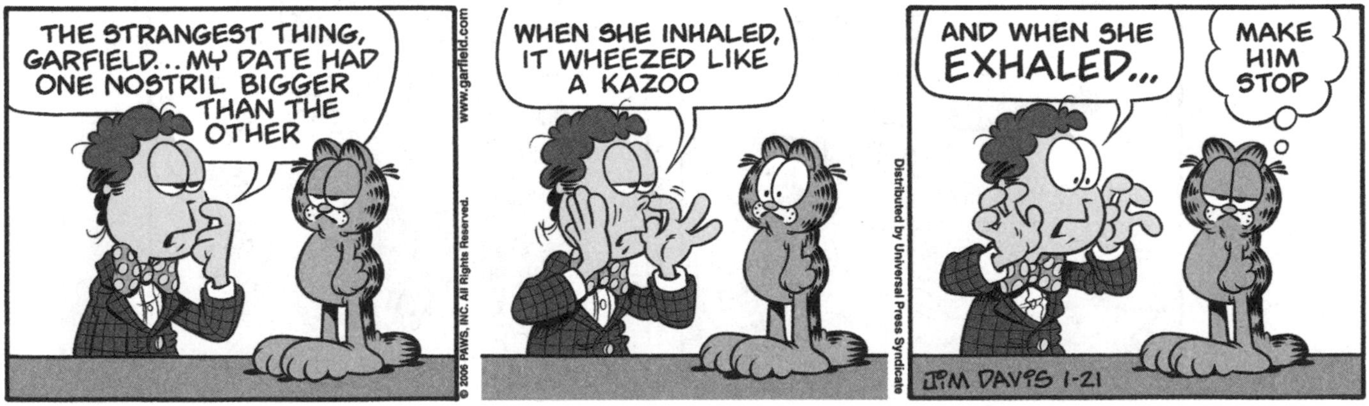
THE STRANGEST THING, GARFIELD... MY DATE HAD ONE NOSTRIL BIGGER THAN THE OTHER
WHEN SHE INHALED, IT WHEEZED LIKE A KAZOO
AND WHEN SHE EXHALED...
MAKE HIM STOP
JIM DAVIS 1-21
© 2006 PAWS, INC. All Rights Reserved. www.garfield.com
Distributed by Universal Press Syndicate

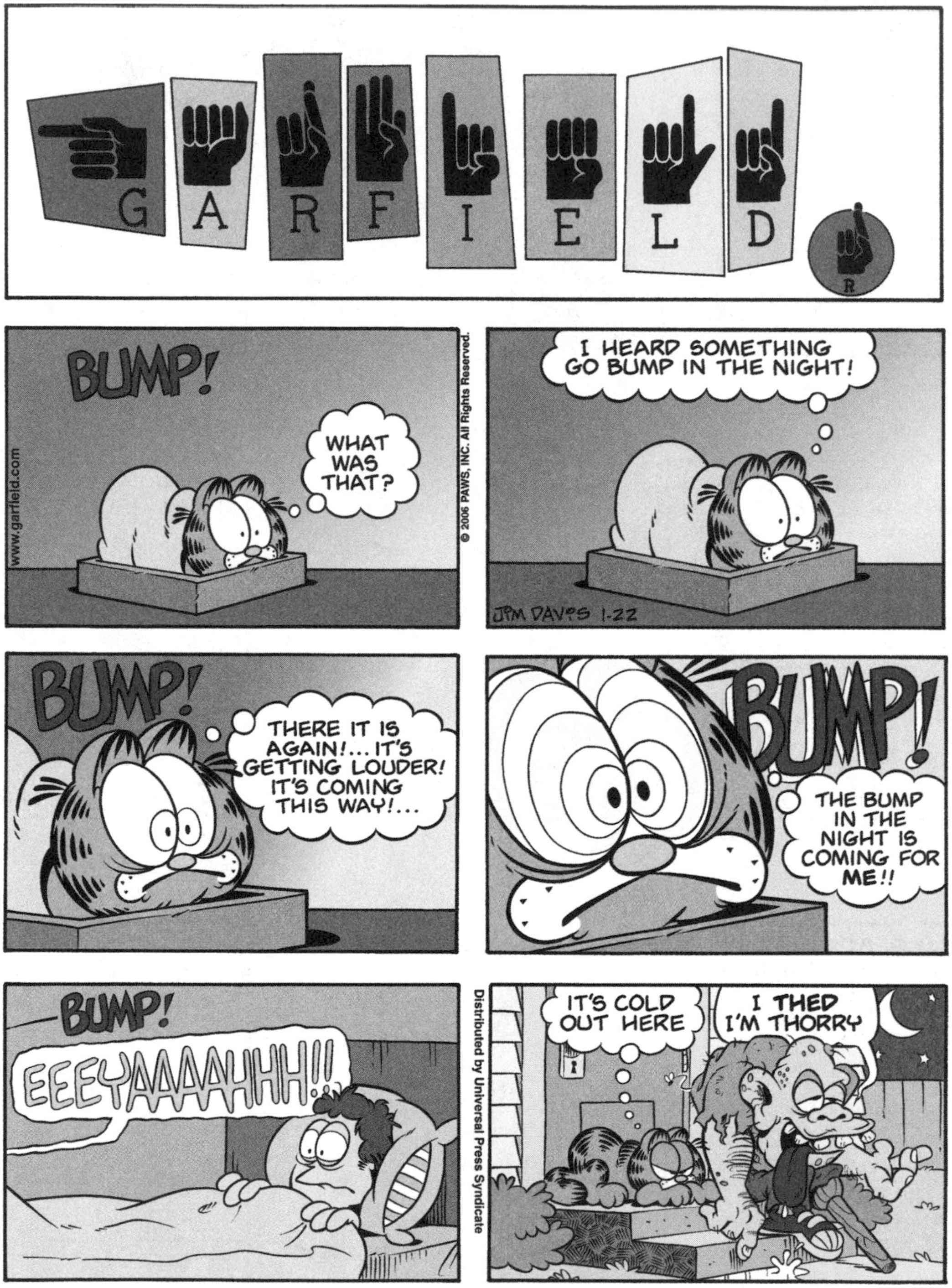
G A R F I E L D
BUMP!
WHAT WAS THAT?
www.garfield.com
© 2006 PAWS, INC. All Rights Reserved.
I HEARD SOMETHING GO BUMP IN THE NIGHT!
JIM DAVIS 1-22
BUMP!
THERE IT IS AGAIN!... IT'S GETTING LOUDER! IT'S COMING THIS WAY!...
BUMP!
THE BUMP IN THE NIGHT IS COMING FOR ME!!
BUMP!
EEEYAAAAHHH!!
Distributed by Universal Press Syndicate
IT'S COLD OUT HERE
I THED I'M THORRY

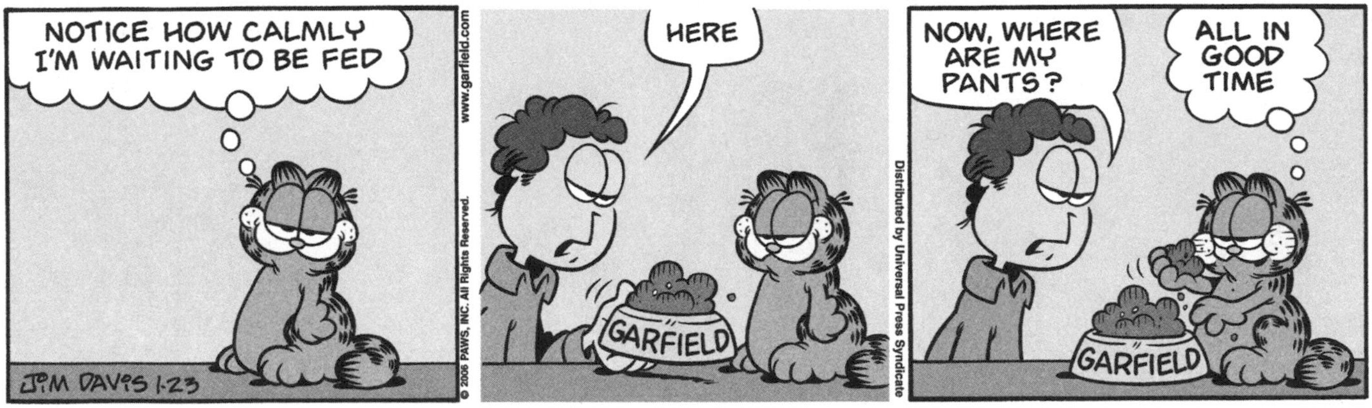
NOTICE HOW CALMLY I'M WAITING TO BE FED
JIM DAVIS 1-23
HERE
© 2006 PAWS, INC. All Rights Reserved. www.garfield.com
NOW, WHERE ARE MY PANTS?
ALL IN GOOD TIME
GARFIELD
Distributed by Universal Press Syndicate

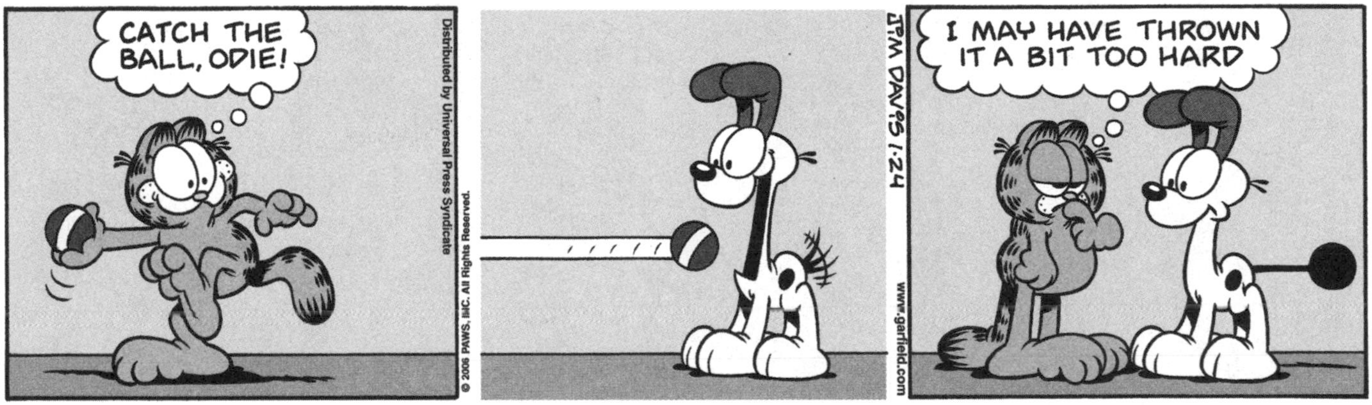
CATCH THE BALL, ODIE!
Distributed by Universal Press Syndicate
© 2006 PAWS, INC. All Rights Reserved.
JIM DAVIS 1-24
www.garfield.com
I MAY HAVE THROWN IT A BIT TOO HARD

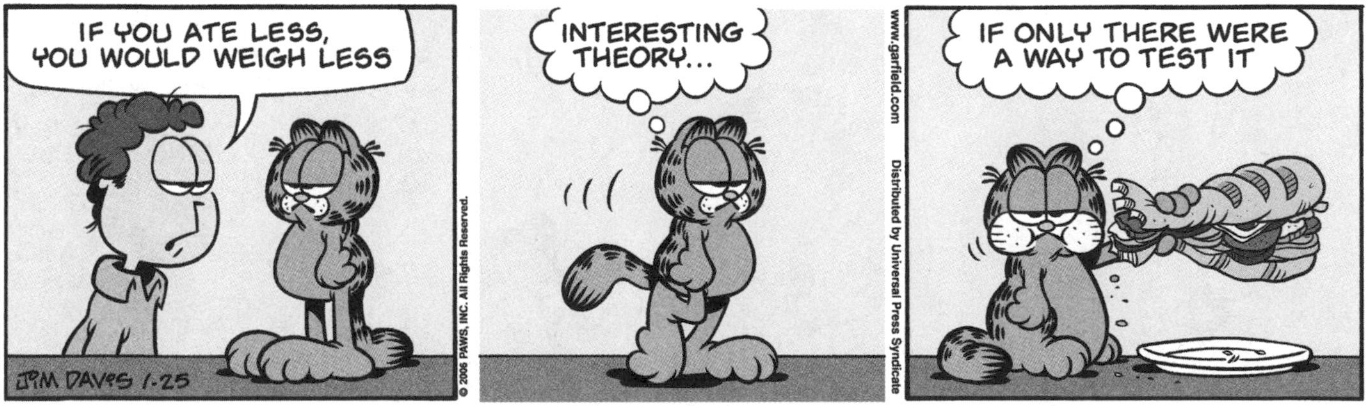
IF YOU ATE LESS, YOU WOULD WEIGH LESS
JIM DAVIS 1-25
© 2006 PAWS, INC. All Rights Reserved.
INTERESTING THEORY...
www.garfield.com
Distributed by Universal Press Syndicate
IF ONLY THERE WERE A WAY TO TEST IT

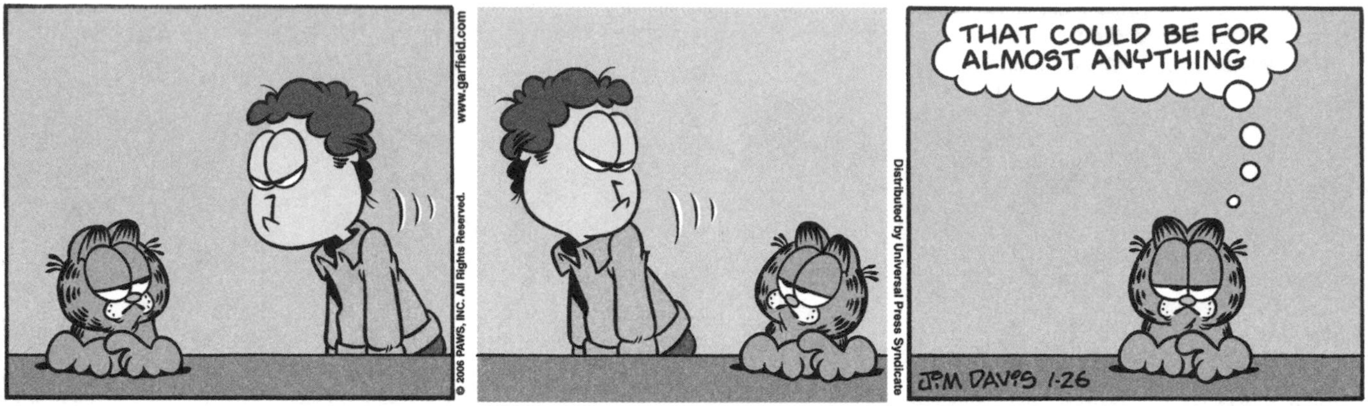

THAT COULD BE FOR ALMOST ANYTHING
JIM DAVIS 1-26
© 2006 PAWS, INC. All Rights Reserved.
www.garfield.com
Distributed by Universal Press Syndicate

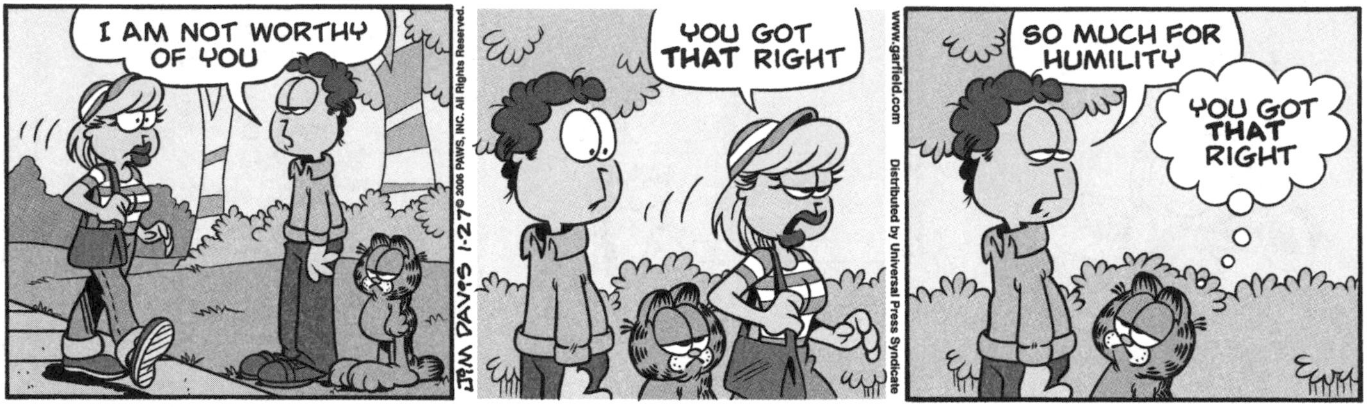

I AM NOT WORTHY OF YOU
YOU GOT THAT RIGHT
SO MUCH FOR HUMILITY
YOU GOT THAT RIGHT
JIM DAVIS 1-27
© 2006 PAWS, INC. All Rights Reserved.
www.garfield.com
Distributed by Universal Press Syndicate

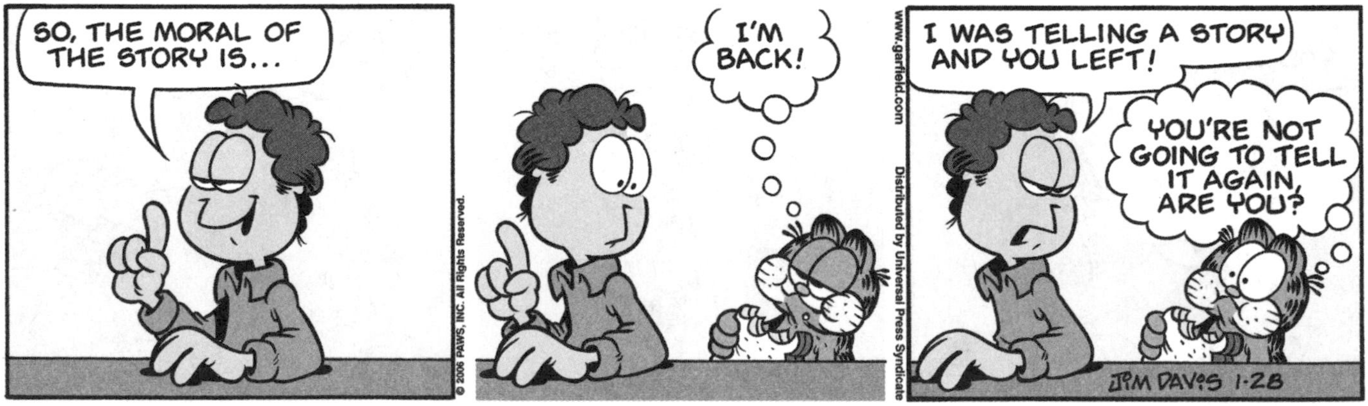

SO, THE MORAL OF THE STORY IS...
I'M BACK!
I WAS TELLING A STORY AND YOU LEFT!
YOU'RE NOT GOING TO TELL IT AGAIN, ARE YOU?
JIM DAVIS 1-28
© 2006 PAWS, INC. All Rights Reserved.
www.garfield.com
Distributed by Universal Press Syndicate

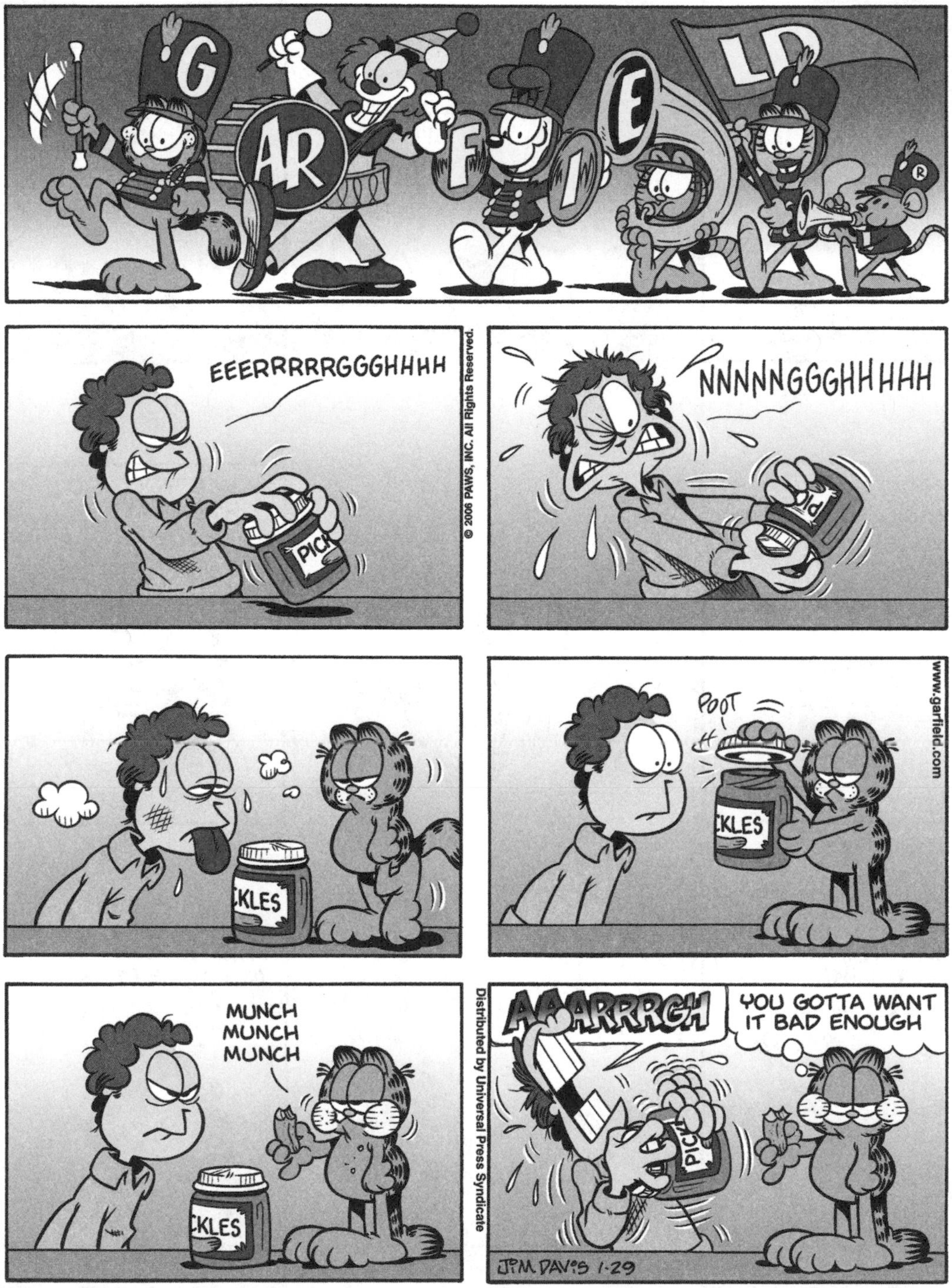
G
AR
F
I
E
LD
© 2006 PAWS, INC. All Rights Reserved.
EEERRRRRGGGHHHH
NNNNNGGGHHHHH
PICK
www.garfield.com
POOT
CKLES
MUNCH
MUNCH
MUNCH
CKLES
Distributed by Universal Press Syndicate
AAARRRGH
YOU GOTTA WANT IT BAD ENOUGH
JIM DAVIS 1-29

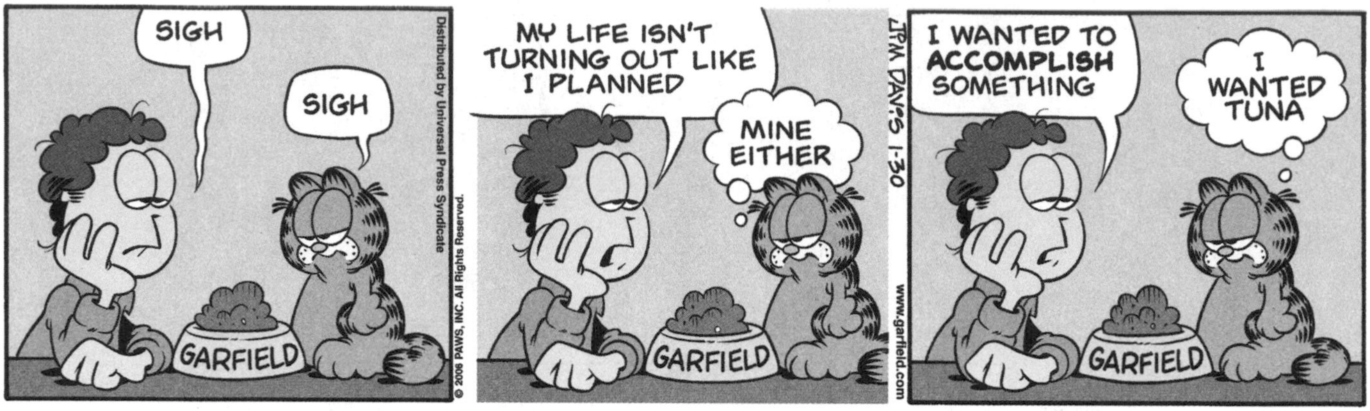
SIGH
SIGH
MY LIFE ISN'T TURNING OUT LIKE I PLANNED
MINE EITHER
I WANTED TO **ACCOMPLISH** SOMETHING
I WANTED TUNA

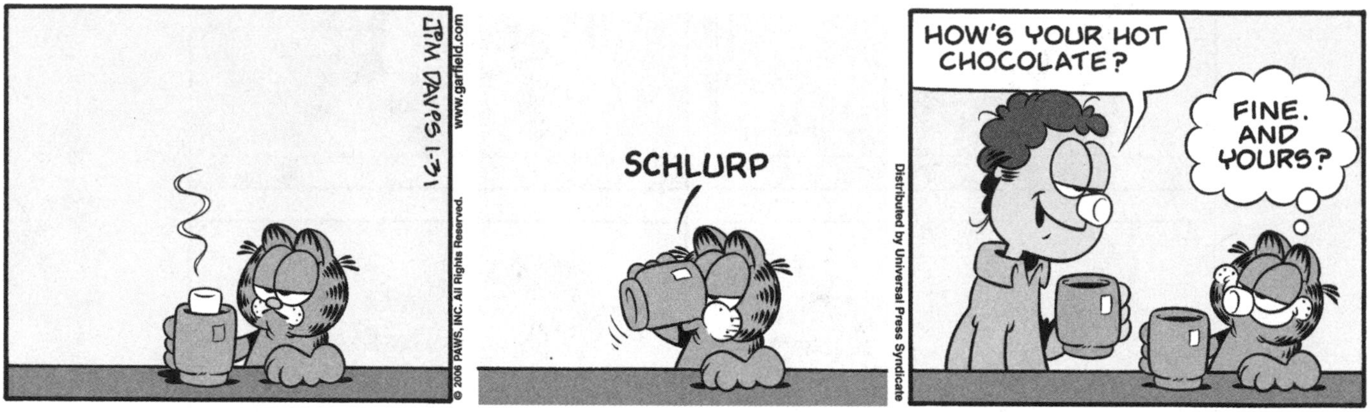
SCHLURP
HOW'S YOUR HOT CHOCOLATE?
FINE. AND YOURS?

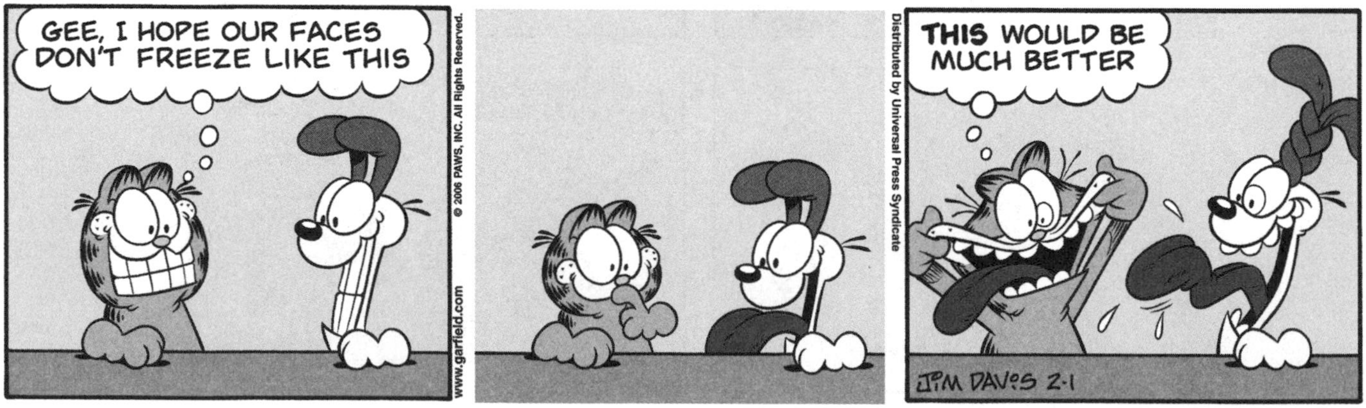
GEE, I HOPE OUR FACES DON'T FREEZE LIKE THIS
THIS WOULD BE MUCH BETTER

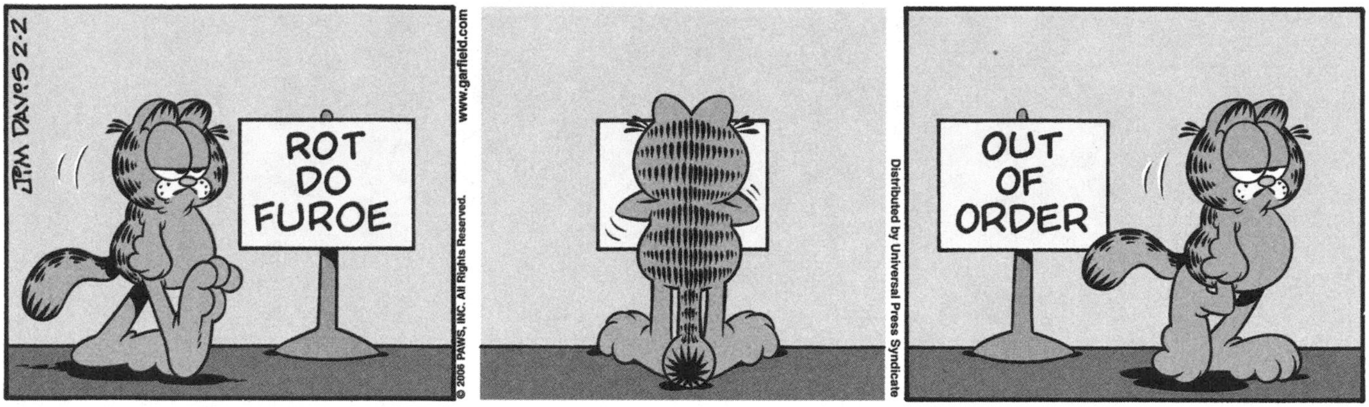
JIM DAVIS 2-2
ROT DO FUROE
OUT OF ORDER
© 2006 PAWS, INC. All Rights Reserved.
www.garfield.com
Distributed by Universal Press Syndicate

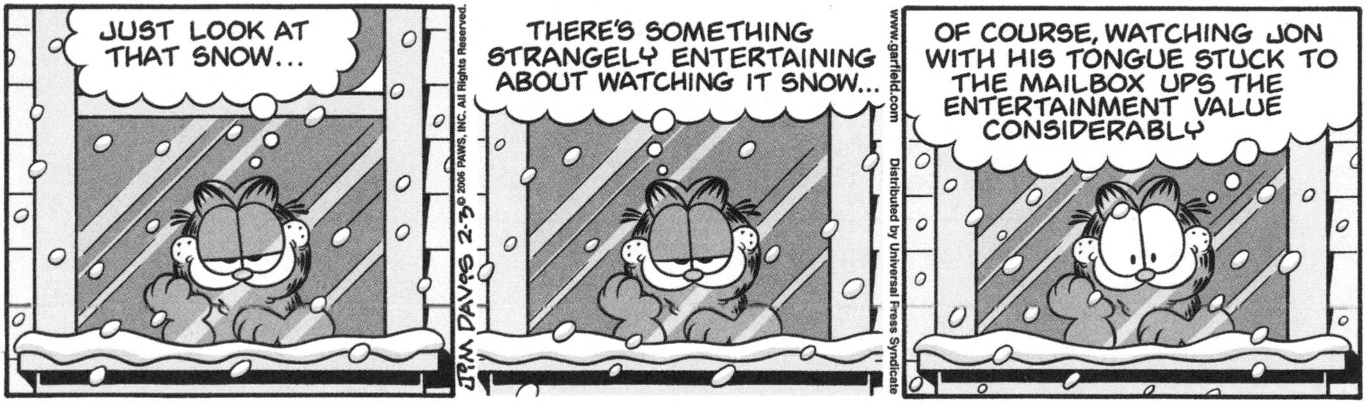
JUST LOOK AT THAT SNOW...
THERE'S SOMETHING STRANGELY ENTERTAINING ABOUT WATCHING IT SNOW...
OF COURSE, WATCHING JON WITH HIS TONGUE STUCK TO THE MAILBOX UPS THE ENTERTAINMENT VALUE CONSIDERABLY
JIM DAVIS 2-3
© 2006 PAWS, INC. All Rights Reserved.
www.garfield.com
Distributed by Universal Press Syndicate

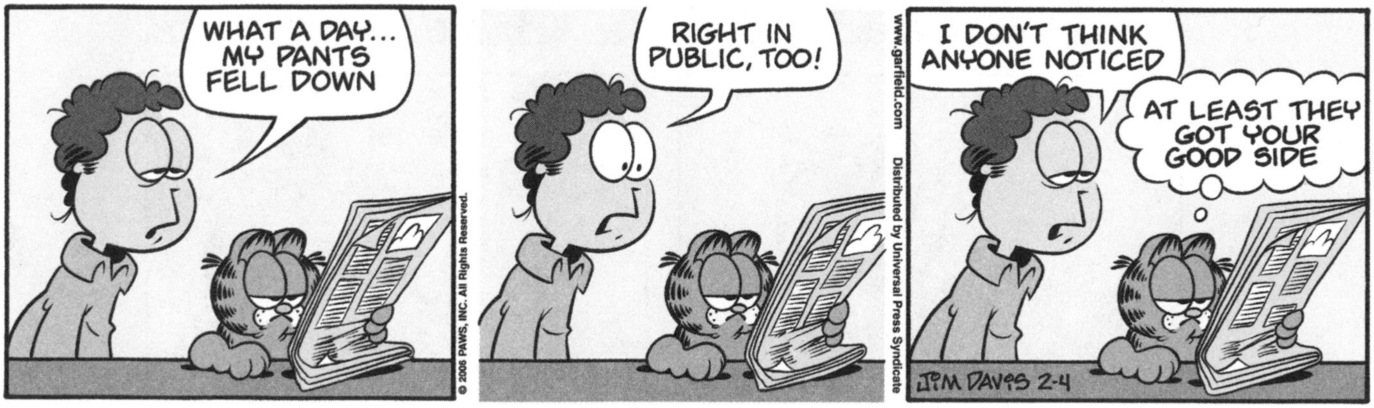
WHAT A DAY... MY PANTS FELL DOWN
RIGHT IN PUBLIC, TOO!
I DON'T THINK ANYONE NOTICED
AT LEAST THEY GOT YOUR GOOD SIDE
JIM DAVIS 2-4
© 2006 PAWS, INC. All Rights Reserved.
www.garfield.com
Distributed by Universal Press Syndicate

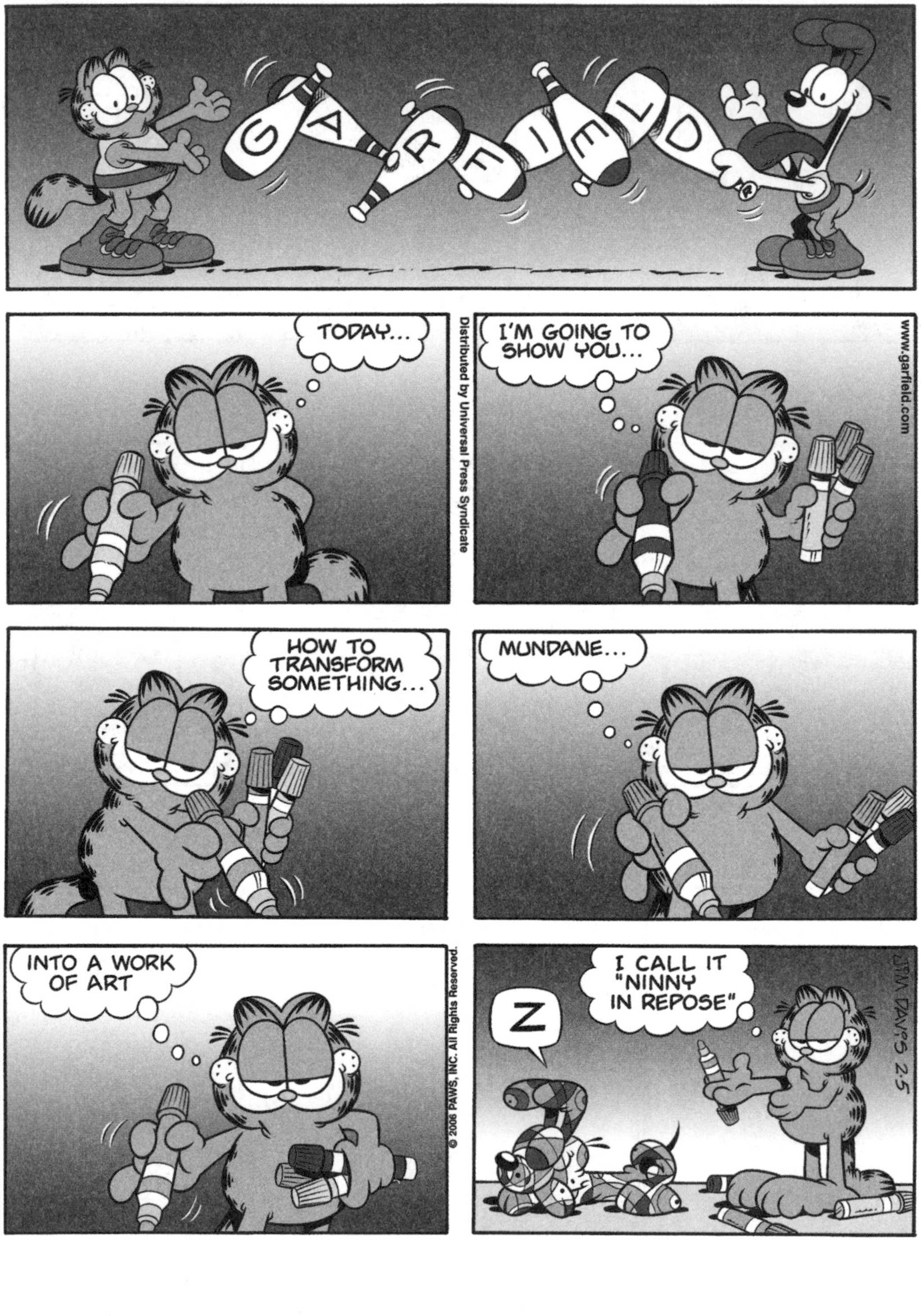
GARFIELD
TODAY...
I'M GOING TO SHOW YOU...
HOW TO TRANSFORM SOMETHING...
MUNDANE...
INTO A WORK OF ART
Z
I CALL IT "NINNY IN REPOSE"
JPM DAVIS 2-5
Distributed by Universal Press Syndicate
www.garfield.com
© 2006 PAWS, INC. All Rights Reserved.

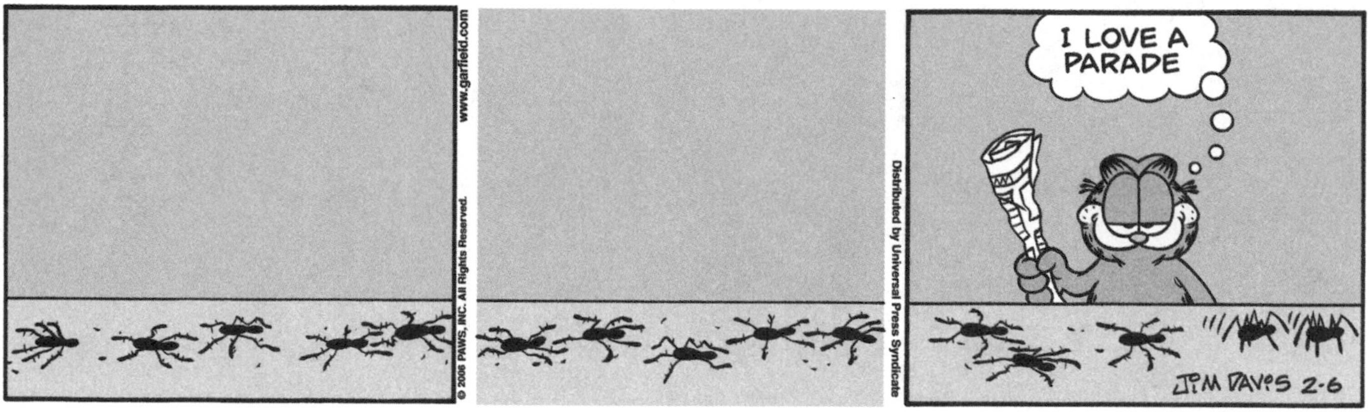
© 2006 PAWS, INC. All Rights Reserved.
www.garfield.com
Distributed by Universal Press Syndicate
I LOVE A PARADE
JIM DAVIS 2-6

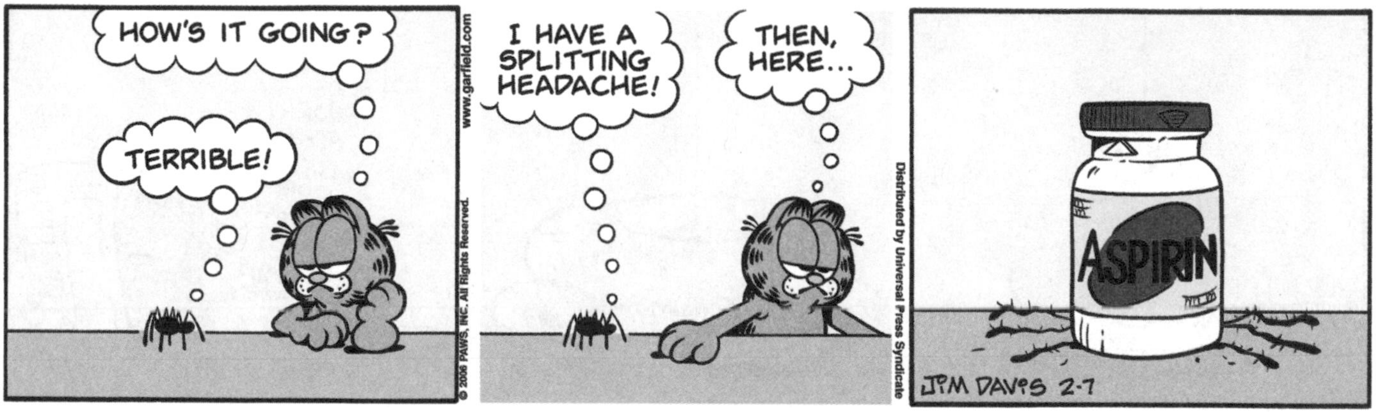
HOW'S IT GOING?
TERRIBLE!
© 2006 PAWS, INC. All Rights Reserved.
www.garfield.com
I HAVE A SPLITTING HEADACHE!
THEN, HERE...
Distributed by Universal Press Syndicate
ASPIRIN
JIM DAVIS 2-7

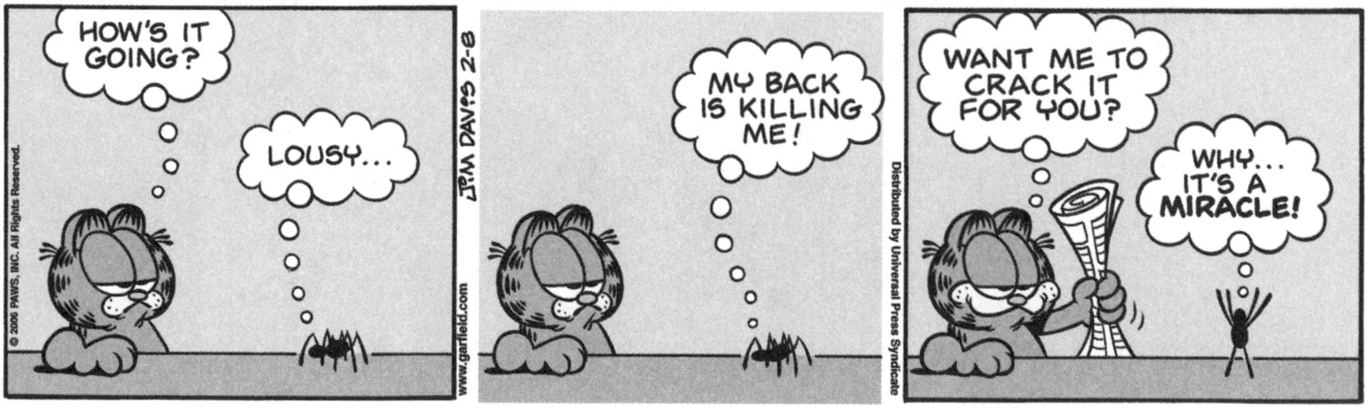
HOW'S IT GOING?
LOUSY...
© 2006 PAWS, INC. All Rights Reserved.
JIM DAVIS 2-8
www.garfield.com
MY BACK IS KILLING ME!
Distributed by Universal Press Syndicate
WANT ME TO CRACK IT FOR YOU?
WHY... IT'S A MIRACLE!

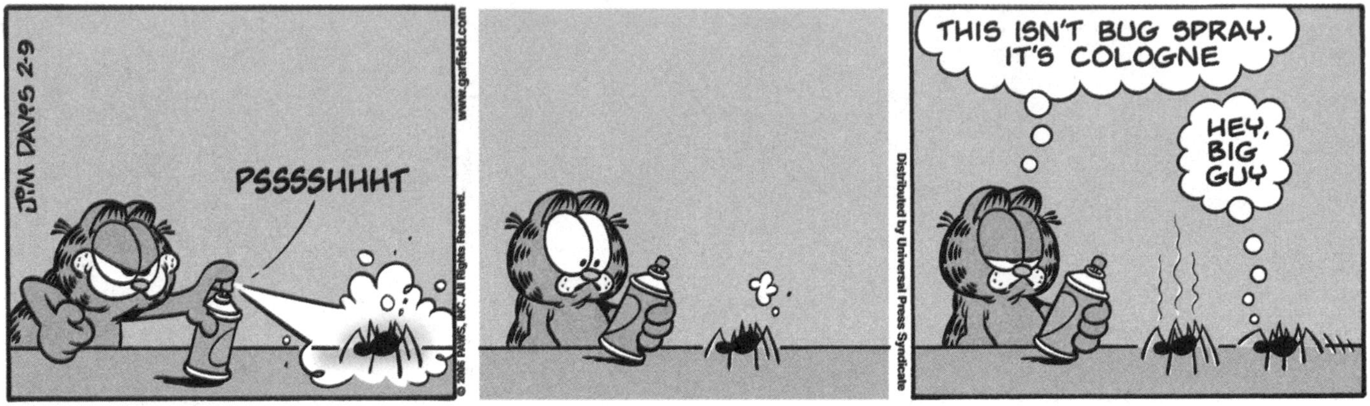
JIM DAVIS 2-9
PSSSSHHHT
www.garfield.com
© 2006 PAWS, INC. All Rights Reserved.
Distributed by Universal Press Syndicate
THIS ISN'T BUG SPRAY. IT'S COLOGNE
HEY, BIG GUY

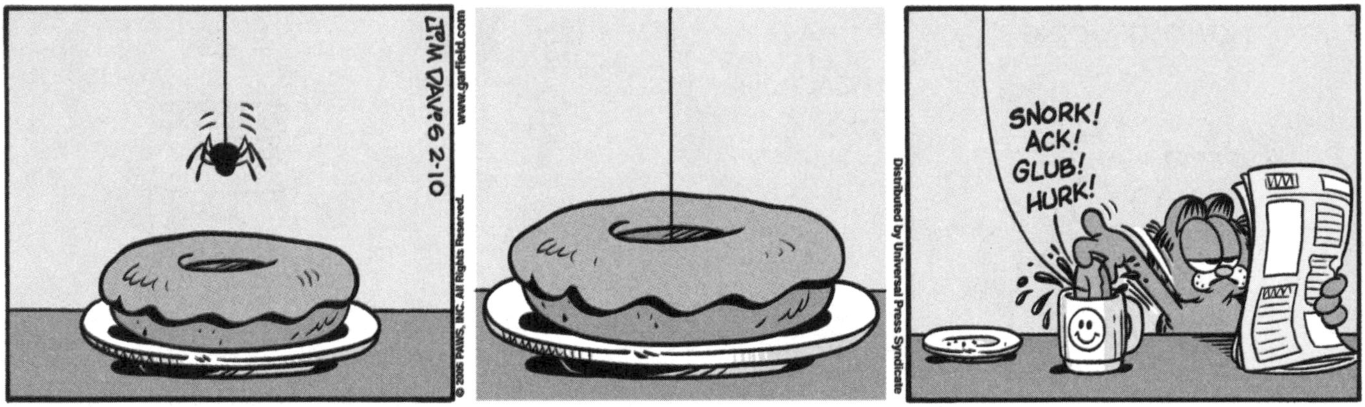
JIM DAVIS 2-10
www.garfield.com
© 2006 PAWS, INC. All Rights Reserved.
Distributed by Universal Press Syndicate
SNORK!
ACK!
GLUB!
HURK!

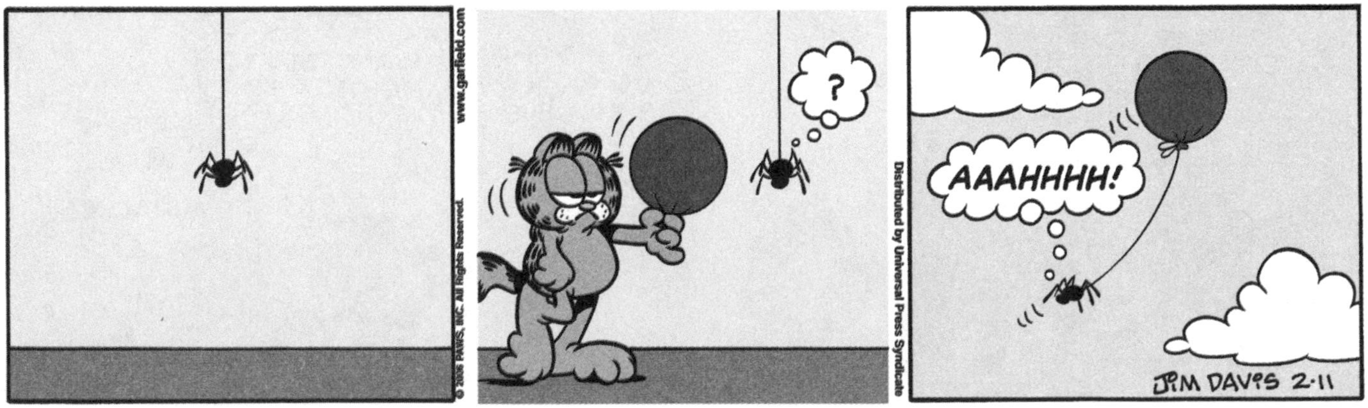
www.garfield.com
© 2006 PAWS, INC. All Rights Reserved.
Distributed by Universal Press Syndicate
?
AAAHHHH!
JIM DAVIS 2-11

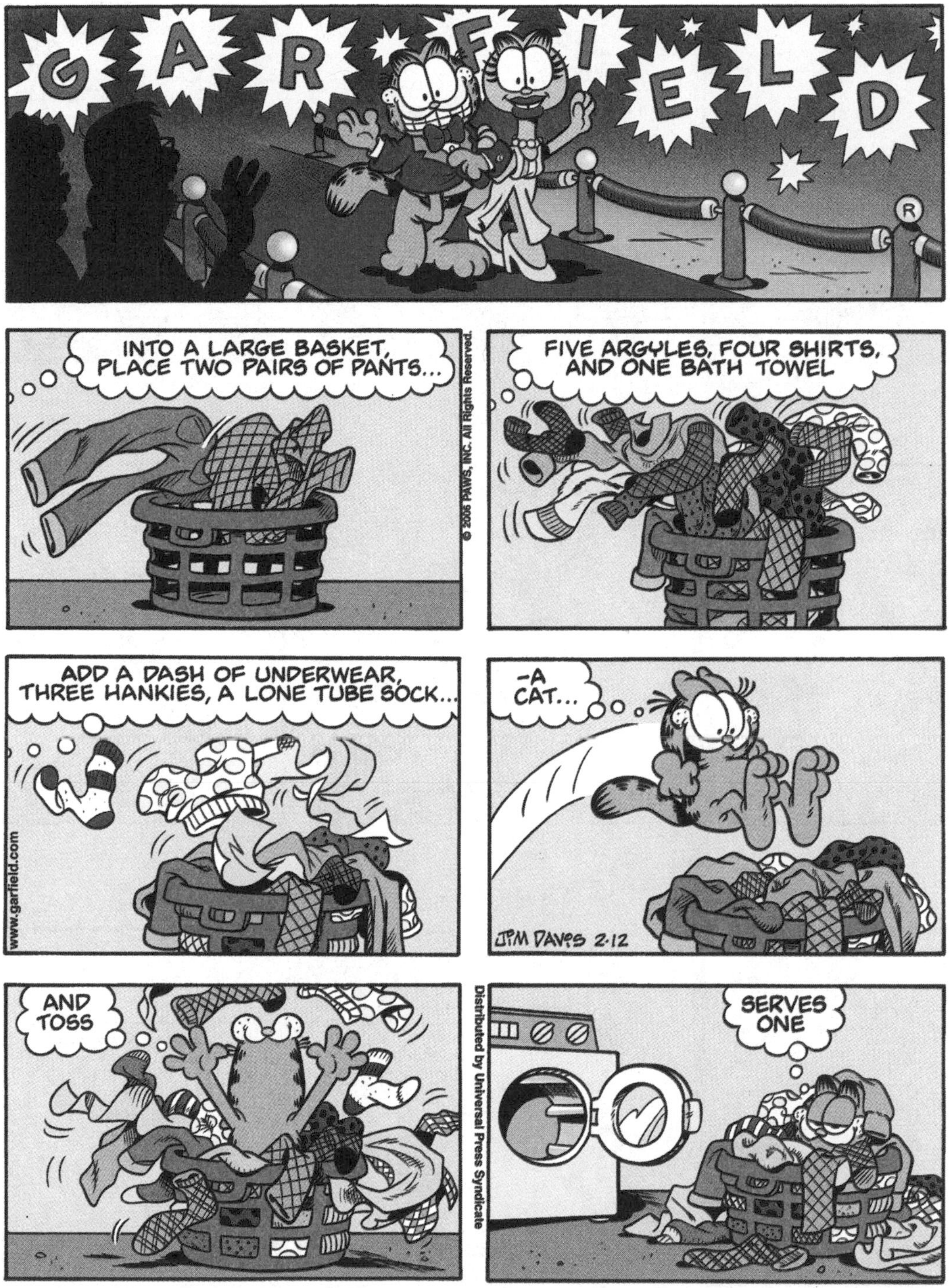
GARFIELD
INTO A LARGE BASKET, PLACE TWO PAIRS OF PANTS...
© 2005 PAWS, INC. All Rights Reserved.
FIVE ARGYLES, FOUR SHIRTS, AND ONE BATH TOWEL
ADD A DASH OF UNDERWEAR, THREE HANKIES, A LONE TUBE SOCK...
www.garfield.com
-A CAT...
JIM DAVIS 2-12
AND TOSS
Distributed by Universal Press Syndicate
SERVES ONE

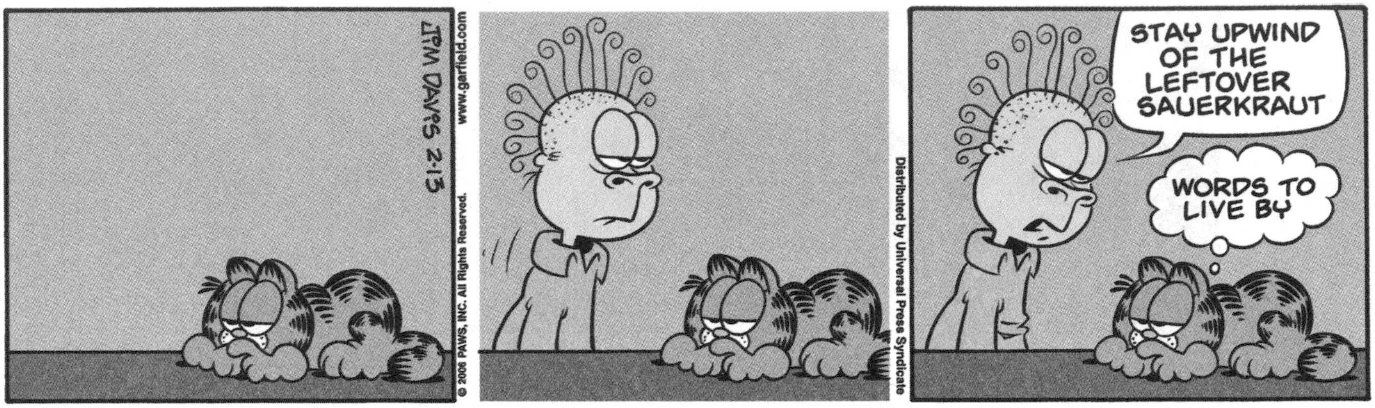
JIM DAVIS 2-13
www.garfield.com
© 2006 PAWS, INC. All Rights Reserved.
Distributed by Universal Press Syndicate
STAY UPWIND OF THE LEFTOVER SAUERKRAUT
WORDS TO LIVE BY

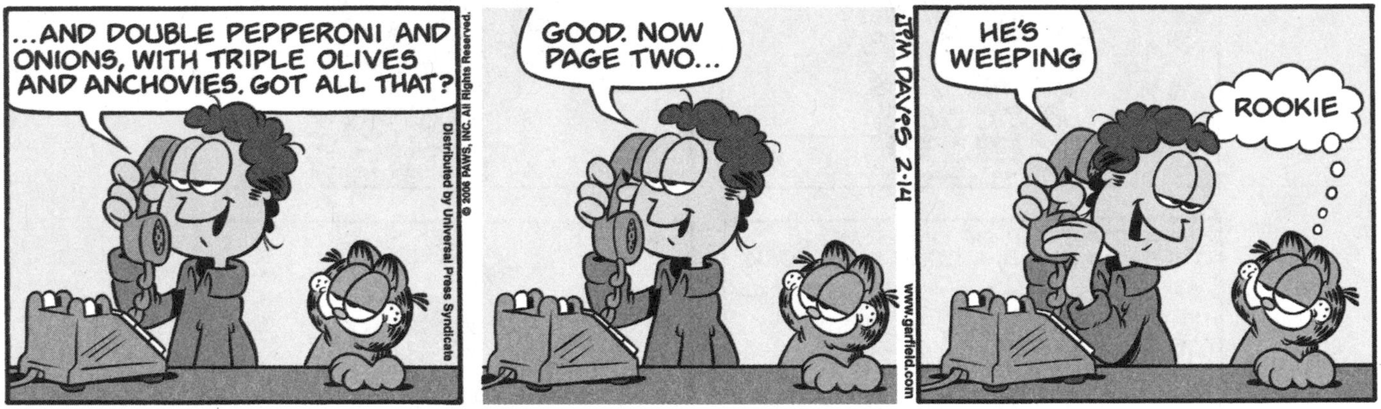
...AND DOUBLE PEPPERONI AND ONIONS, WITH TRIPLE OLIVES AND ANCHOVIES. GOT ALL THAT?
© 2006 PAWS, INC. All Rights Reserved.
Distributed by Universal Press Syndicate
GOOD. NOW PAGE TWO...
JIM DAVIS 2-14
www.garfield.com
HE'S WEEPING
ROOKIE

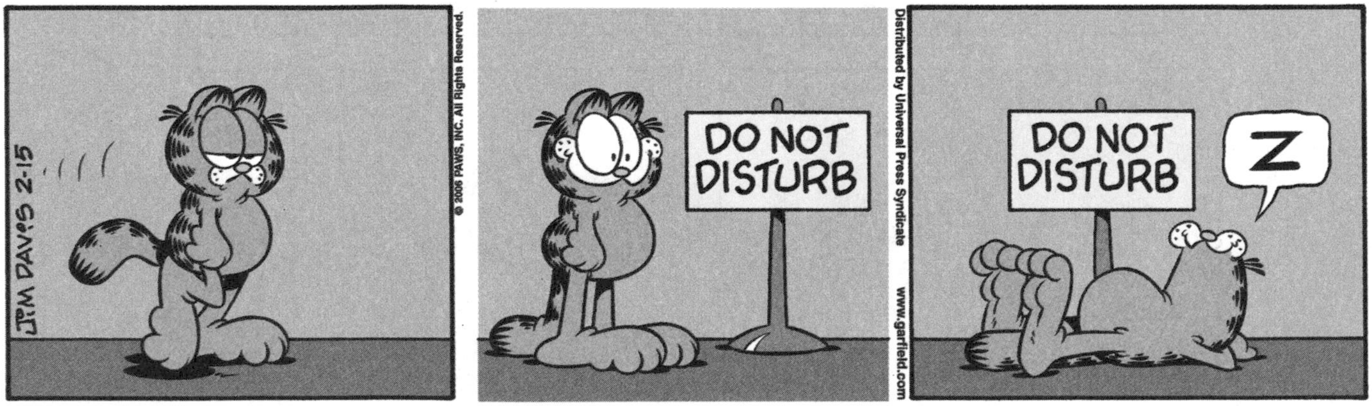
JIM DAVIS 2-15
© 2006 PAWS, INC. All Rights Reserved.
Distributed by Universal Press Syndicate
DO NOT DISTURB
www.garfield.com
DO NOT DISTURB
Z

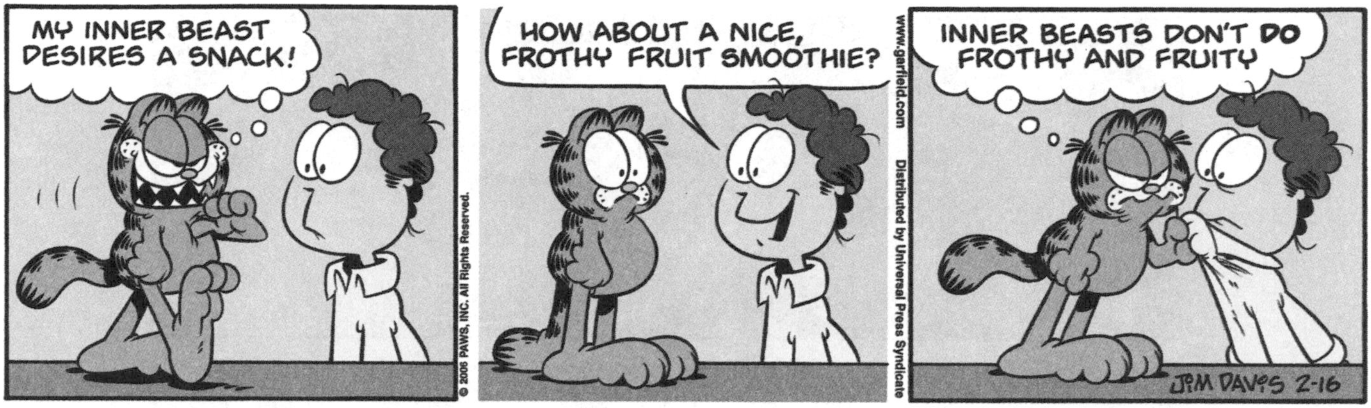
MY INNER BEAST DESIRES A SNACK!
HOW ABOUT A NICE, FROTHY FRUIT SMOOTHIE?
INNER BEASTS DON'T DO FROTHY AND FRUITY
JIM DAVIS 2-16
© 2006 PAWS, INC. All Rights Reserved.
www.garfield.com Distributed by Universal Press Syndicate

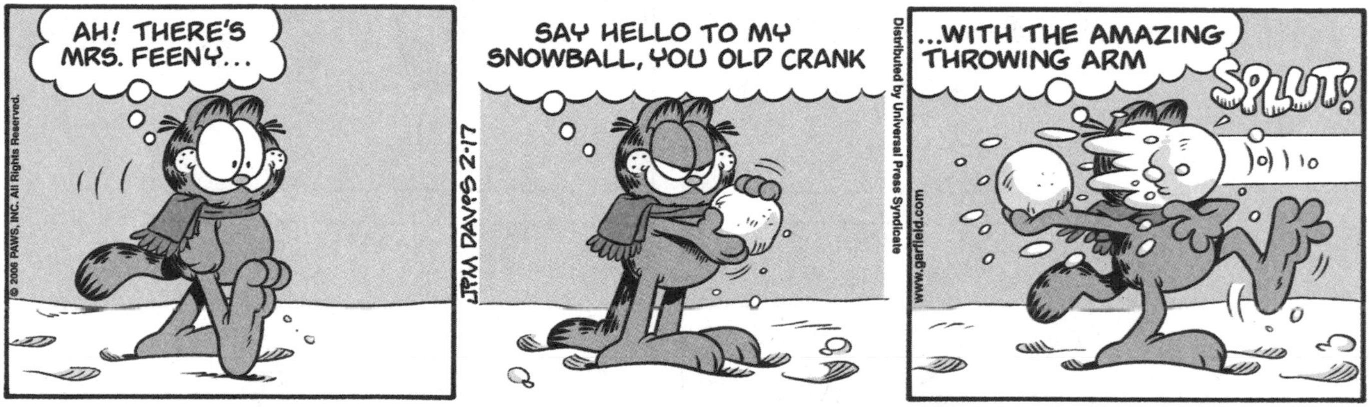
AH! THERE'S MRS. FEENY...
SAY HELLO TO MY SNOWBALL, YOU OLD CRANK
...WITH THE AMAZING THROWING ARM
SPLUT!
JIM DAVIS 2-17
© 2006 PAWS, INC. All Rights Reserved.
Distributed by Universal Press Syndicate www.garfield.com

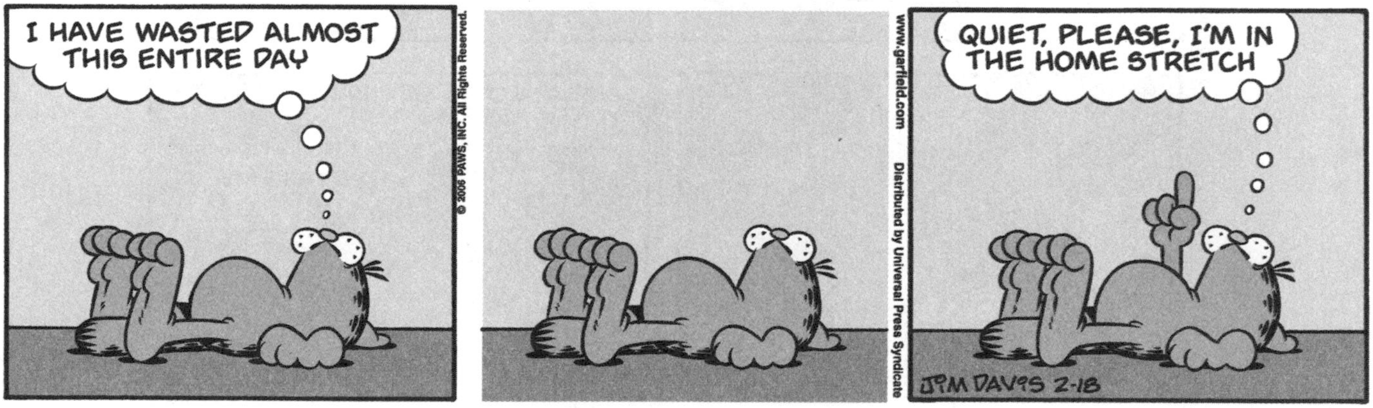
I HAVE WASTED ALMOST THIS ENTIRE DAY
QUIET, PLEASE, I'M IN THE HOME STRETCH
JIM DAVIS 2-18
© 2006 PAWS, INC. All Rights Reserved.
www.garfield.com Distributed by Universal Press Syndicate

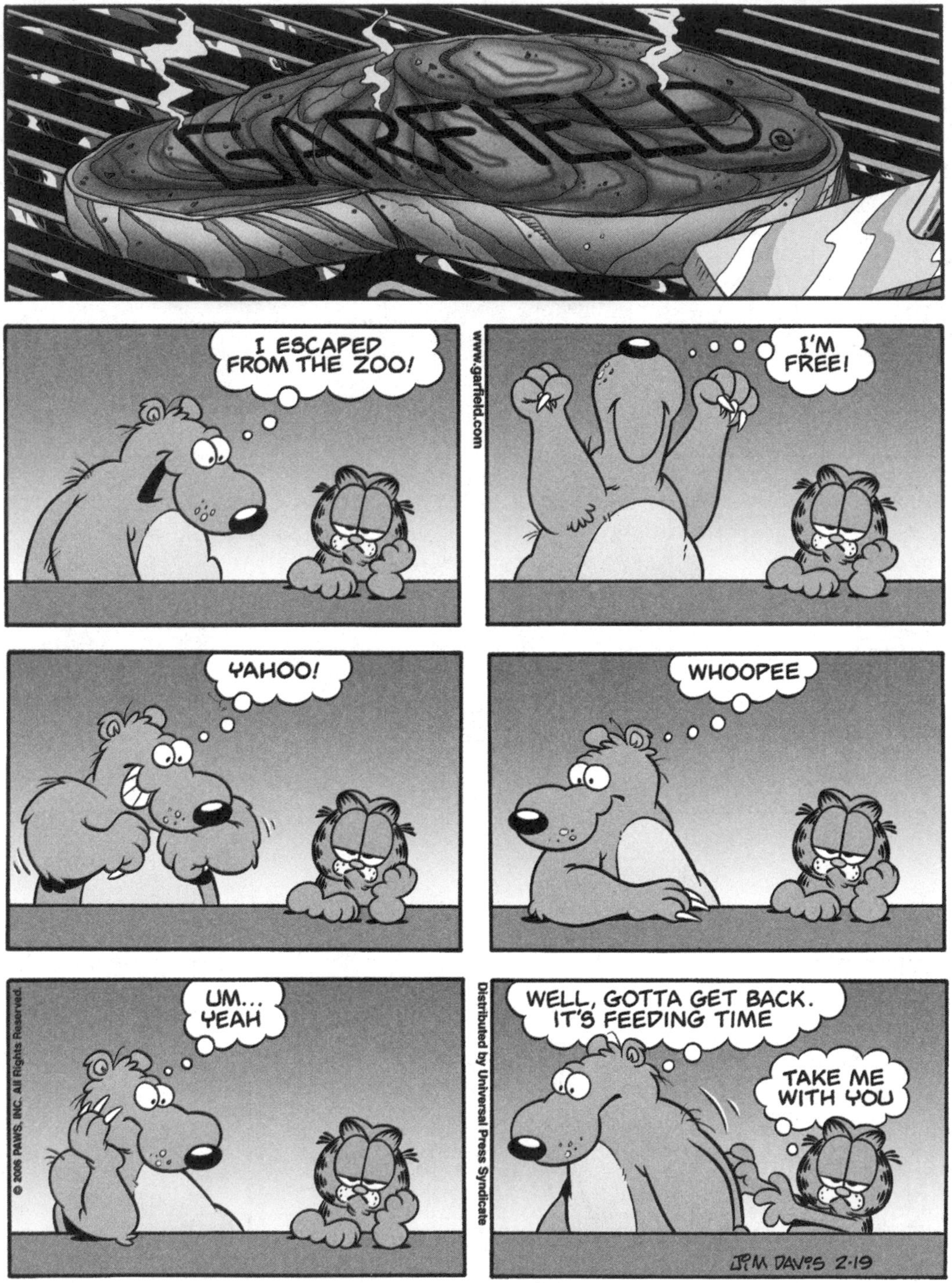
GARFIELD®
www.garfield.com
I ESCAPED FROM THE ZOO!
I'M FREE!
YAHOO!
WHOOPEE
UM... YEAH
© 2006 PAWS, INC. All Rights Reserved.
Distributed by Universal Press Syndicate
WELL, GOTTA GET BACK. IT'S FEEDING TIME
TAKE ME WITH YOU
JIM DAVIS 2-19

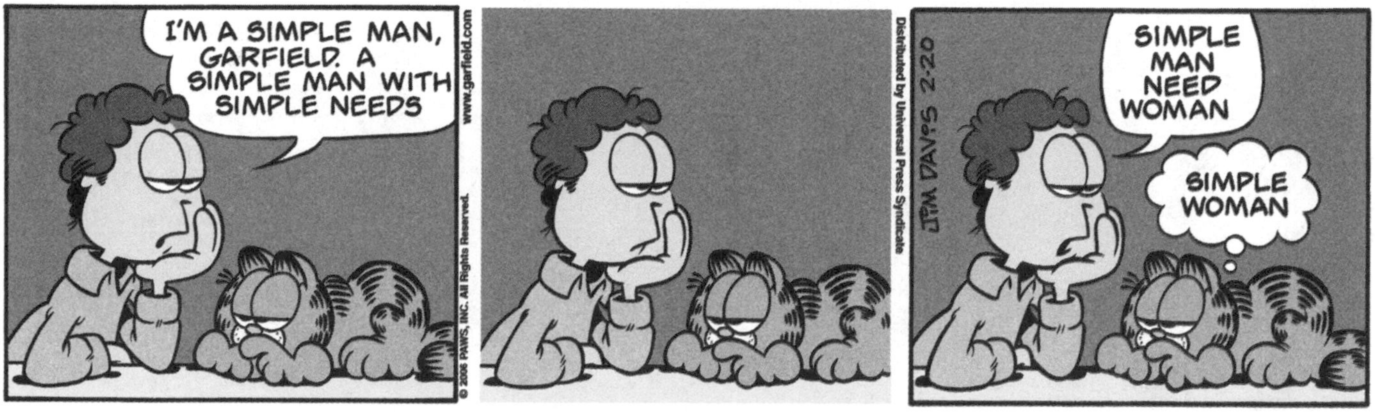
I'M A SIMPLE MAN, GARFIELD. A SIMPLE MAN WITH SIMPLE NEEDS
SIMPLE MAN NEED WOMAN
SIMPLE WOMAN
JIM DAVIS 2-20
© 2006 PAWS, INC. All Rights Reserved. www.garfield.com
Distributed by Universal Press Syndicate

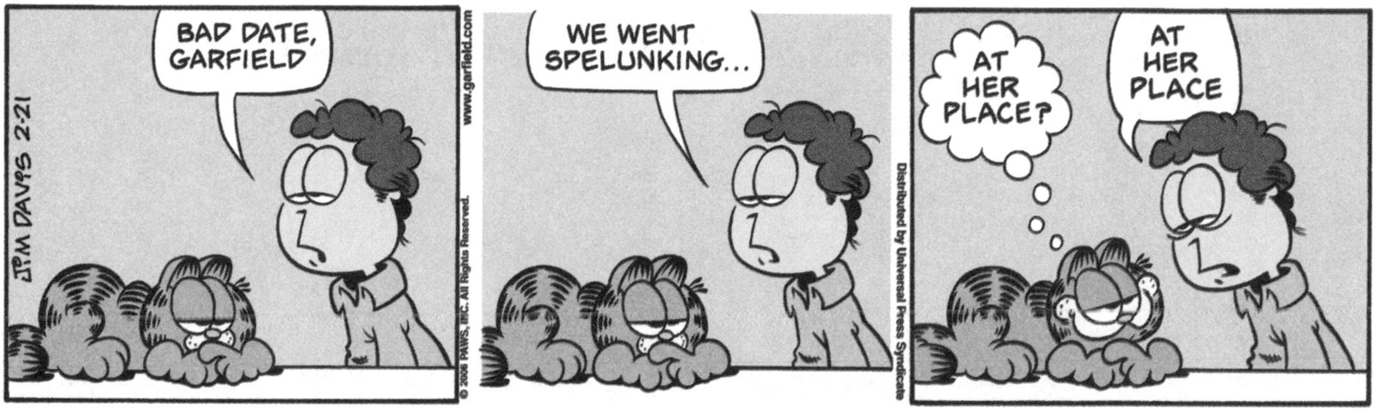
BAD DATE, GARFIELD
WE WENT SPELUNKING...
AT HER PLACE?
AT HER PLACE
JIM DAVIS 2-21
© 2006 PAWS, INC. All Rights Reserved. www.garfield.com
Distributed by Universal Press Syndicate

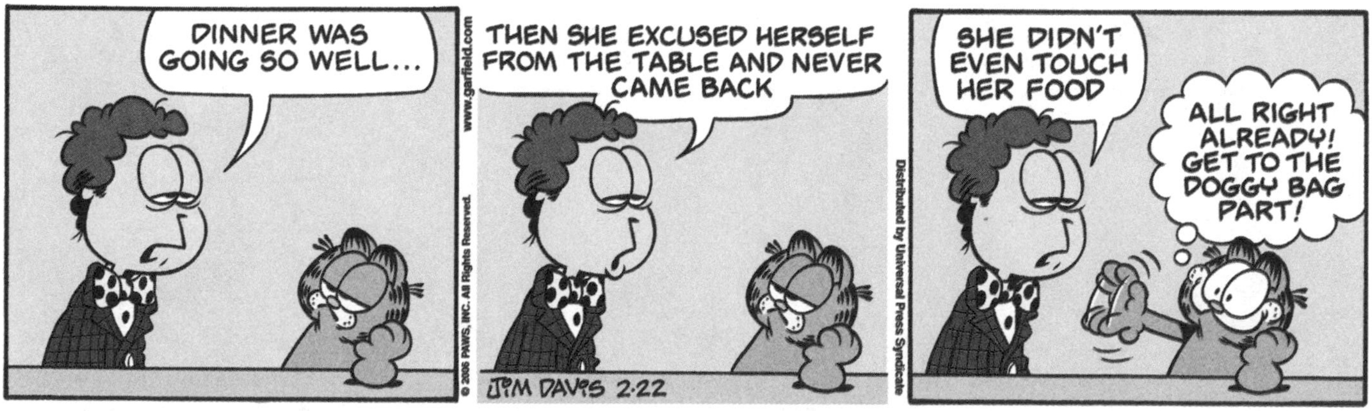
DINNER WAS GOING SO WELL...
THEN SHE EXCUSED HERSELF FROM THE TABLE AND NEVER CAME BACK
SHE DIDN'T EVEN TOUCH HER FOOD
ALL RIGHT ALREADY! GET TO THE DOGGY BAG PART!
JIM DAVIS 2-22
© 2006 PAWS, INC. All Rights Reserved. www.garfield.com
Distributed by Universal Press Syndicate

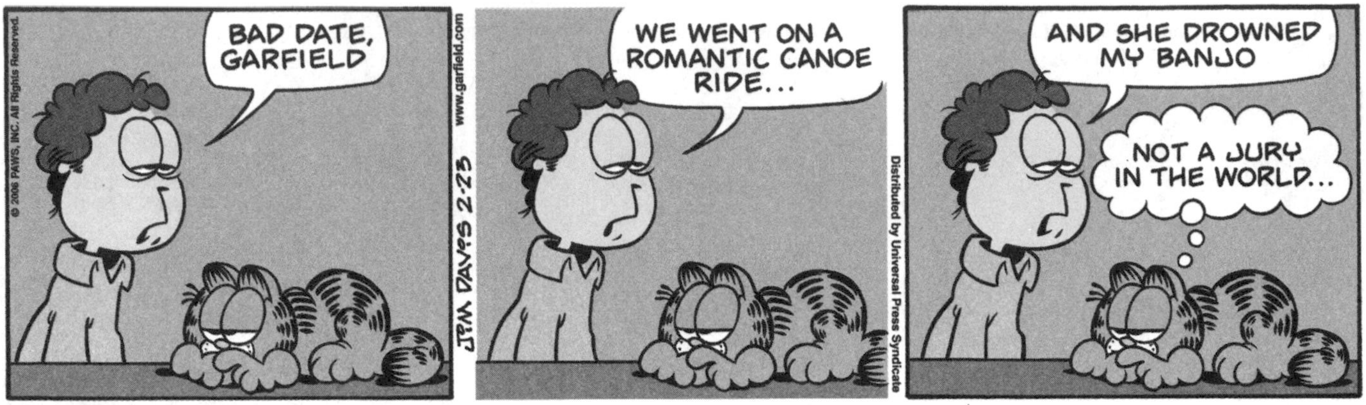
BAD DATE, GARFIELD
WE WENT ON A ROMANTIC CANOE RIDE...
AND SHE DROWNED MY BANJO
NOT A JURY IN THE WORLD...
© 2006 PAWS, INC. All Rights Reserved.
www.garfield.com
Distributed by Universal Press Syndicate

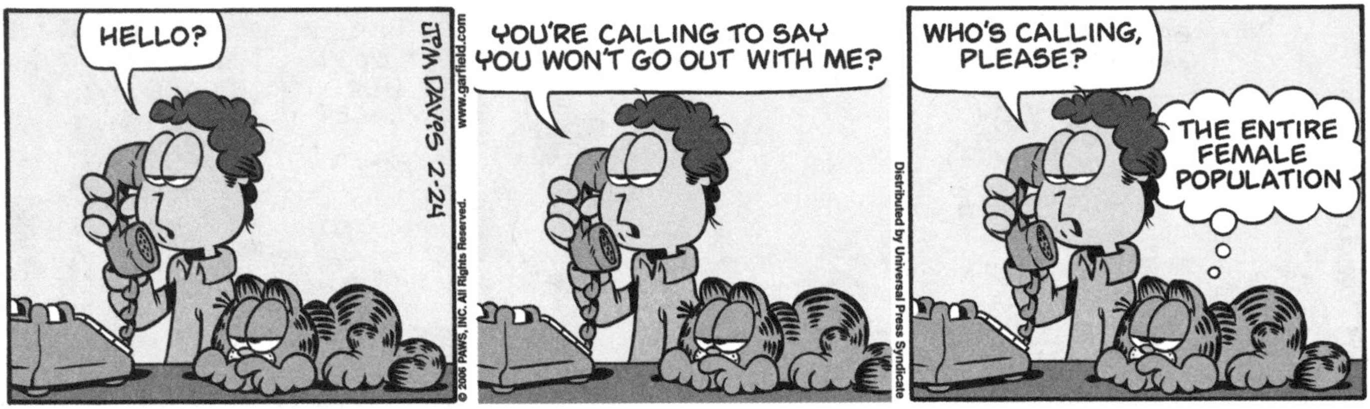
HELLO?
YOU'RE CALLING TO SAY YOU WON'T GO OUT WITH ME?
WHO'S CALLING, PLEASE?
THE ENTIRE FEMALE POPULATION
© 2006 PAWS, INC. All Rights Reserved.
www.garfield.com
Distributed by Universal Press Syndicate

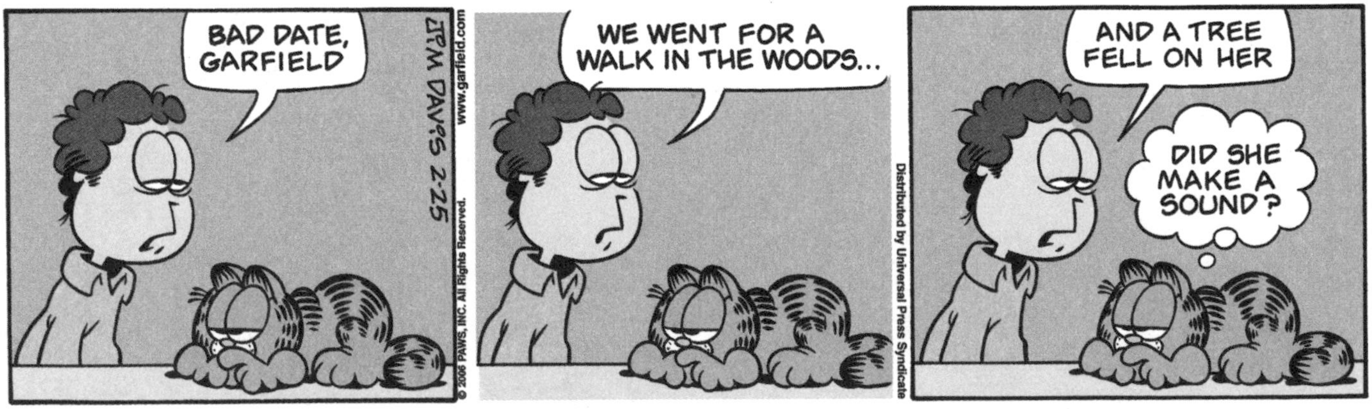
BAD DATE, GARFIELD
WE WENT FOR A WALK IN THE WOODS...
AND A TREE FELL ON HER
DID SHE MAKE A SOUND?
© 2006 PAWS, INC. All Rights Reserved.
www.garfield.com
Distributed by Universal Press Syndicate

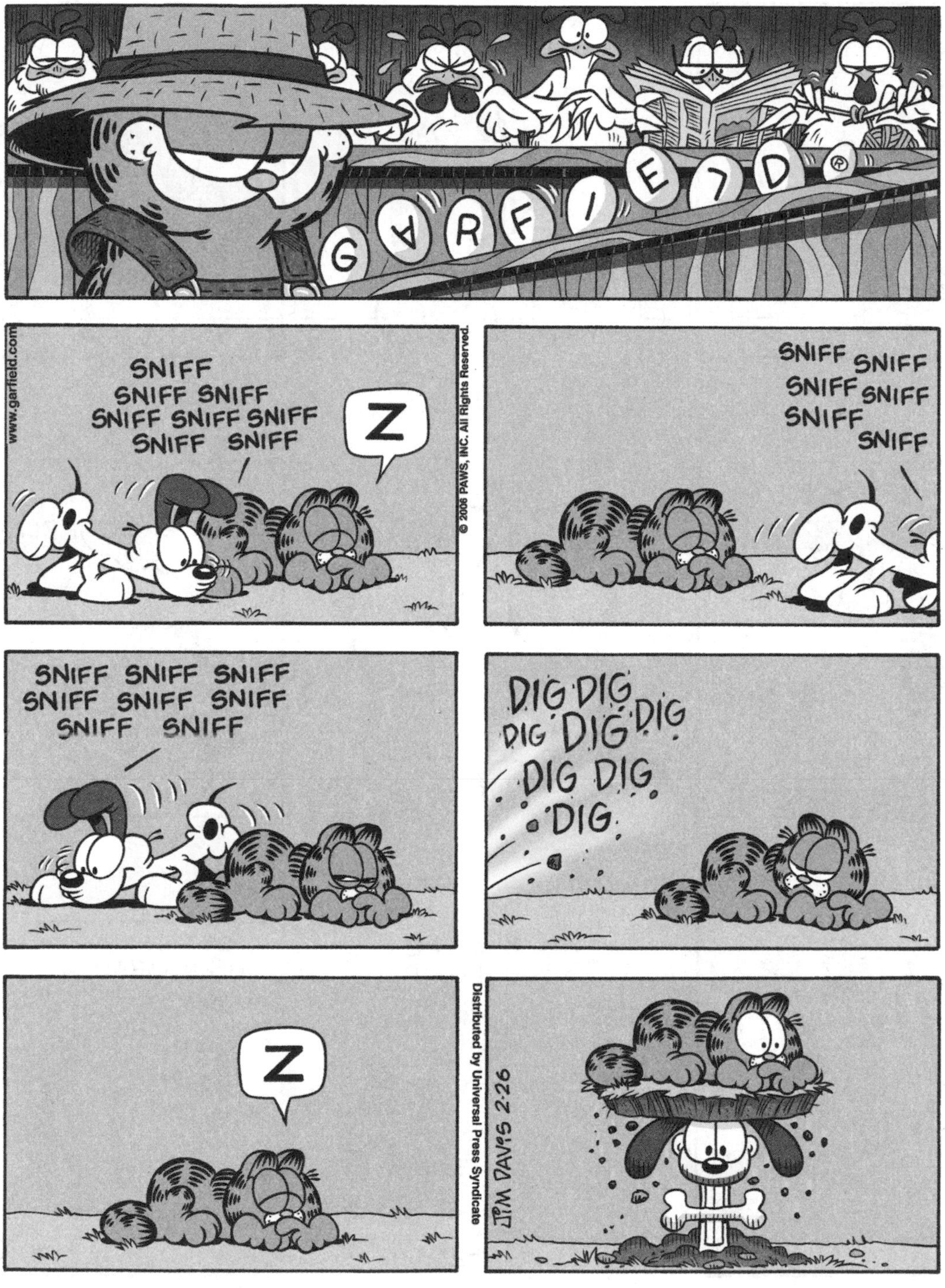
GARFIELD®
www.garfield.com
SNIFF SNIFF SNIFF SNIFF SNIFF SNIFF SNIFF SNIFF
Z
© 2006 PAWS, INC. All Rights Reserved.
SNIFF SNIFF SNIFF SNIFF SNIFF SNIFF
SNIFF SNIFF SNIFF SNIFF SNIFF SNIFF SNIFF SNIFF
DIG DIG DIG DIG DIG DIG DIG DIG
Z
Distributed by Universal Press Syndicate
JIM DAVIS 2-26

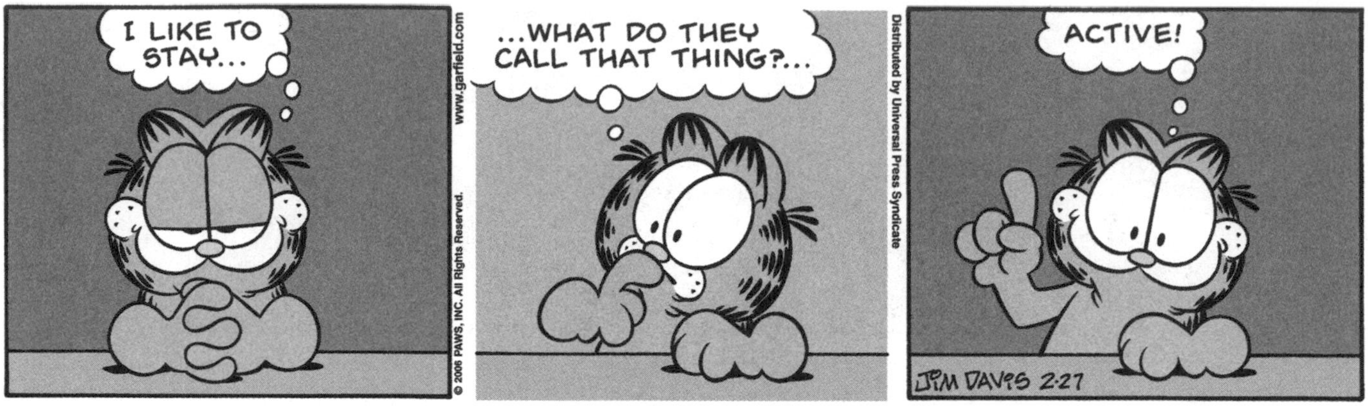
I LIKE TO STAY...
...WHAT DO THEY CALL THAT THING?...
ACTIVE!
JIM DAVIS 2-27
© 2006 PAWS, INC. All Rights Reserved. www.garfield.com
Distributed by Universal Press Syndicate

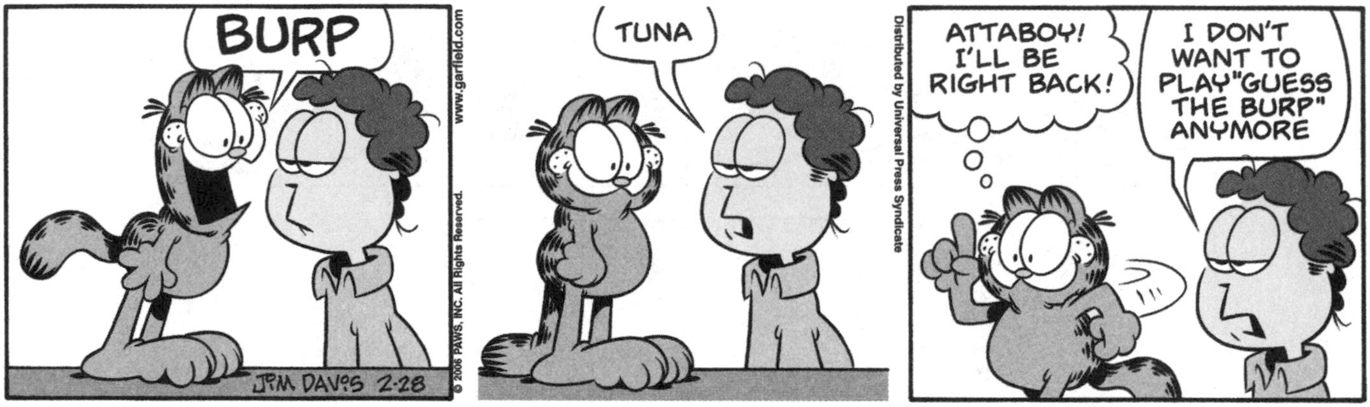
BURP
TUNA
ATTABOY! I'LL BE RIGHT BACK!
I DON'T WANT TO PLAY "GUESS THE BURP" ANYMORE
JIM DAVIS 2-28
© 2006 PAWS, INC. All Rights Reserved. www.garfield.com
Distributed by Universal Press Syndicate

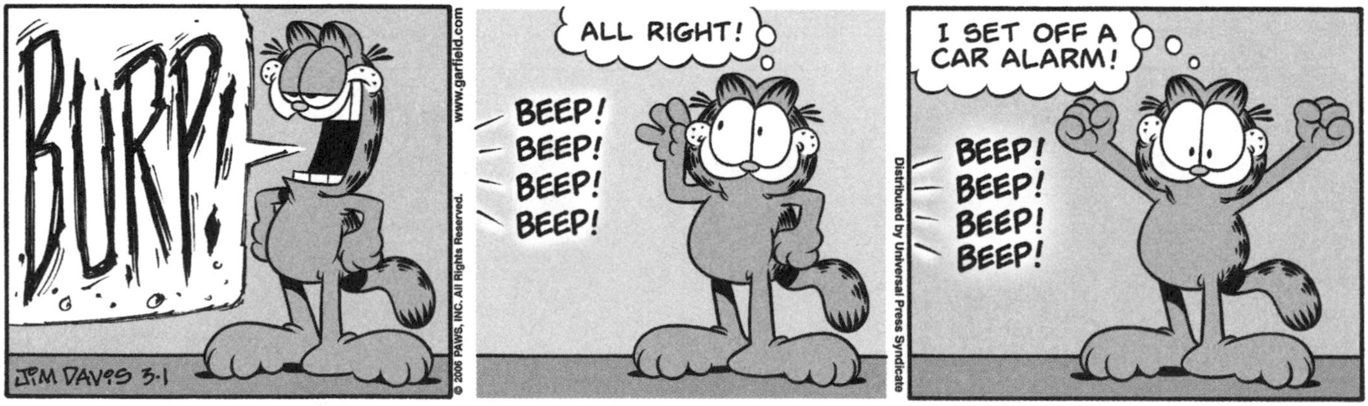
BURP!
ALL RIGHT!
BEEP! BEEP! BEEP! BEEP!
I SET OFF A CAR ALARM!
BEEP! BEEP! BEEP! BEEP!
JIM DAVIS 3-1
© 2006 PAWS, INC. All Rights Reserved. www.garfield.com
Distributed by Universal Press Syndicate

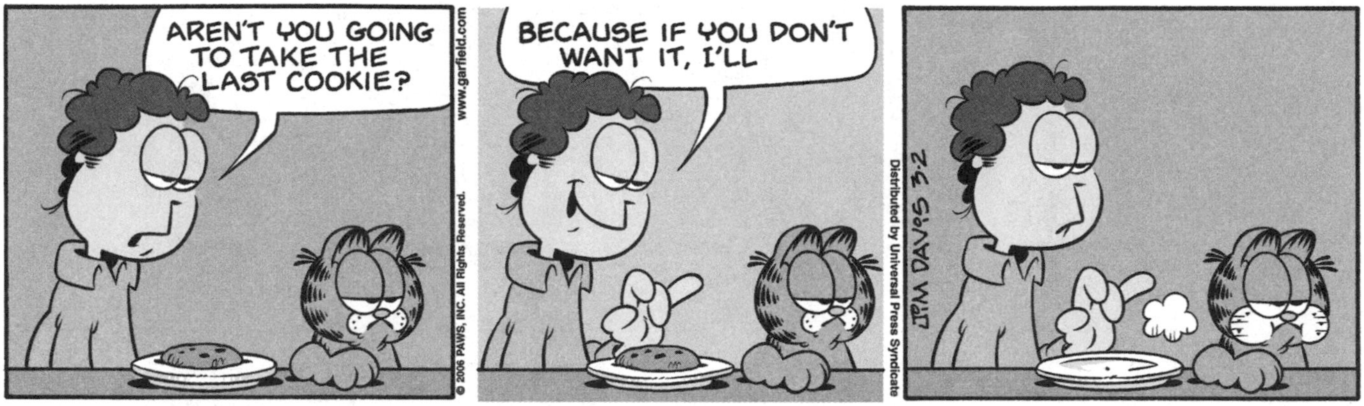
ARENT'T YOU GOING TO TAKE THE LAST COOKIE?
© 2006 PAWS, INC. All Rights Reserved. www.garfield.com
BECAUSE IF YOU DON'T WANT IT, I'LL
Distributed by Universal Press Syndicate
JIM DAVIS 3.2

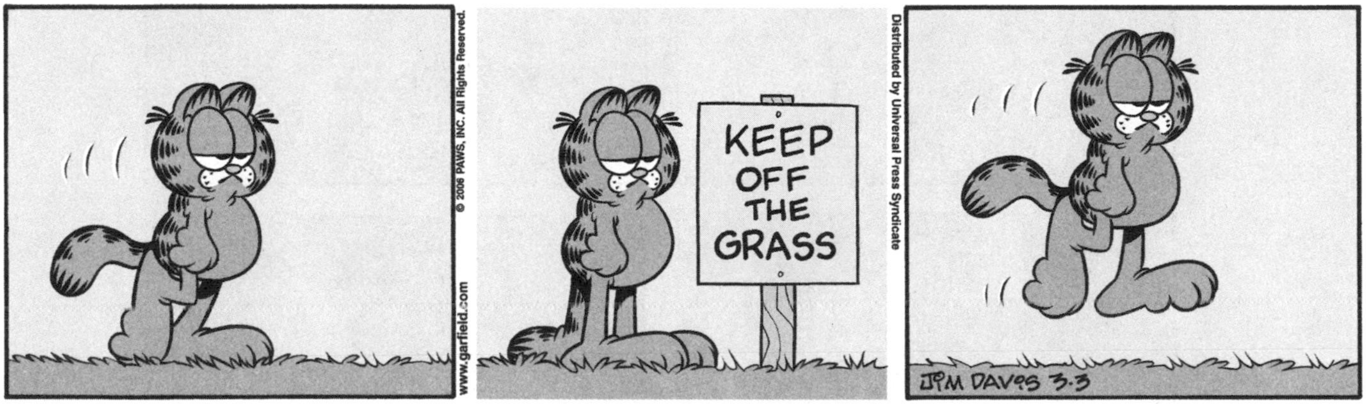
© 2006 PAWS, INC. All Rights Reserved. www.garfield.com
KEEP OFF THE GRASS
Distributed by Universal Press Syndicate
JIM DAVIS 3.3

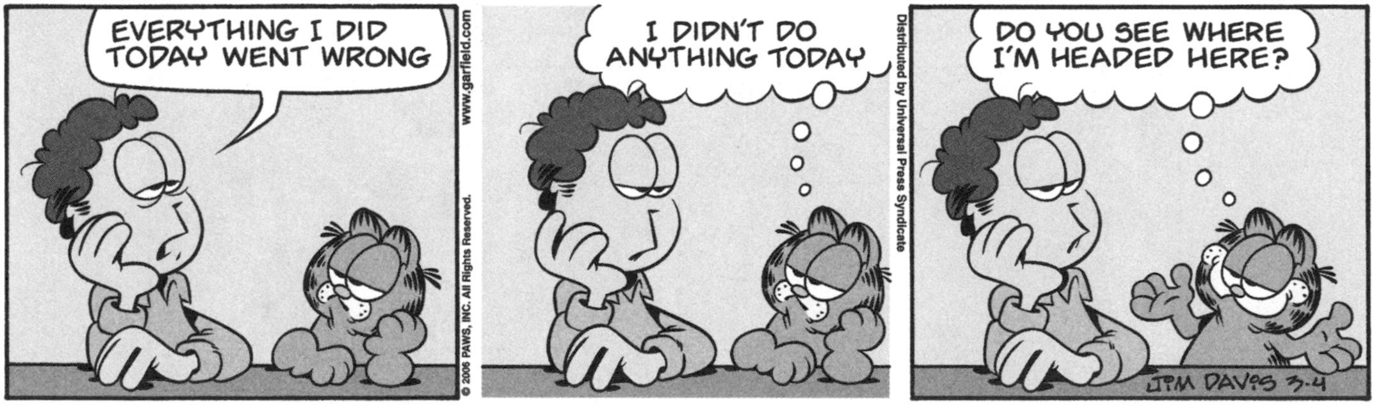
EVERYTHING I DID TODAY WENT WRONG
© 2006 PAWS, INC. All Rights Reserved. www.garfield.com
I DIDN'T DO ANYTHING TODAY
Distributed by Universal Press Syndicate
DO YOU SEE WHERE I'M HEADED HERE?
JIM DAVIS 3.4

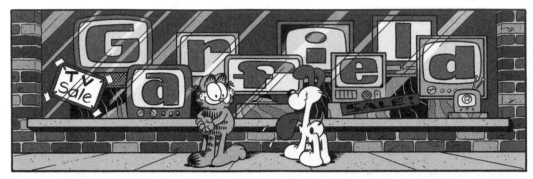

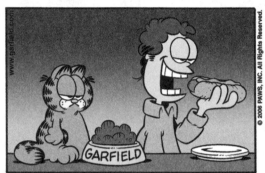

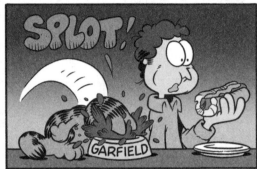

Garfield
TV Sale
SALE!
www.garfield.com
© 2006 PAWS, INC. All Rights Reserved.
GARFIELD
SPLOT!
GARFIELD
MUNCH
MUNCH
MUNCH
MUNCH
POO
CLONK
JIM DAVIS 3-5
Distributed by Universal Press Syndicate
GARFIELD
YOU'VE GOT A LITTLE MUSTARD RIIIGHT THERE
GARFIELD

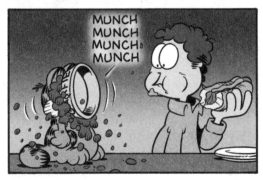

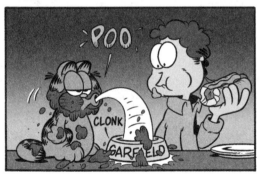

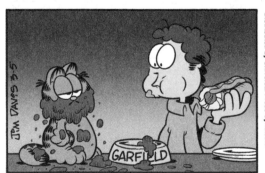

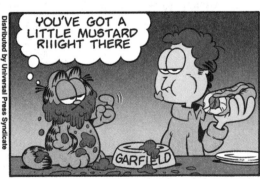

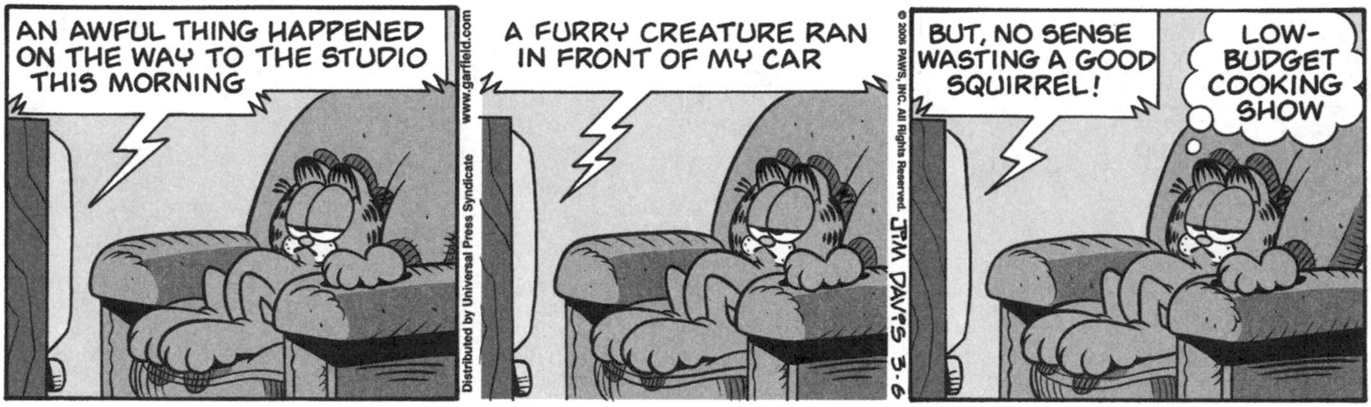
AN AWFUL THING HAPPENED ON THE WAY TO THE STUDIO THIS MORNING
A FURRY CREATURE RAN IN FRONT OF MY CAR
BUT, NO SENSE WASTING A GOOD SQUIRREL!
LOW-BUDGET COOKING SHOW

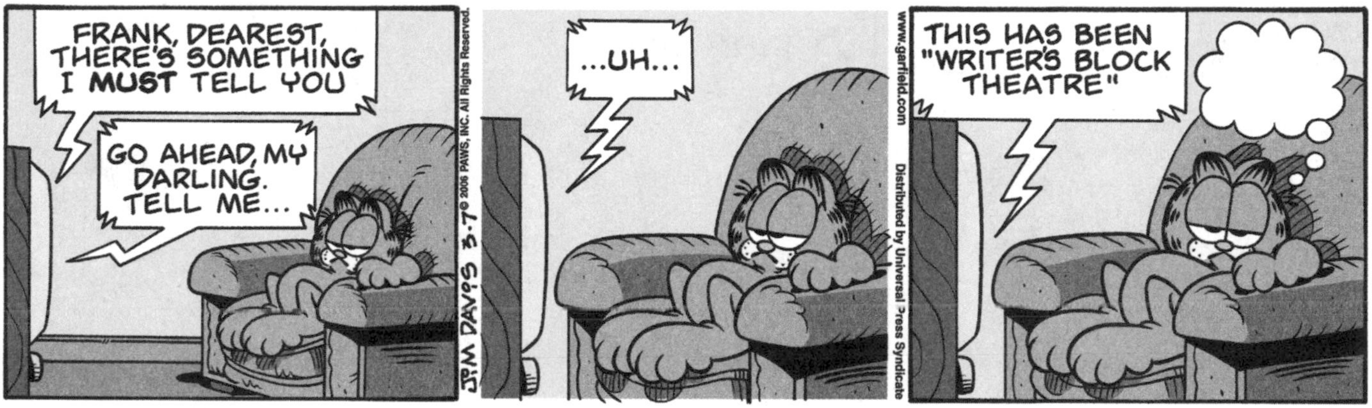
FRANK, DEAREST, THERE'S SOMETHING I **MUST** TELL YOU
GO AHEAD, MY DARLING. TELL ME...
...UH...
THIS HAS BEEN "WRITER'S BLOCK THEATRE"

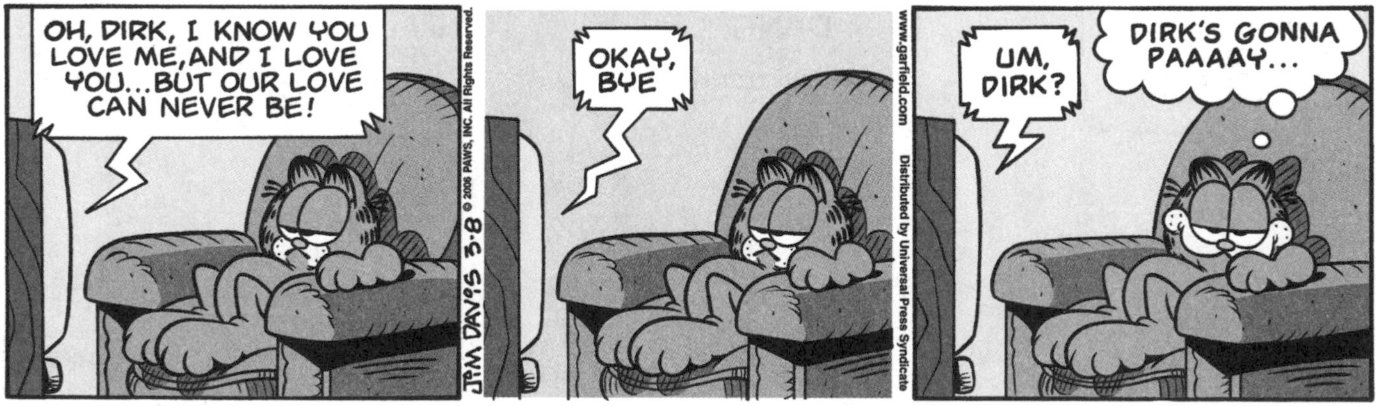
OH, DIRK, I KNOW YOU LOVE ME, AND I LOVE YOU...BUT OUR LOVE CAN NEVER BE!
OKAY, BYE
UM, DIRK?
DIRK'S GONNA PAAAAY...

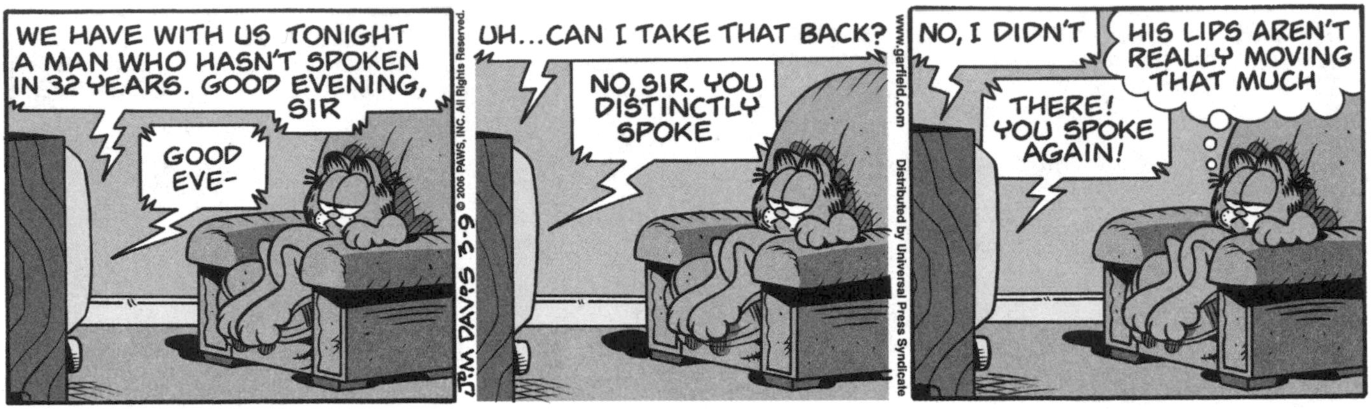
WE HAVE WITH US TONIGHT A MAN WHO HASN'T SPOKEN IN 32 YEARS. GOOD EVENING, SIR
GOOD EVE-
JIM DAVIS 3-9
© 2006 PAWS, INC. All Rights Reserved.
UH... CAN I TAKE THAT BACK?
NO, SIR. YOU DISTINCTLY SPOKE
www.garfield.com
Distributed by Universal Press Syndicate
NO, I DIDN'T
THERE! YOU SPOKE AGAIN!
HIS LIPS AREN'T REALLY MOVING THAT MUCH

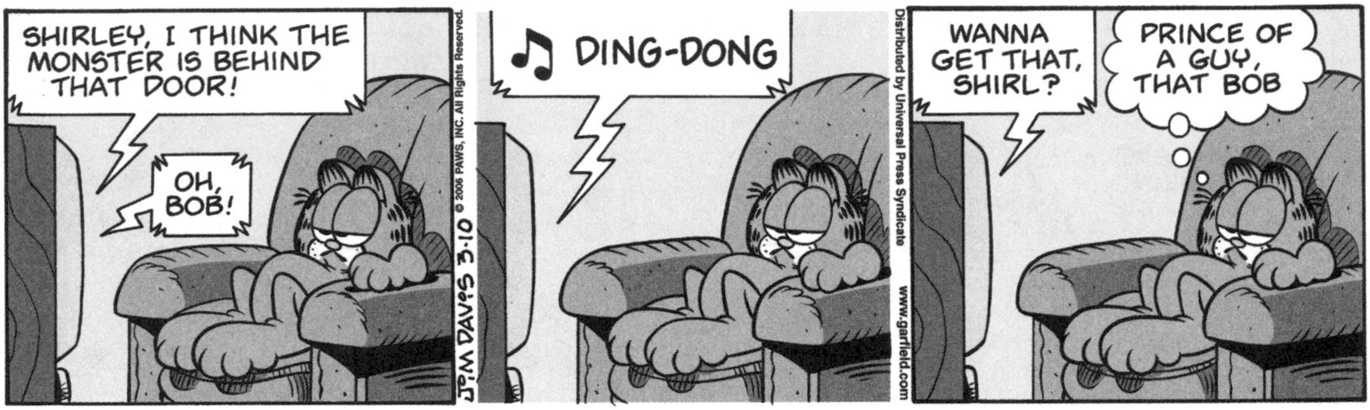
SHIRLEY, I THINK THE MONSTER IS BEHIND THAT DOOR!
OH, BOB!
JIM DAVIS 3-10
© 2006 PAWS, INC. All Rights Reserved.
♫ DING-DONG
Distributed by Universal Press Syndicate
www.garfield.com
WANNA GET THAT, SHIRL?
PRINCE OF A GUY, THAT BOB

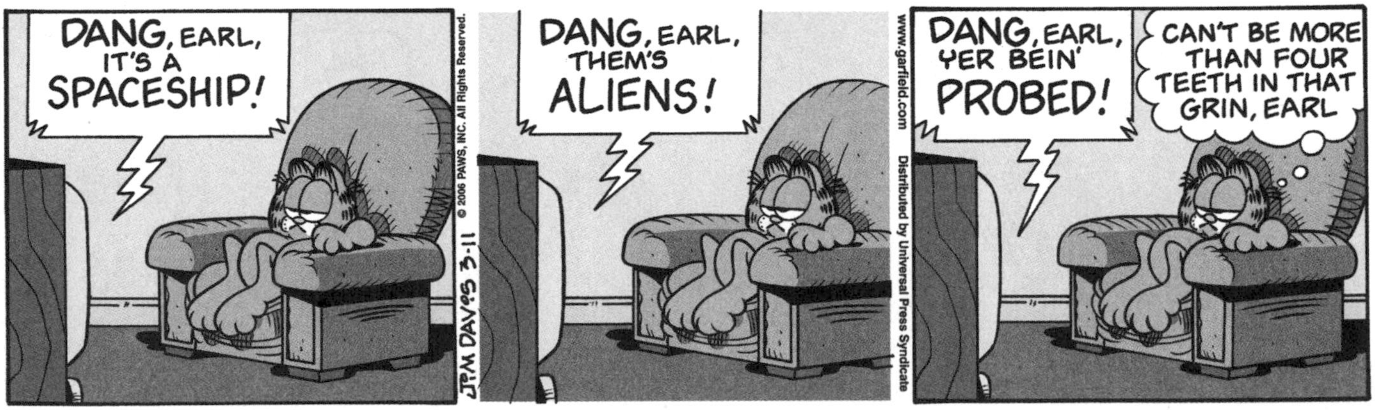
DANG, EARL, IT'S A SPACESHIP!
JIM DAVIS 3-11
© 2006 PAWS, INC. All Rights Reserved.
DANG, EARL, THEM'S ALIENS!
www.garfield.com
Distributed by Universal Press Syndicate
DANG, EARL, YER BEIN' PROBED!
CAN'T BE MORE THAN FOUR TEETH IN THAT GRIN, EARL

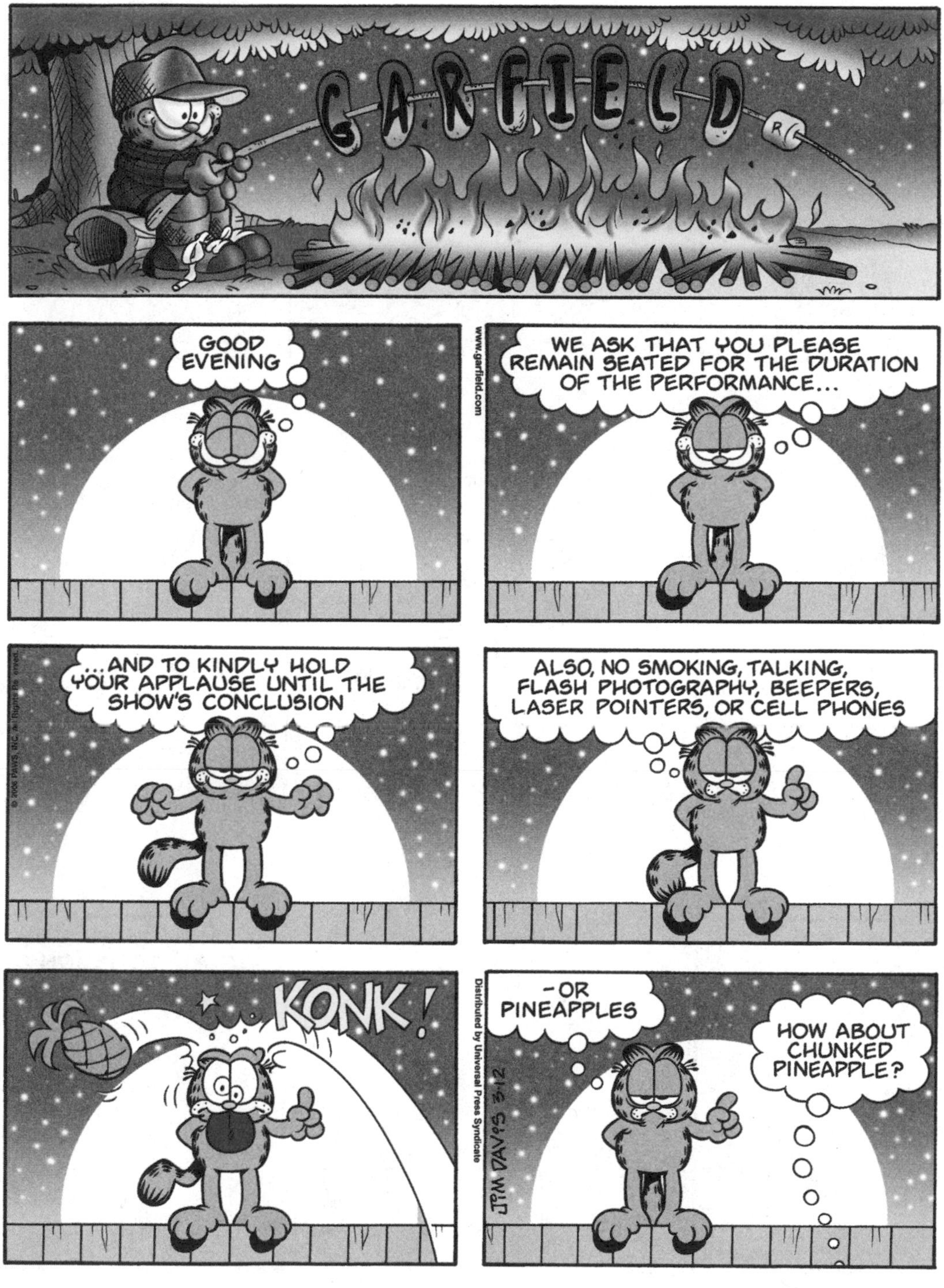
GARFIELD
www.garfield.com
GOOD EVENING
WE ASK THAT YOU PLEASE REMAIN SEATED FOR THE DURATION OF THE PERFORMANCE...
© 2006 PAWS, INC. All Rights Reserved.
...AND TO KINDLY HOLD YOUR APPLAUSE UNTIL THE SHOW'S CONCLUSION
ALSO, NO SMOKING, TALKING, FLASH PHOTOGRAPHY, BEEPERS, LASER POINTERS, OR CELL PHONES
KONK!
Distributed by Universal Press Syndicate
JIM DAVIS 3-12
-OR PINEAPPLES
HOW ABOUT CHUNKED PINEAPPLE?

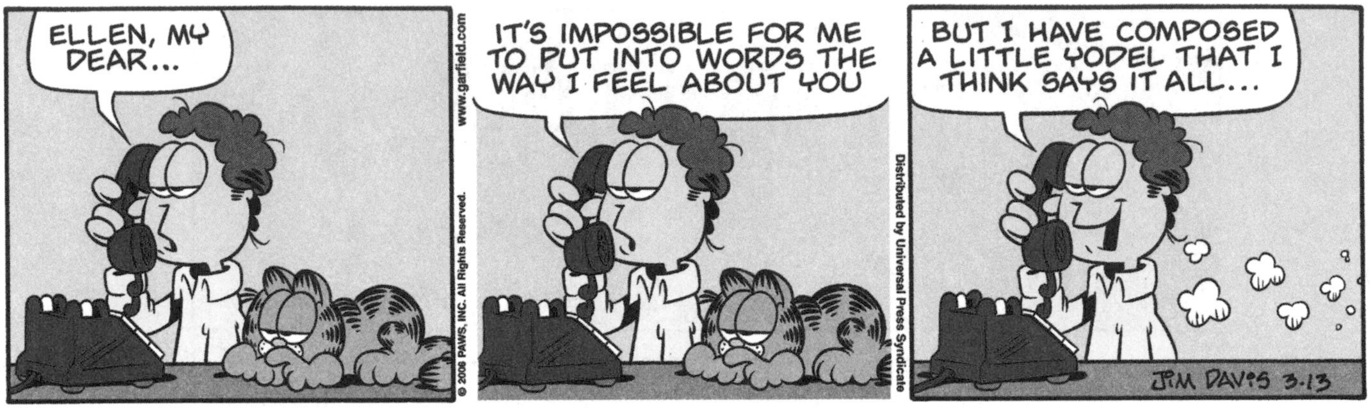
ELLEN, MY DEAR...
IT'S IMPOSSIBLE FOR ME TO PUT INTO WORDS THE WAY I FEEL ABOUT YOU
BUT I HAVE COMPOSED A LITTLE YODEL THAT I THINK SAYS IT ALL...
JIM DAVIS 3-13
© 2006 PAWS, INC. All Rights Reserved.
www.garfield.com
Distributed by Universal Press Syndicate

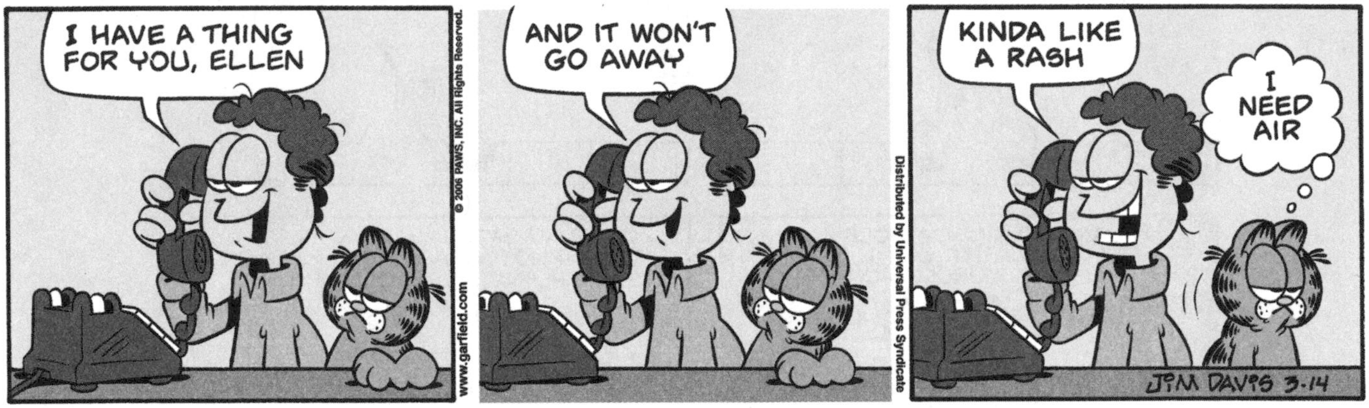
I HAVE A THING FOR YOU, ELLEN
AND IT WON'T GO AWAY
KINDA LIKE A RASH
I NEED AIR
JIM DAVIS 3-14
© 2006 PAWS, INC. All Rights Reserved.
www.garfield.com
Distributed by Universal Press Syndicate

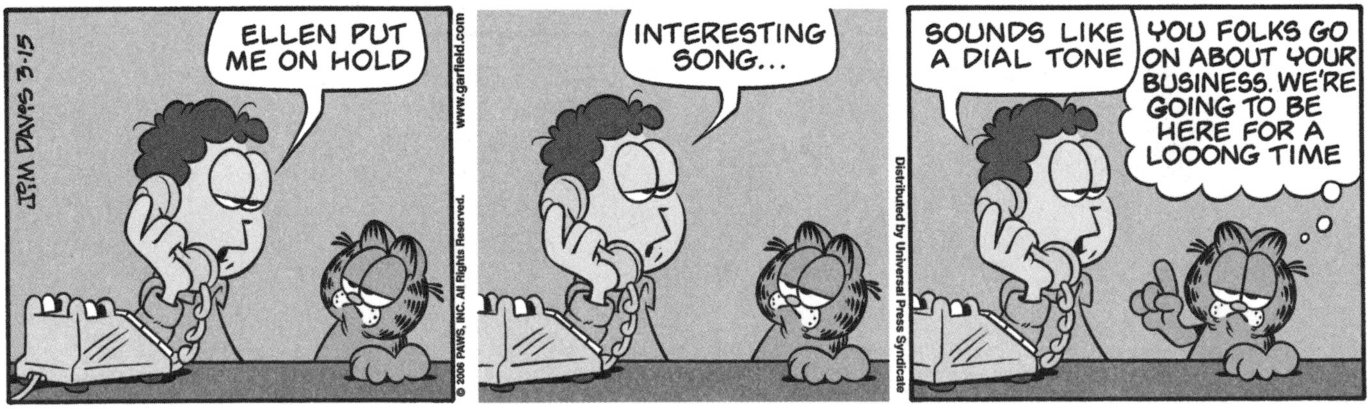
JIM DAVIS 3-15
ELLEN PUT ME ON HOLD
INTERESTING SONG...
SOUNDS LIKE A DIAL TONE
YOU FOLKS GO ON ABOUT YOUR BUSINESS. WE'RE GOING TO BE HERE FOR A LOOONG TIME
© 2006 PAWS, INC. All Rights Reserved.
www.garfield.com
Distributed by Universal Press Syndicate

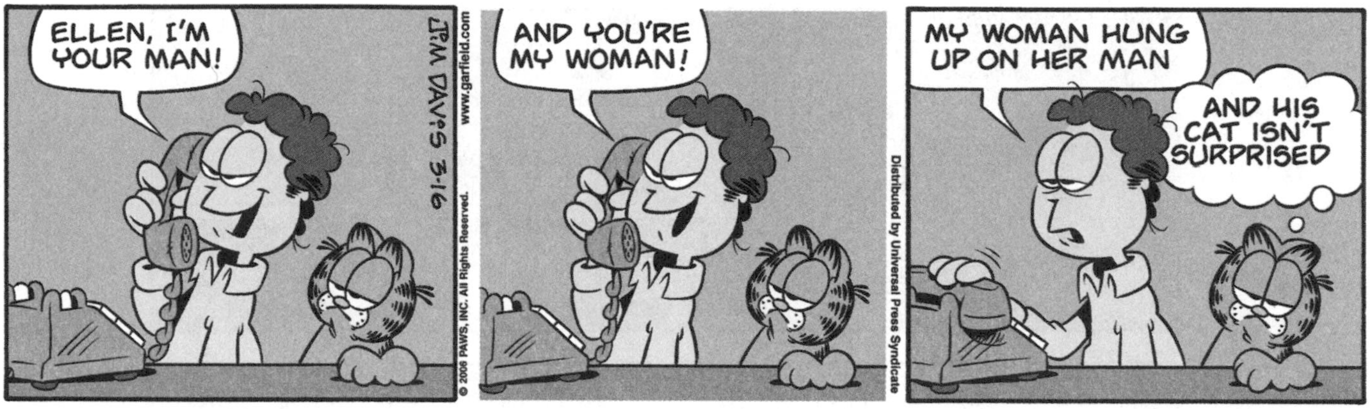
ELLEN, I'M YOUR MAN!
JIM DAVIS 3-16
www.garfield.com
© 2006 PAWS, INC. All Rights Reserved.
AND YOU'RE MY WOMAN!
Distributed by Universal Press Syndicate
MY WOMAN HUNG UP ON HER MAN
AND HIS CAT ISN'T SURPRISED

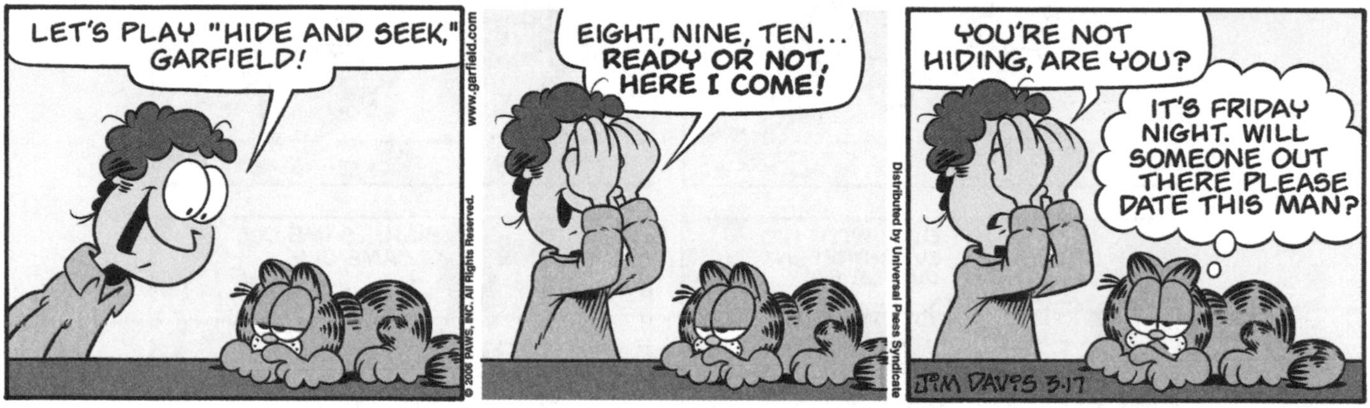
LET'S PLAY "HIDE AND SEEK," GARFIELD!
www.garfield.com
© 2006 PAWS, INC. All Rights Reserved.
EIGHT, NINE, TEN... READY OR NOT, HERE I COME!
Distributed by Universal Press Syndicate
YOU'RE NOT HIDING, ARE YOU?
IT'S FRIDAY NIGHT. WILL SOMEONE OUT THERE PLEASE DATE THIS MAN?
JIM DAVIS 3-17

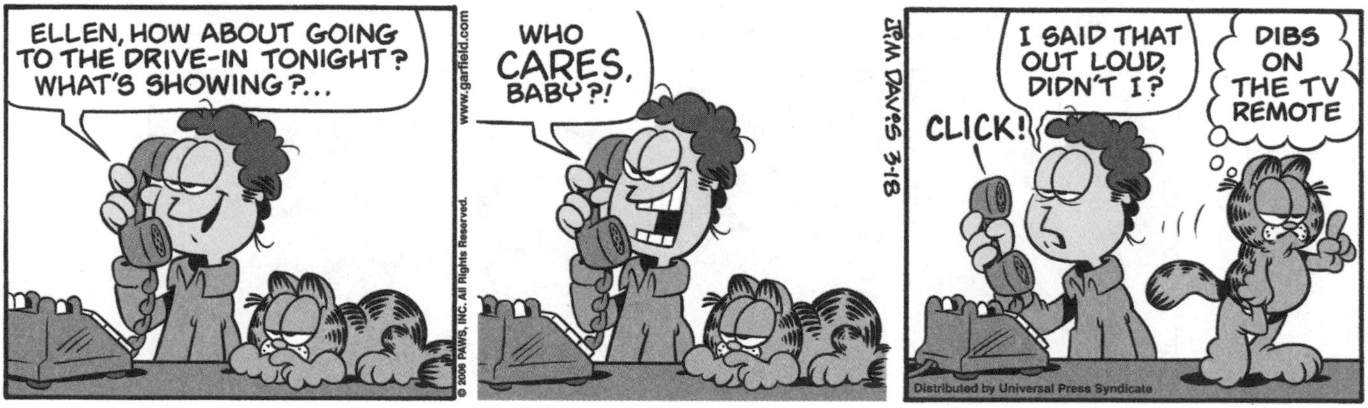
ELLEN, HOW ABOUT GOING TO THE DRIVE-IN TONIGHT? WHAT'S SHOWING?...
www.garfield.com
© 2006 PAWS, INC. All Rights Reserved.
WHO CARES, BABY?!
JIM DAVIS 3-18
CLICK!
I SAID THAT OUT LOUD, DIDN'T I?
DIBS ON THE TV REMOTE
Distributed by Universal Press Syndicate

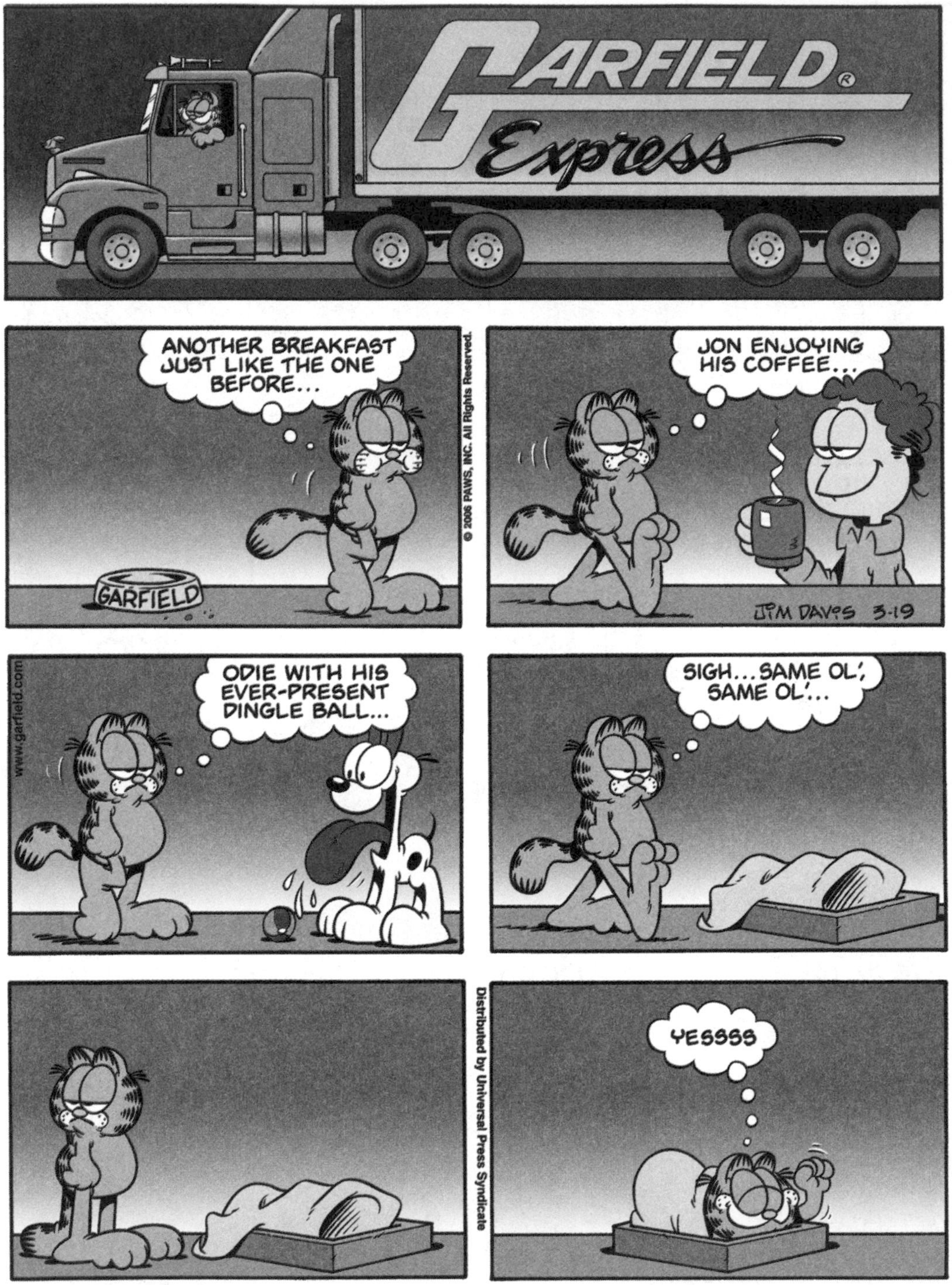
GARFIELD®
Express
ANOTHER BREAKFAST JUST LIKE THE ONE BEFORE...
GARFIELD
© 2006 PAWS, INC. All Rights Reserved.
JON ENJOYING HIS COFFEE...
JIM DAVIS 3-19
www.garfield.com
ODIE WITH HIS EVER-PRESENT DINGLE BALL...
SIGH... SAME OL', SAME OL'...
Distributed by Universal Press Syndicate
YESSSS

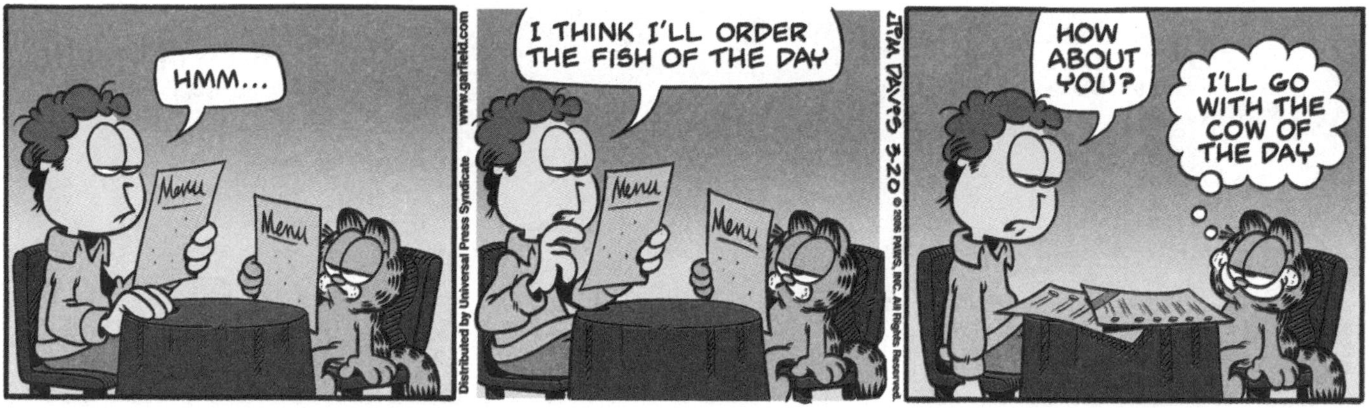
HMM...
www.garfield.com
Distributed by Universal Press Syndicate
I THINK I'LL ORDER THE FISH OF THE DAY
JPM DAVIS 3-20
© 2006 PAWS, INC. All Rights Reserved.
HOW ABOUT YOU?
I'LL GO WITH THE COW OF THE DAY

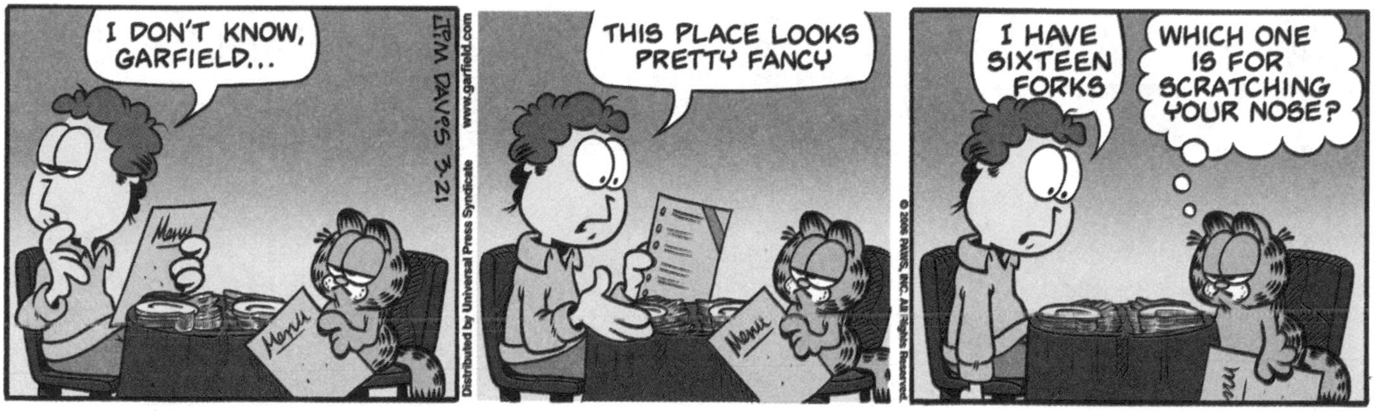
I DON'T KNOW, GARFIELD...
JPM DAVIS 3-21
www.garfield.com
Distributed by Universal Press Syndicate
THIS PLACE LOOKS PRETTY FANCY
© 2006 PAWS, INC. All Rights Reserved.
I HAVE SIXTEEN FORKS
WHICH ONE IS FOR SCRATCHING YOUR NOSE?

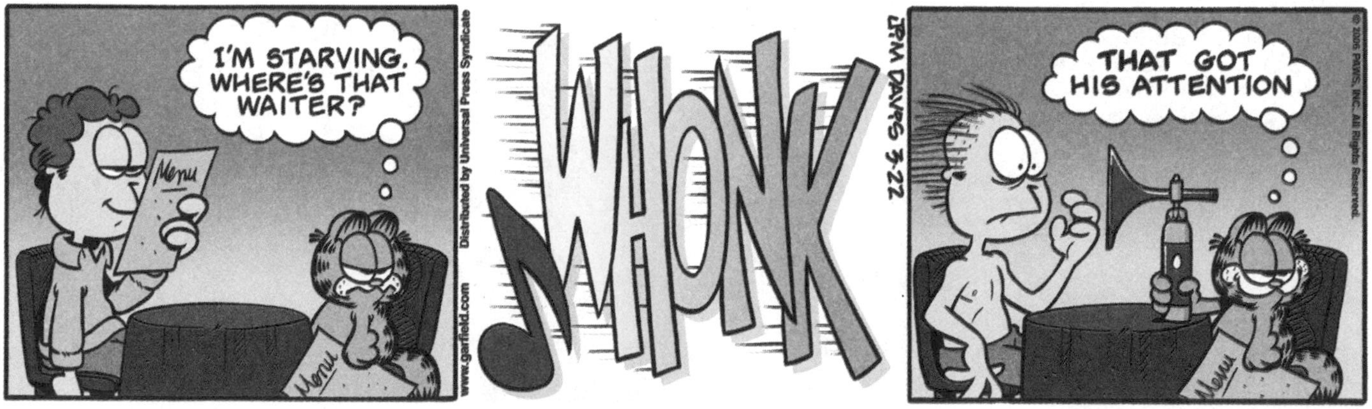
I'M STARVING. WHERE'S THAT WAITER?
Distributed by Universal Press Syndicate
www.garfield.com
WHONK
JPM DAVIS 3-22
THAT GOT HIS ATTENTION
© 2006 PAWS, INC. All Rights Reserved.

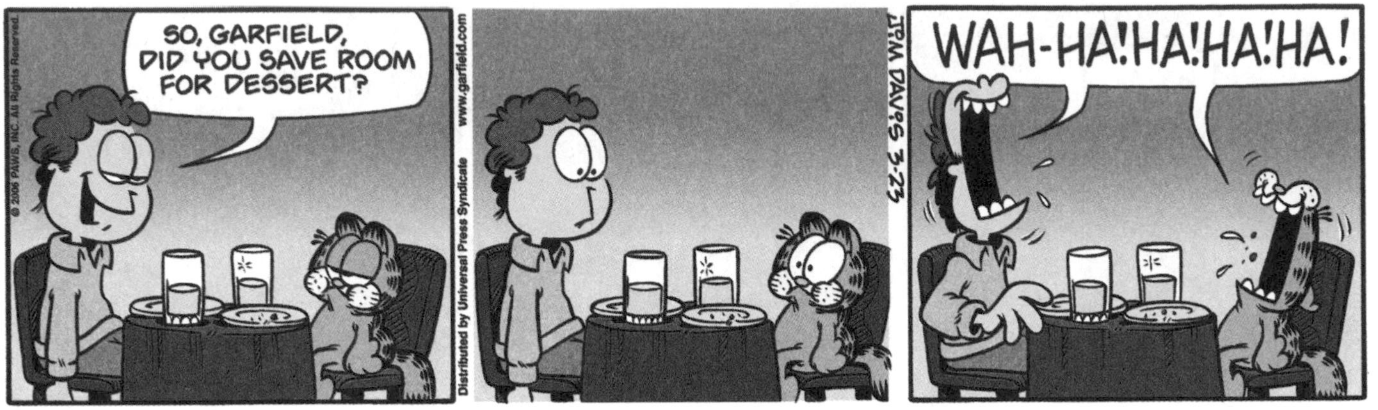
SO, GARFIELD, DID YOU SAVE ROOM FOR DESSERT?
WAH-HA! HA! HA! HA!
© 2006 PAWS, INC. All Rights Reserved.
Distributed by Universal Press Syndicate www.garfield.com
JIM DAVIS 3-23

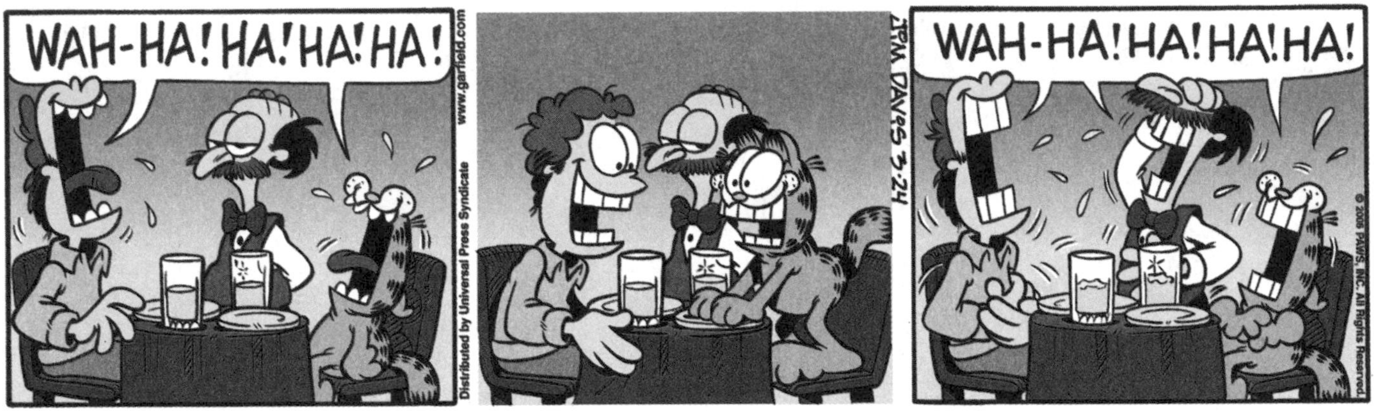
WAH-HA! HA! HA! HA!
WAH-HA! HA! HA! HA!
Distributed by Universal Press Syndicate www.garfield.com
JIM DAVIS 3-24
© 2006 PAWS, INC. All Rights Reserved.

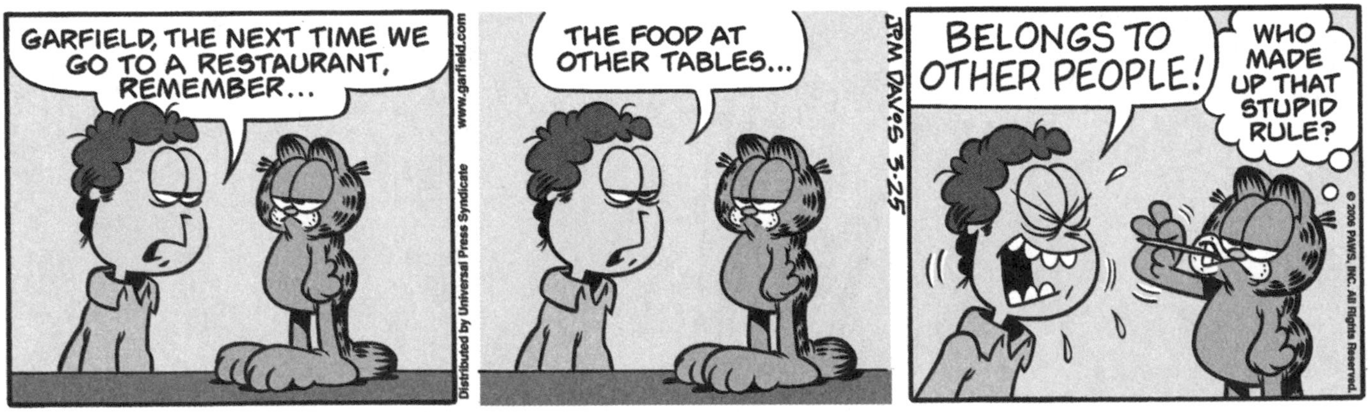
GARFIELD, THE NEXT TIME WE GO TO A RESTAURANT, REMEMBER...
THE FOOD AT OTHER TABLES...
BELONGS TO OTHER PEOPLE!
WHO MADE UP THAT STUPID RULE?
Distributed by Universal Press Syndicate www.garfield.com
JIM DAVIS 3-25
© 2006 PAWS, INC. All Rights Reserved.

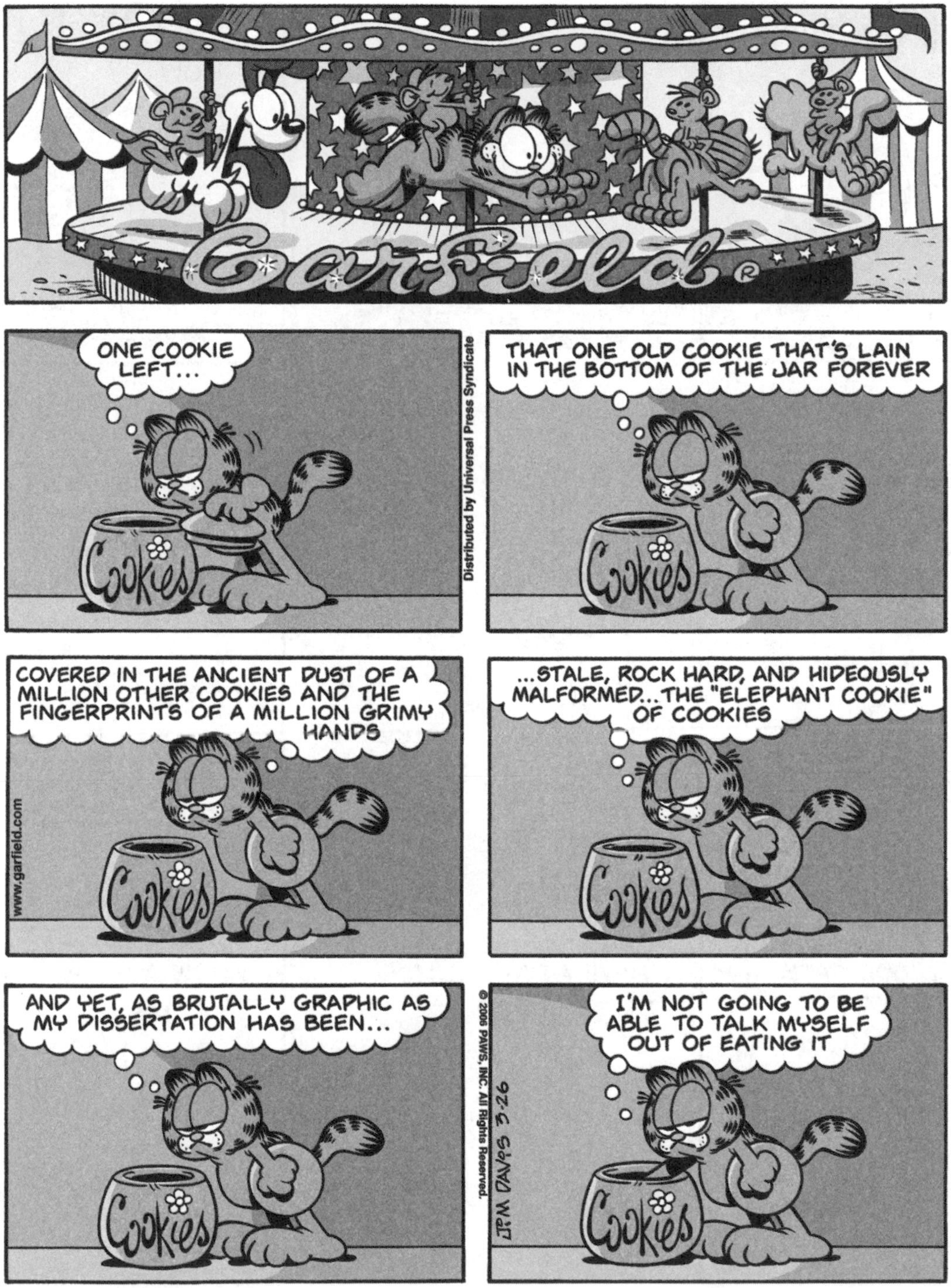
Garfield
ONE COOKIE LEFT...
Distributed by Universal Press Syndicate
THAT ONE OLD COOKIE THAT'S LAIN IN THE BOTTOM OF THE JAR FOREVER
COVERED IN THE ANCIENT DUST OF A MILLION OTHER COOKIES AND THE FINGERPRINTS OF A MILLION GRIMY HANDS
www.garfield.com
...STALE, ROCK HARD, AND HIDEOUSLY MALFORMED...THE "ELEPHANT COOKIE" OF COOKIES
AND YET, AS BRUTALLY GRAPHIC AS MY DISSERTATION HAS BEEN...
© 2006 PAWS, INC. All Rights Reserved.
JIM DAVIS 3-26
I'M NOT GOING TO BE ABLE TO TALK MYSELF OUT OF EATING IT

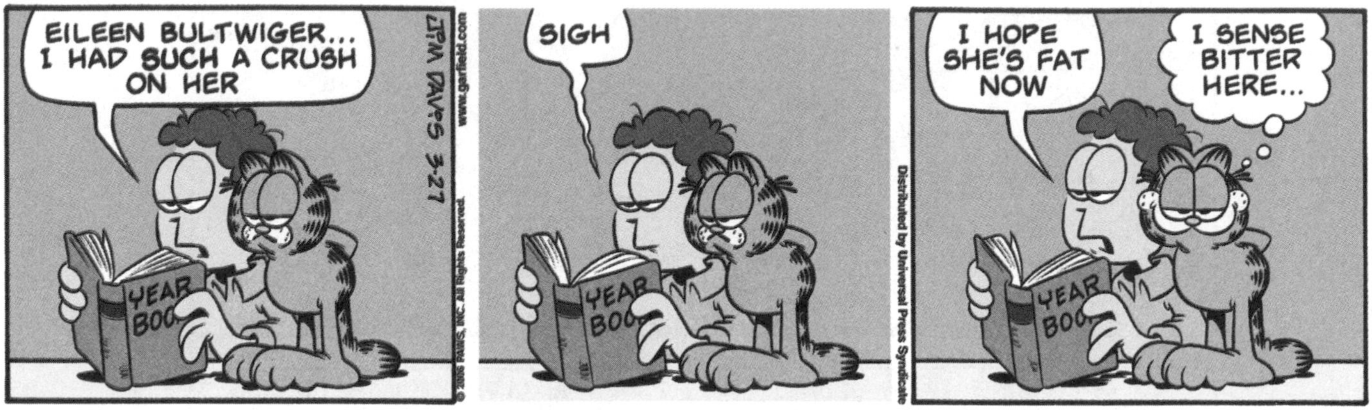
EILEEN BULTWIGER... I HAD SUCH A CRUSH ON HER
JIM DAVIS 3-27
SIGH
I HOPE SHE'S FAT NOW
I SENSE BITTER HERE...

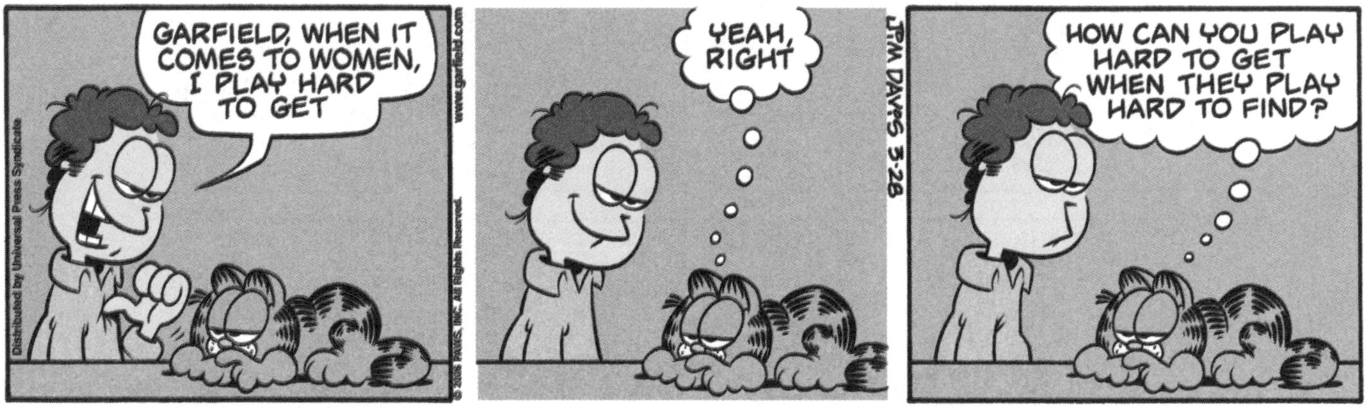
GARFIELD, WHEN IT COMES TO WOMEN, I PLAY HARD TO GET
YEAH, RIGHT
JIM DAVIS 3-28
HOW CAN YOU PLAY HARD TO GET WHEN THEY PLAY HARD TO FIND?

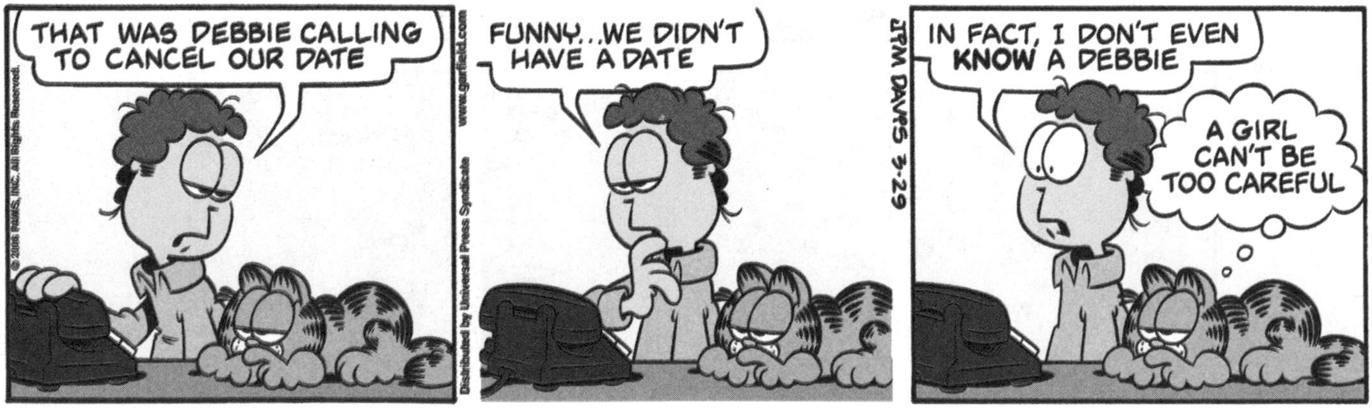
THAT WAS DEBBIE CALLING TO CANCEL OUR DATE
FUNNY...WE DIDN'T HAVE A DATE
JIM DAVIS 3-29
IN FACT, I DON'T EVEN KNOW A DEBBIE
A GIRL CAN'T BE TOO CAREFUL

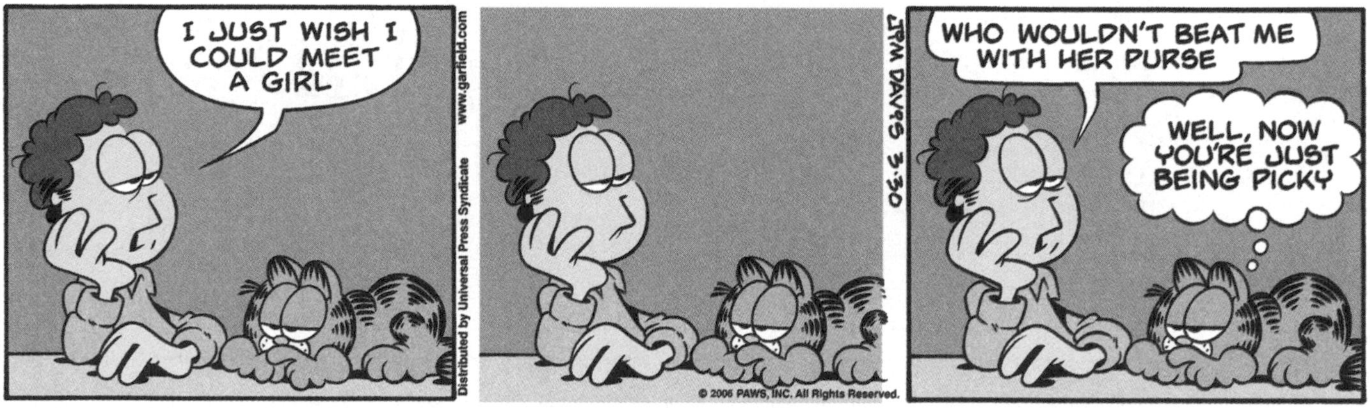
I JUST WISH I COULD MEET A GIRL
www.garfield.com
Distributed by Universal Press Syndicate
JIM DAVIS 3.30
WHO WOULDN'T BEAT ME WITH HER PURSE
WELL, NOW YOU'RE JUST BEING PICKY
© 2006 PAWS, INC. All Rights Reserved.

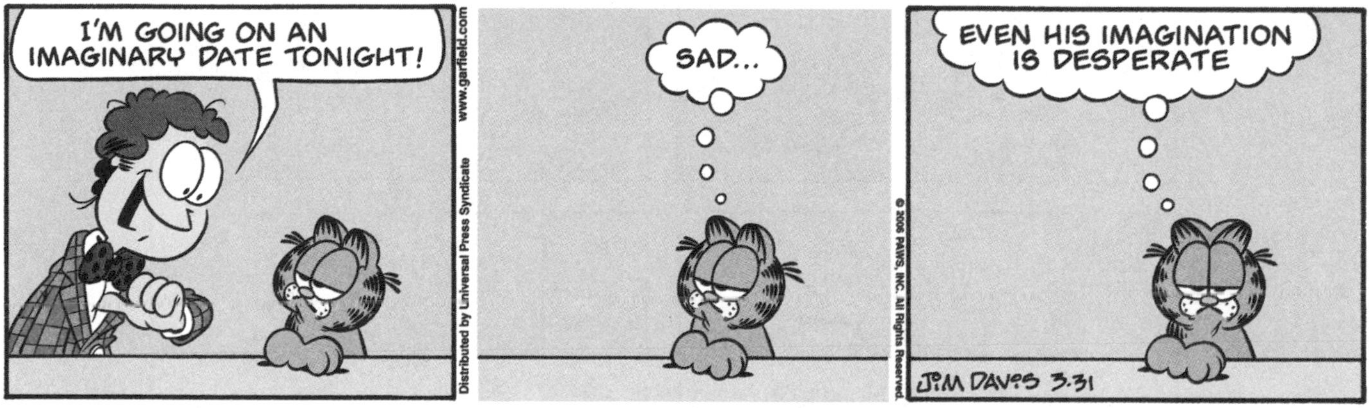
I'M GOING ON AN IMAGINARY DATE TONIGHT!
www.garfield.com
Distributed by Universal Press Syndicate
SAD...
© 2006 PAWS, INC. All Rights Reserved.
EVEN HIS IMAGINATION IS DESPERATE
JIM DAVIS 3.31

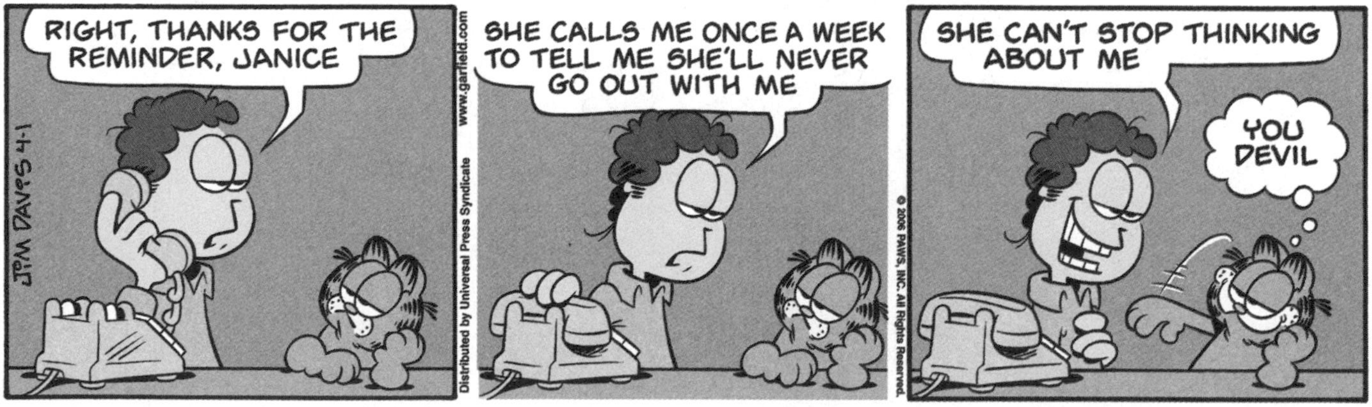
RIGHT, THANKS FOR THE REMINDER, JANICE
JIM DAVIS 4-1
www.garfield.com
Distributed by Universal Press Syndicate
SHE CALLS ME ONCE A WEEK TO TELL ME SHE'LL NEVER GO OUT WITH ME
© 2006 PAWS, INC. All Rights Reserved.
SHE CAN'T STOP THINKING ABOUT ME
YOU DEVIL

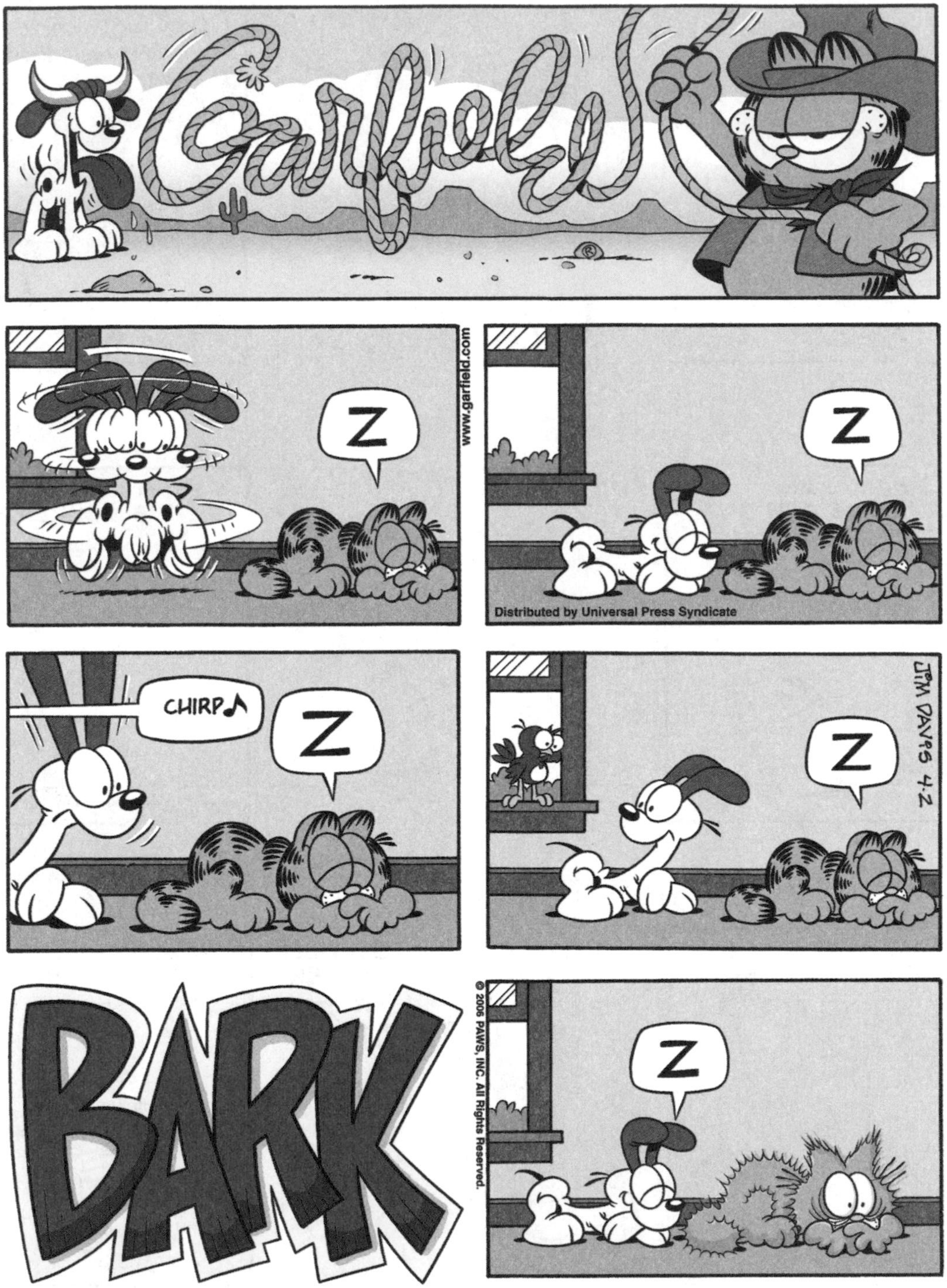
Garfield
Z
www.garfield.com
Z
Distributed by Universal Press Syndicate
CHIRP♪
Z
Z
JIM DAVIS 4-2
BARK
© 2006 PAWS, INC. All Rights Reserved.
Z

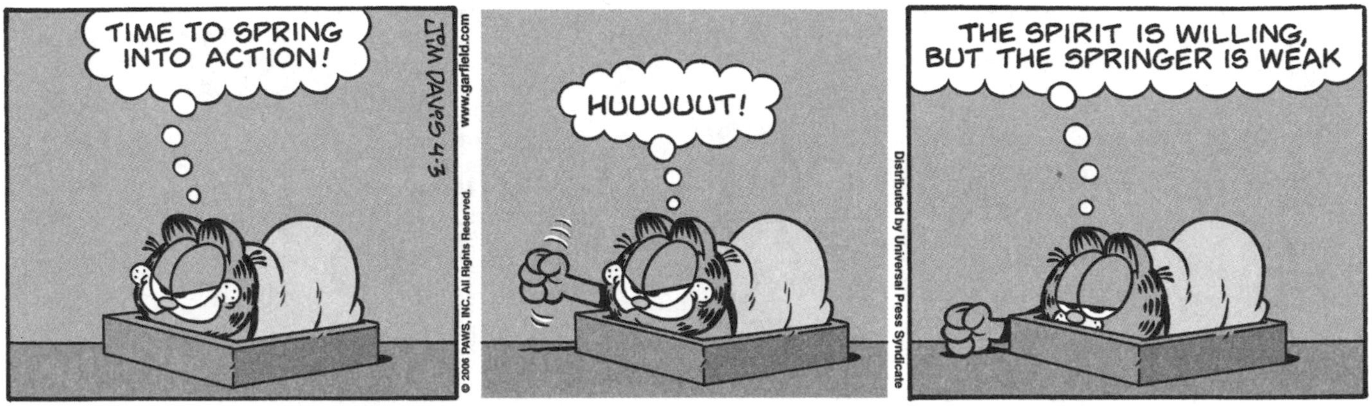
TIME TO SPRING INTO ACTION!
JIM DAVIS 4-3
www.garfield.com
© 2006 PAWS, INC. All Rights Reserved.
HUUUUUT!
Distributed by Universal Press Syndicate
THE SPIRIT IS WILLING, BUT THE SPRINGER IS WEAK

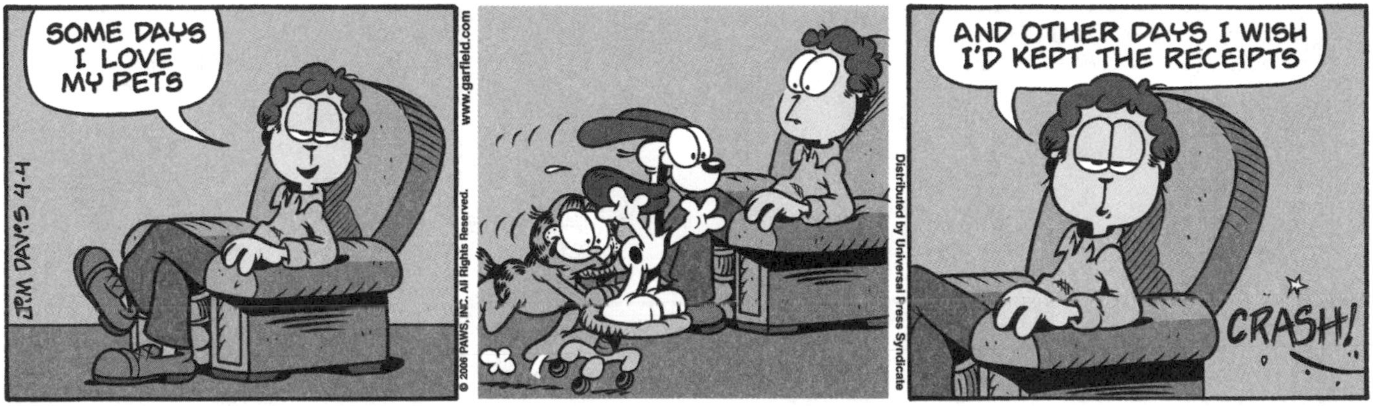
SOME DAYS I LOVE MY PETS
JIM DAVIS 4-4
www.garfield.com
© 2006 PAWS, INC. All Rights Reserved.
Distributed by Universal Press Syndicate
AND OTHER DAYS I WISH I'D KEPT THE RECEIPTS
CRASH!

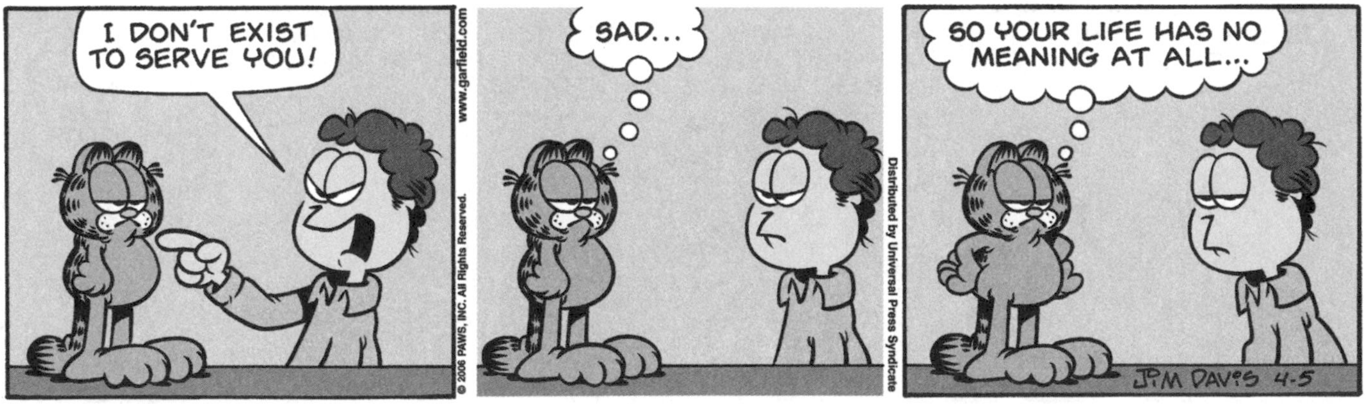
I DON'T EXIST TO SERVE YOU!
www.garfield.com
© 2006 PAWS, INC. All Rights Reserved.
SAD...
Distributed by Universal Press Syndicate
SO YOUR LIFE HAS NO MEANING AT ALL...
JIM DAVIS 4-5

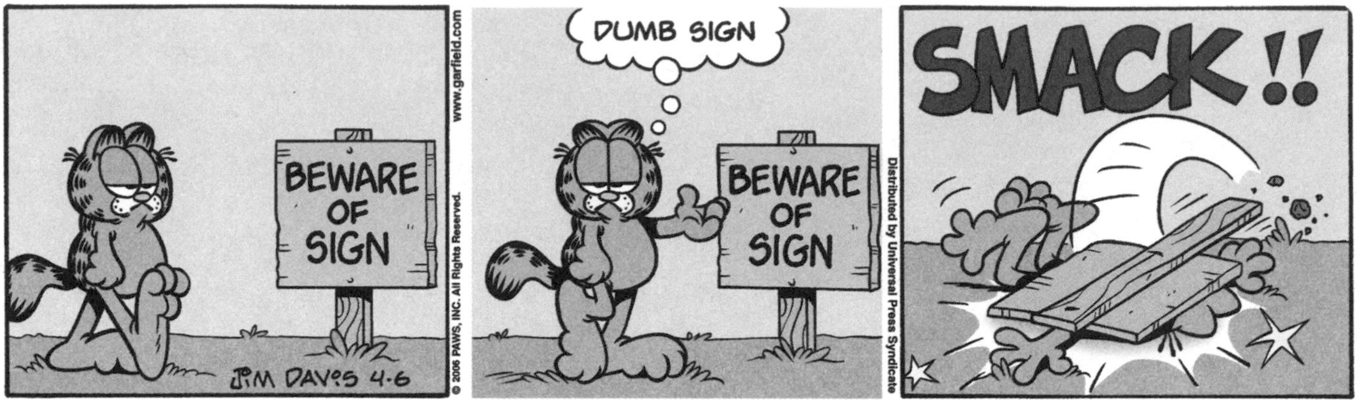
BEWARE OF SIGN
JIM DAVIS 4-6
© 2006 PAWS, INC. All Rights Reserved. www.garfield.com
DUMB SIGN
BEWARE OF SIGN
Distributed by Universal Press Syndicate
SMACK!!

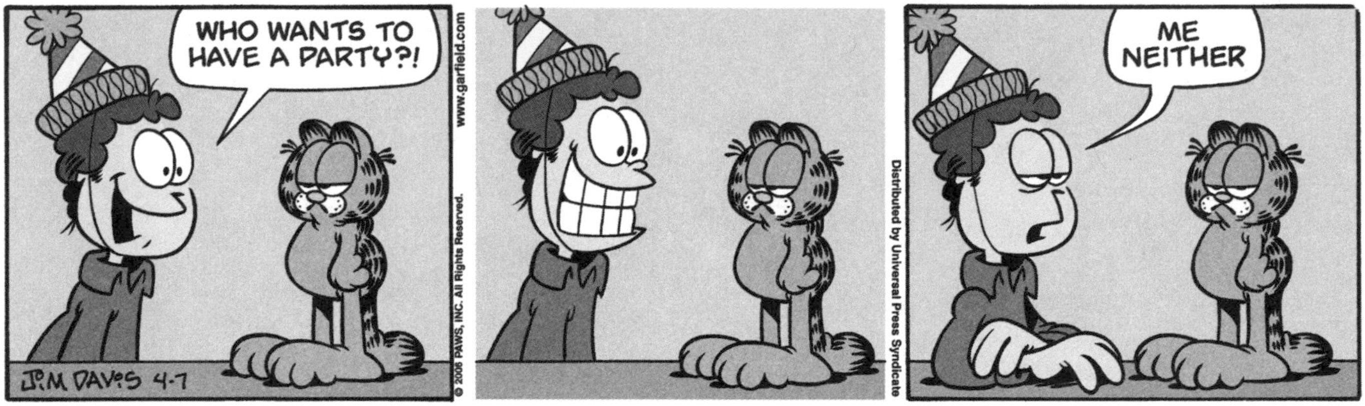
WHO WANTS TO HAVE A PARTY?!
JIM DAVIS 4-7
© 2006 PAWS, INC. All Rights Reserved. www.garfield.com
Distributed by Universal Press Syndicate
ME NEITHER

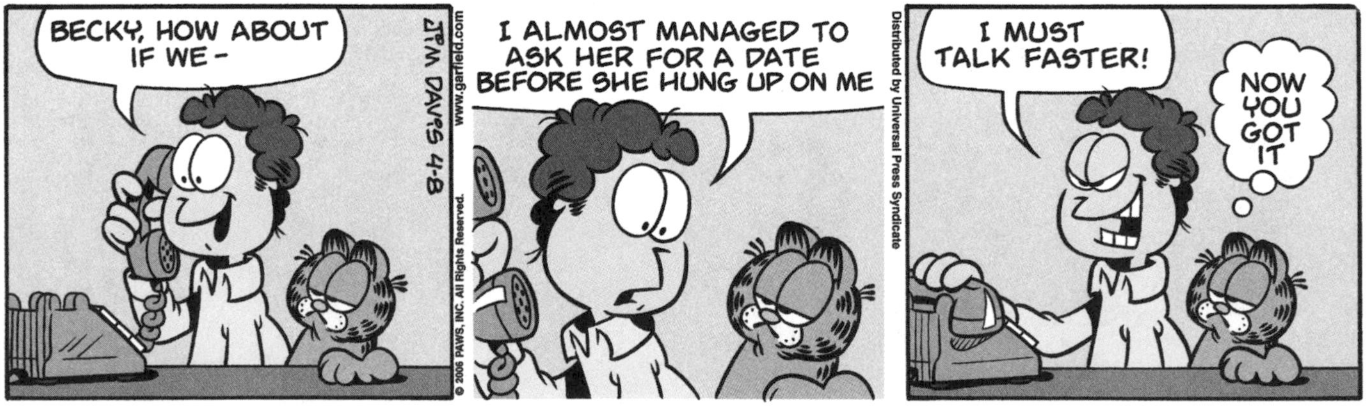
BECKY, HOW ABOUT IF WE -
JIM DAVIS 4-8
© 2006 PAWS, INC. All Rights Reserved. www.garfield.com
I ALMOST MANAGED TO ASK HER FOR A DATE BEFORE SHE HUNG UP ON ME
Distributed by Universal Press Syndicate
I MUST TALK FASTER!
NOW YOU GOT IT

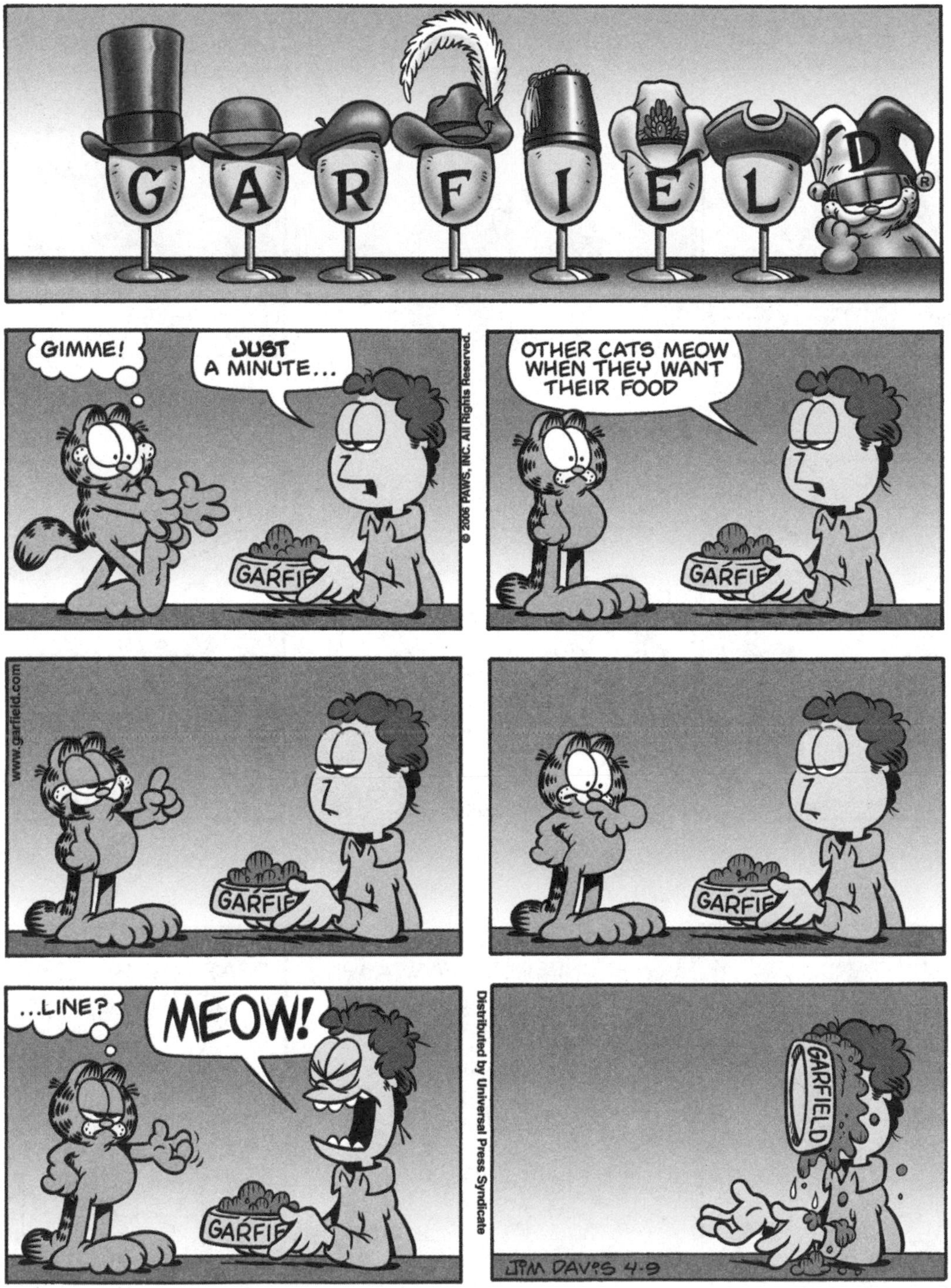
GARFIELD
GIMME!
JUST A MINUTE...
© 2006 PAWS, INC. All Rights Reserved.
OTHER CATS MEOW WHEN THEY WANT THEIR FOOD
www.garfield.com
...LINE?
MEOW!
Distributed by Universal Press Syndicate
GARFIELD
JIM DAVIS 4-9

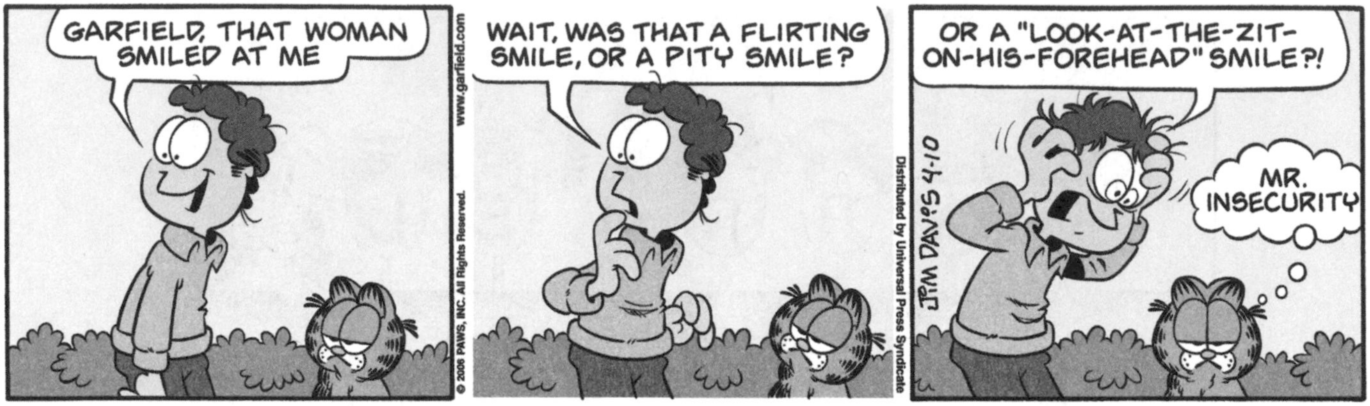
GARFIELD, THAT WOMAN SMILED AT ME
WAIT, WAS THAT A FLIRTING SMILE, OR A PITY SMILE?
OR A "LOOK-AT-THE-ZIT-ON-HIS-FOREHEAD" SMILE?!
MR. INSECURITY
© 2006 PAWS, INC. All Rights Reserved. www.garfield.com
Distributed by Universal Press Syndicate
JPM DAVIS 4-10

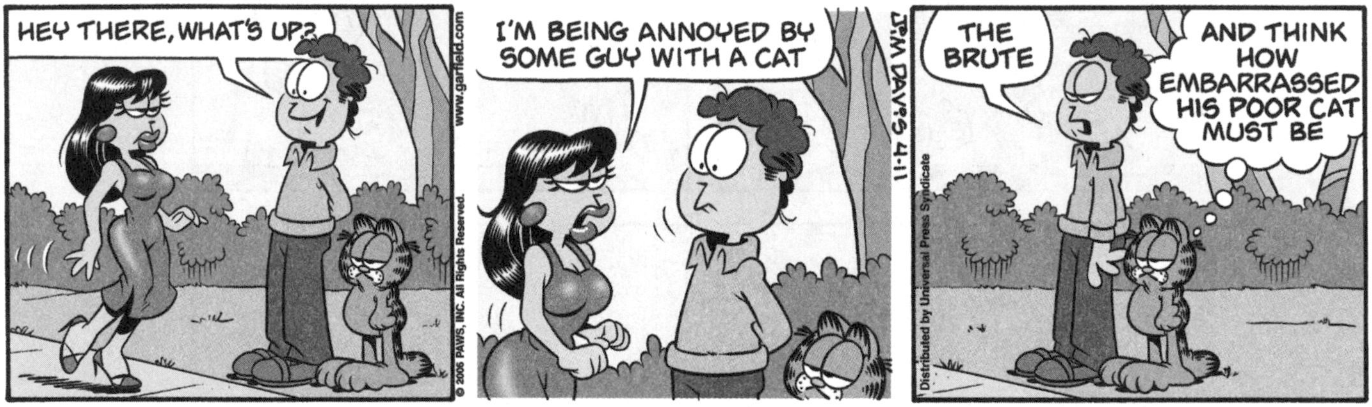
HEY THERE, WHAT'S UP?
I'M BEING ANNOYED BY SOME GUY WITH A CAT
THE BRUTE
AND THINK HOW EMBARRASSED HIS POOR CAT MUST BE
© 2006 PAWS, INC. All Rights Reserved. www.garfield.com
Distributed by Universal Press Syndicate
JPM DAVIS 4-11

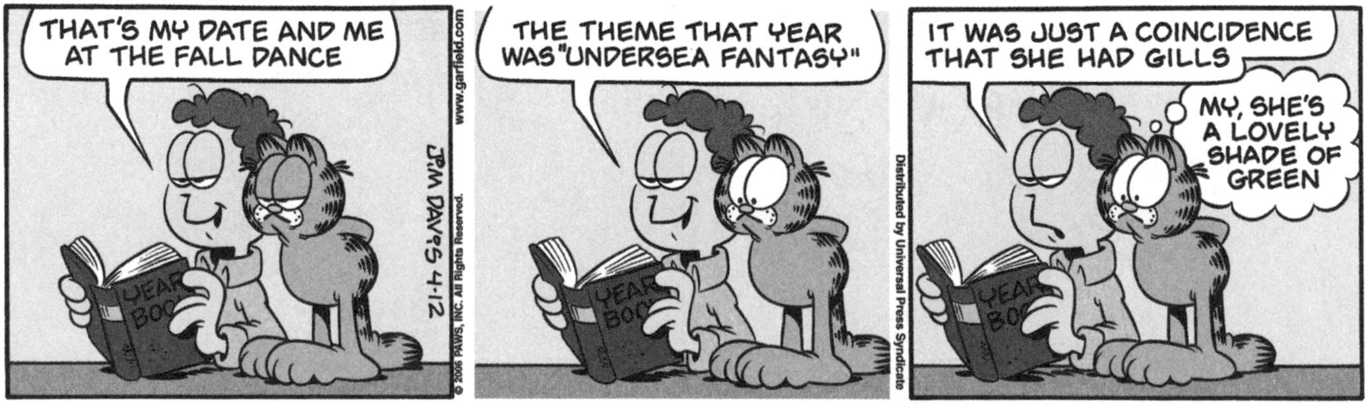
THAT'S MY DATE AND ME AT THE FALL DANCE
THE THEME THAT YEAR WAS "UNDERSEA FANTASY"
IT WAS JUST A COINCIDENCE THAT SHE HAD GILLS
MY, SHE'S A LOVELY SHADE OF GREEN
YEAR BOOK
© 2006 PAWS, INC. All Rights Reserved. www.garfield.com
Distributed by Universal Press Syndicate
JPM DAVIS 4-12

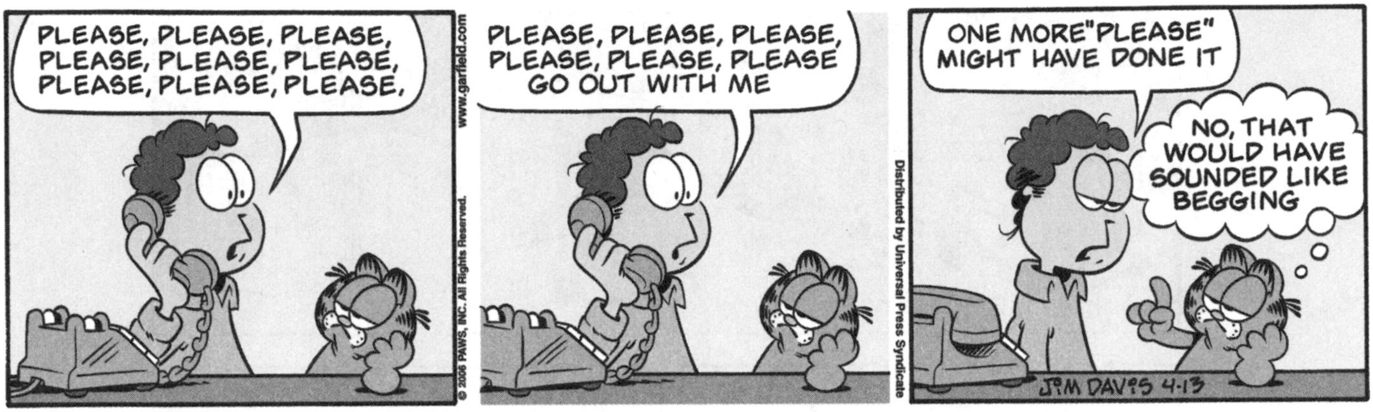
PLEASE, PLEASE, PLEASE, PLEASE, PLEASE, PLEASE, PLEASE, PLEASE, PLEASE,
www.garfield.com
© 2006 PAWS, INC. All Rights Reserved.
PLEASE, PLEASE, PLEASE, PLEASE, PLEASE, PLEASE GO OUT WITH ME
Distributed by Universal Press Syndicate
ONE MORE "PLEASE" MIGHT HAVE DONE IT
NO, THAT WOULD HAVE SOUNDED LIKE BEGGING
JIM DAVIS 4-13

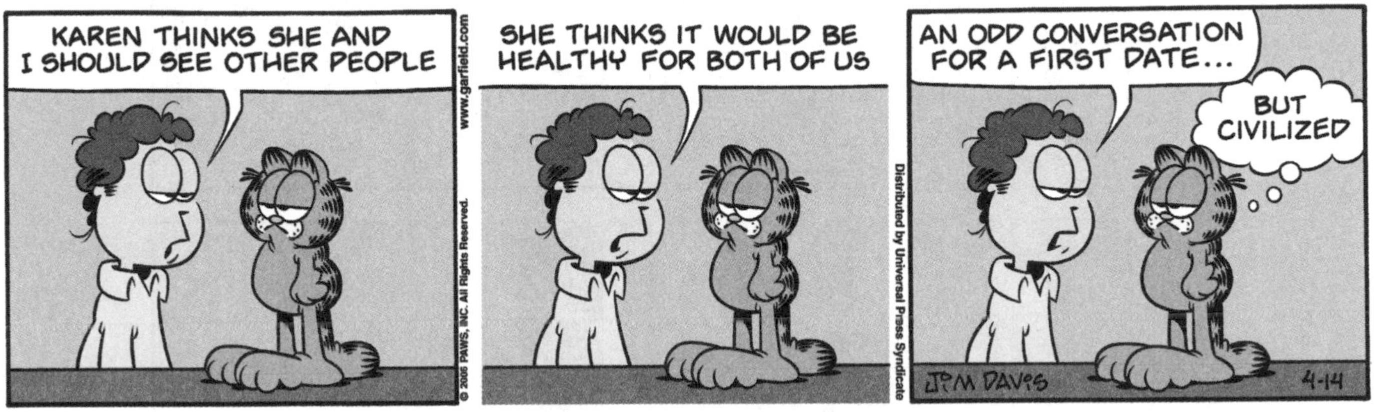
KAREN THINKS SHE AND I SHOULD SEE OTHER PEOPLE
www.garfield.com
© 2006 PAWS, INC. All Rights Reserved.
SHE THINKS IT WOULD BE HEALTHY FOR BOTH OF US
Distributed by Universal Press Syndicate
AN ODD CONVERSATION FOR A FIRST DATE...
BUT CIVILIZED
JIM DAVIS
4-14

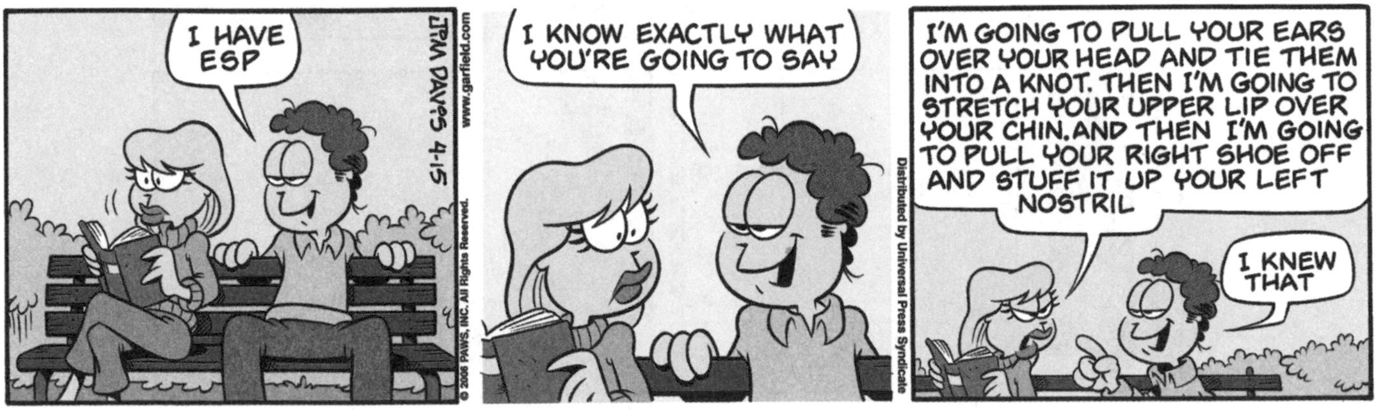
I HAVE ESP
JIM DAVIS 4-15
www.garfield.com
© 2006 PAWS, INC. All Rights Reserved.
I KNOW EXACTLY WHAT YOU'RE GOING TO SAY
Distributed by Universal Press Syndicate
I'M GOING TO PULL YOUR EARS OVER YOUR HEAD AND TIE THEM INTO A KNOT. THEN I'M GOING TO STRETCH YOUR UPPER LIP OVER YOUR CHIN. AND THEN I'M GOING TO PULL YOUR RIGHT SHOE OFF AND STUFF IT UP YOUR LEFT NOSTRIL
I KNEW THAT

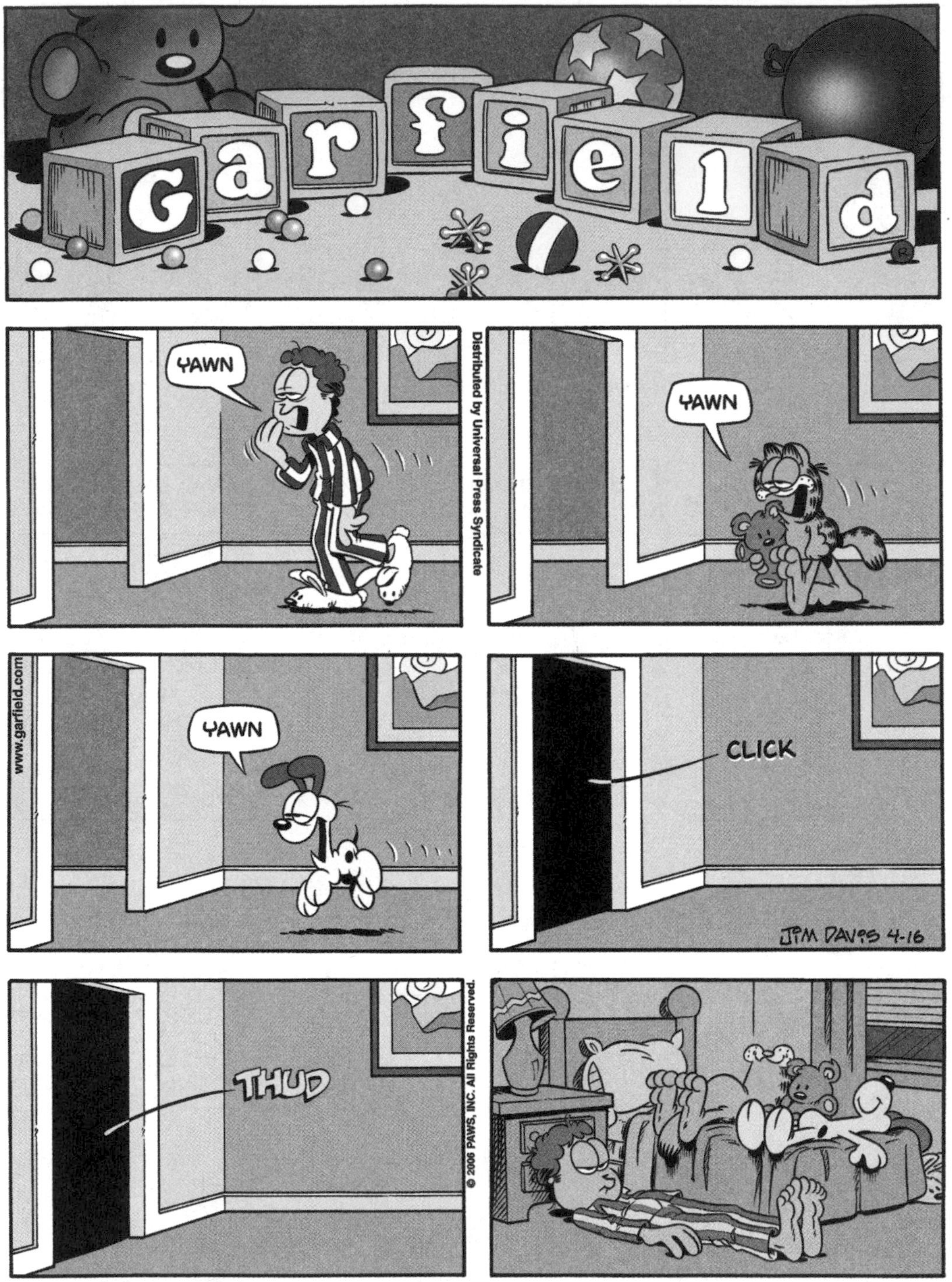
Garfield
YAWN
Distributed by Universal Press Syndicate
YAWN
www.garfield.com
YAWN
CLICK
JIM DAVIS 4-16
THUD
© 2006 PAWS, INC. All Rights Reserved.

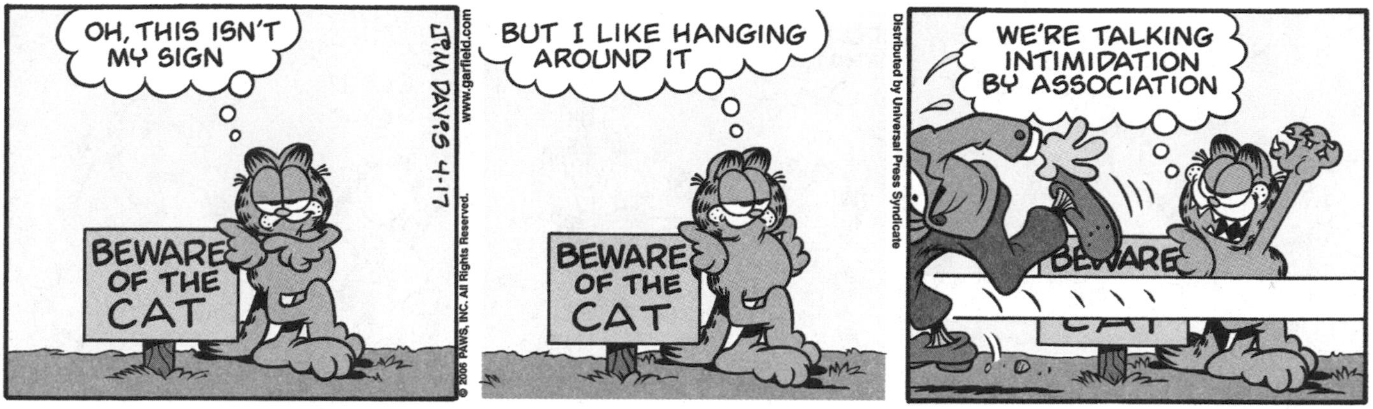
OH, THIS ISN'T MY SIGN
BEWARE OF THE CAT
JIM DAVIS 4-17
© 2006 PAWS, INC. All Rights Reserved. www.garfield.com
BUT I LIKE HANGING AROUND IT
BEWARE OF THE CAT
Distributed by Universal Press Syndicate
WE'RE TALKING INTIMIDATION BY ASSOCIATION
BEWARE

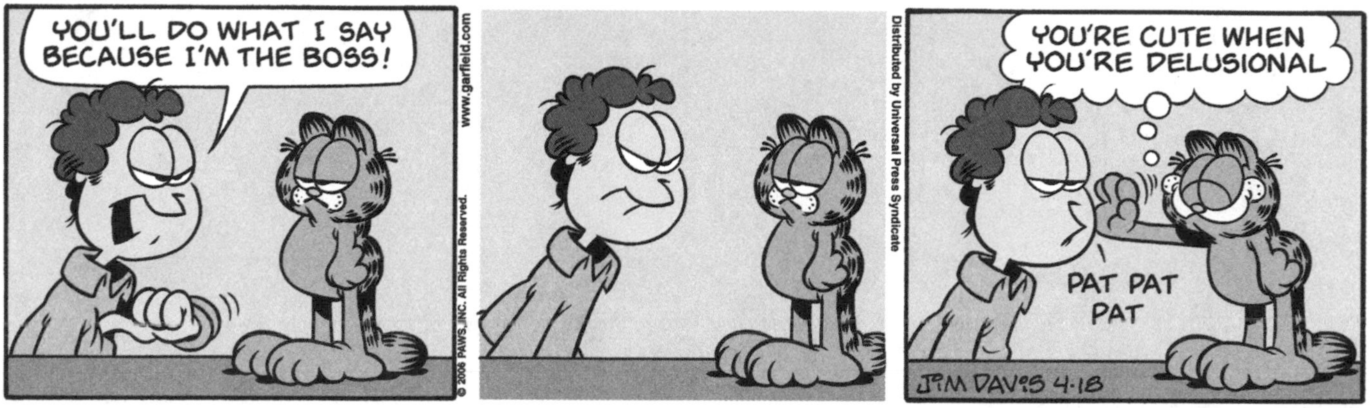
YOU'LL DO WHAT I SAY BECAUSE I'M THE BOSS!
© 2006 PAWS, INC. All Rights Reserved. www.garfield.com
Distributed by Universal Press Syndicate
YOU'RE CUTE WHEN YOU'RE DELUSIONAL
PAT PAT PAT
JIM DAVIS 4-18

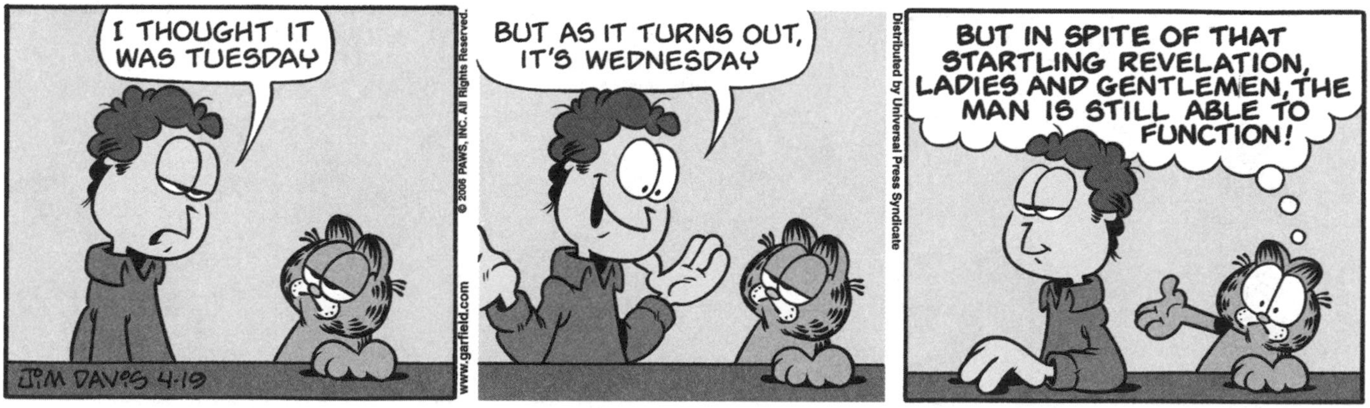
I THOUGHT IT WAS TUESDAY
JIM DAVIS 4-19
© 2006 PAWS, INC. All Rights Reserved. www.garfield.com
BUT AS IT TURNS OUT, IT'S WEDNESDAY
Distributed by Universal Press Syndicate
BUT IN SPITE OF THAT STARTLING REVELATION, LADIES AND GENTLEMEN, THE MAN IS STILL ABLE TO FUNCTION!

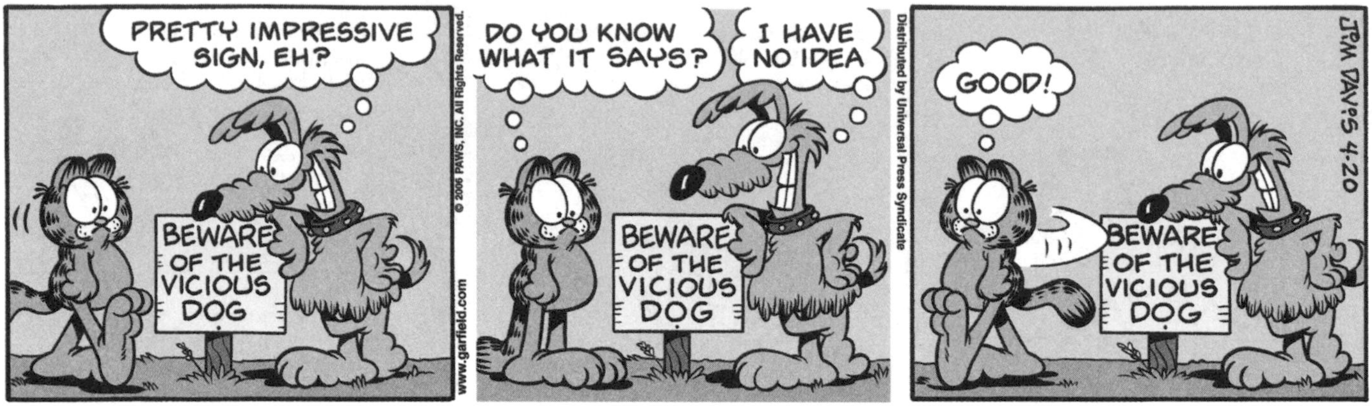
PRETTY IMPRESSIVE SIGN, EH?
BEWARE OF THE VICIOUS DOG
© 2006 PAWS, INC. All Rights Reserved. www.garfield.com
DO YOU KNOW WHAT IT SAYS?
I HAVE NO IDEA
BEWARE OF THE VICIOUS DOG
Distributed by Universal Press Syndicate
GOOD!
BEWARE OF THE VICIOUS DOG
JPM DAVIS 4-20

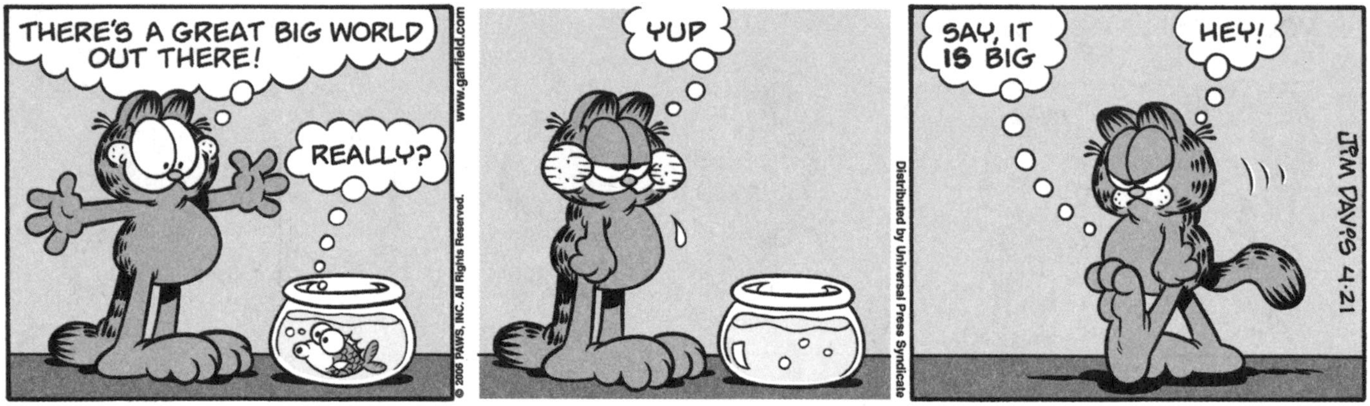
THERE'S A GREAT BIG WORLD OUT THERE!
REALLY?
www.garfield.com © 2006 PAWS, INC. All Rights Reserved.
YUP
Distributed by Universal Press Syndicate
SAY, IT IS BIG
HEY!
JPM DAVIS 4-21

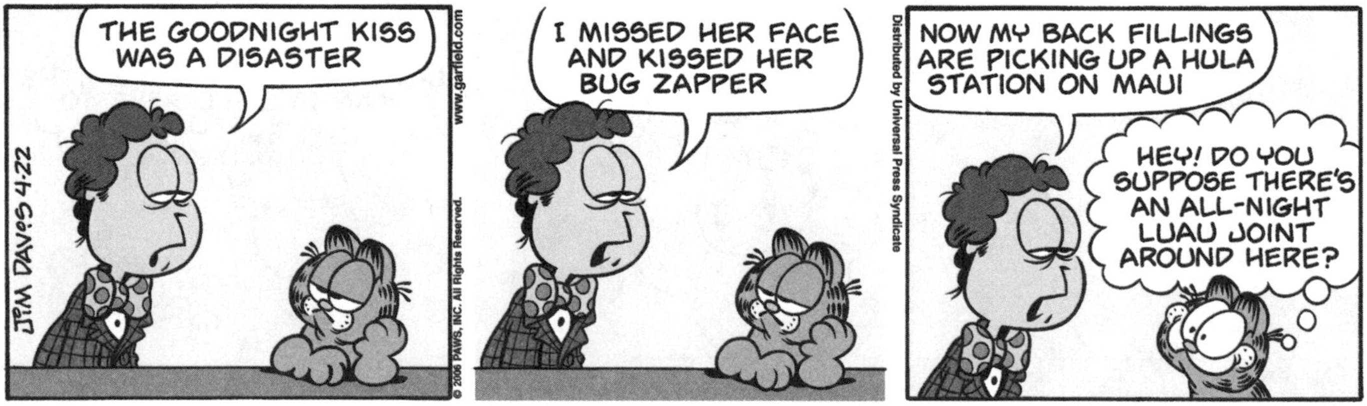
JPM DAVIS 4-22
THE GOODNIGHT KISS WAS A DISASTER
www.garfield.com © 2006 PAWS, INC. All Rights Reserved.
I MISSED HER FACE AND KISSED HER BUG ZAPPER
Distributed by Universal Press Syndicate
NOW MY BACK FILLINGS ARE PICKING UP A HULA STATION ON MAUI
HEY! DO YOU SUPPOSE THERE'S AN ALL-NIGHT LUAU JOINT AROUND HERE?

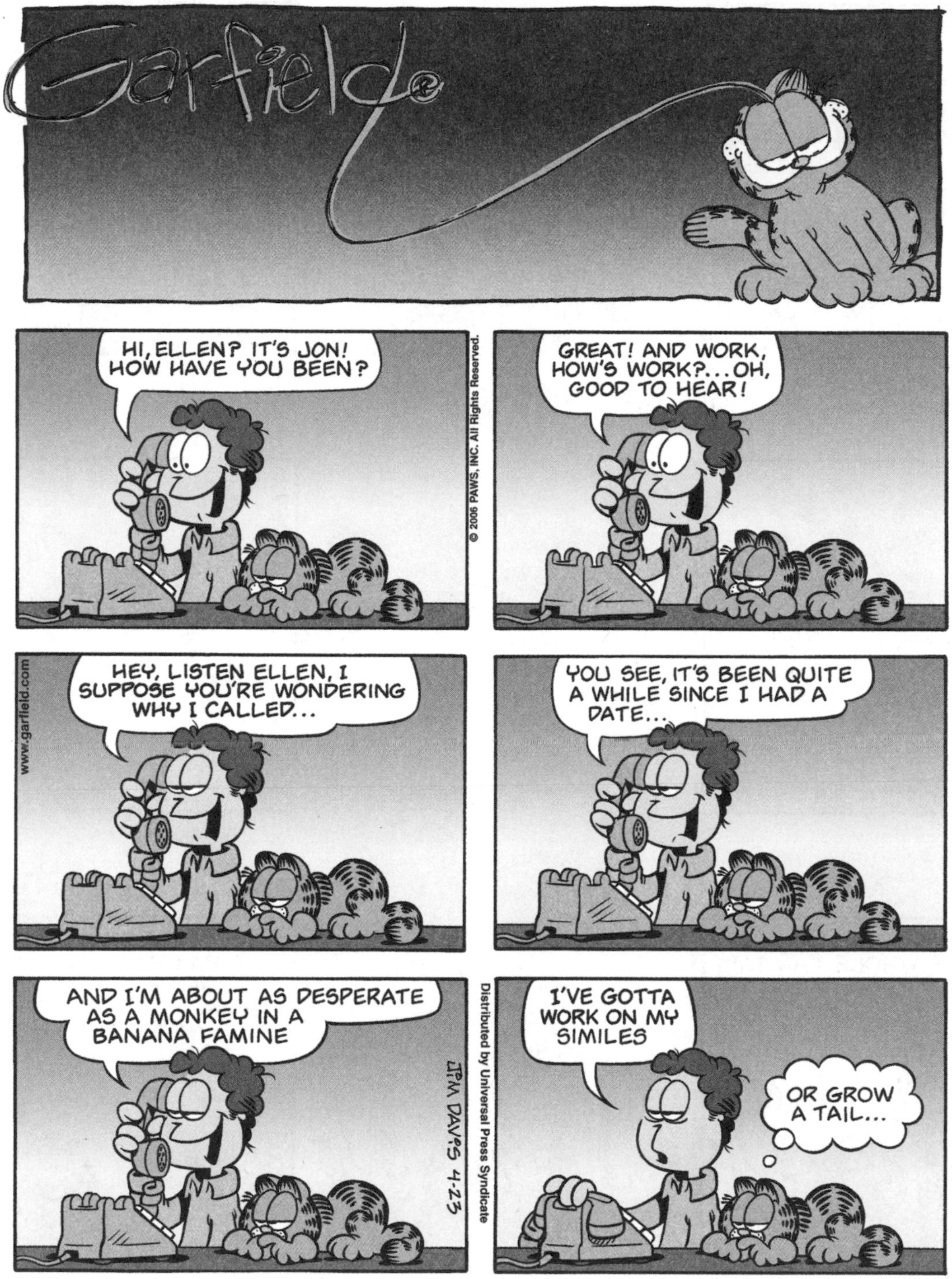
Garfield
HI, ELLEN? IT'S JON! HOW HAVE YOU BEEN?
© 2006 PAWS, INC. All Rights Reserved.
GREAT! AND WORK, HOW'S WORK?...OH, GOOD TO HEAR!
www.garfield.com
HEY, LISTEN ELLEN, I SUPPOSE YOU'RE WONDERING WHY I CALLED...
YOU SEE, IT'S BEEN QUITE A WHILE SINCE I HAD A DATE...
AND I'M ABOUT AS DESPERATE AS A MONKEY IN A BANANA FAMINE
JIM DAVIS 4-23
Distributed by Universal Press Syndicate
I'VE GOTTA WORK ON MY SIMILES
OR GROW A TAIL...

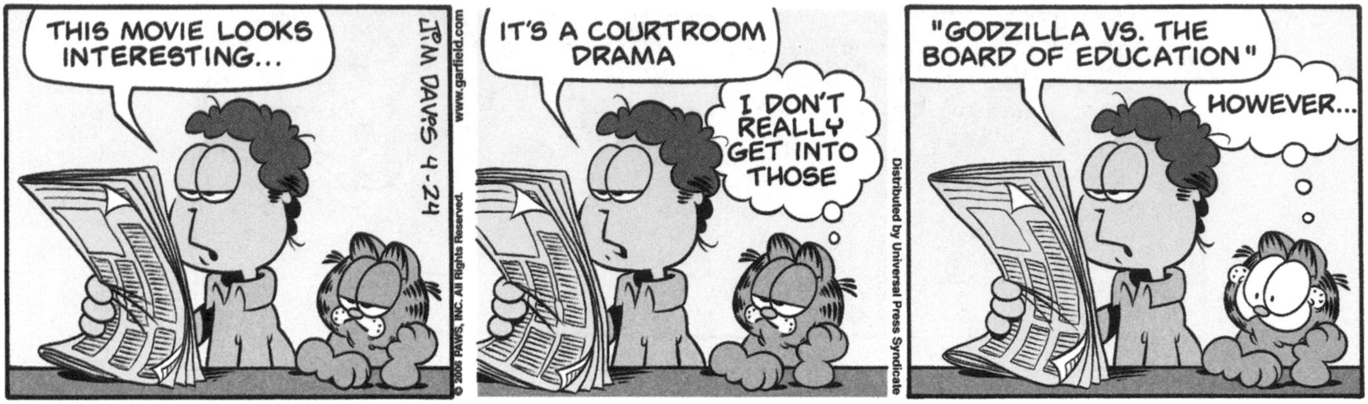
THIS MOVIE LOOKS INTERESTING...
JPM DAVIS 4-24
www.garfield.com
© 2006 PAWS, INC. All Rights Reserved.
IT'S A COURTROOM DRAMA
I DON'T REALLY GET INTO THOSE
Distributed by Universal Press Syndicate
"GODZILLA VS. THE BOARD OF EDUCATION"
HOWEVER...

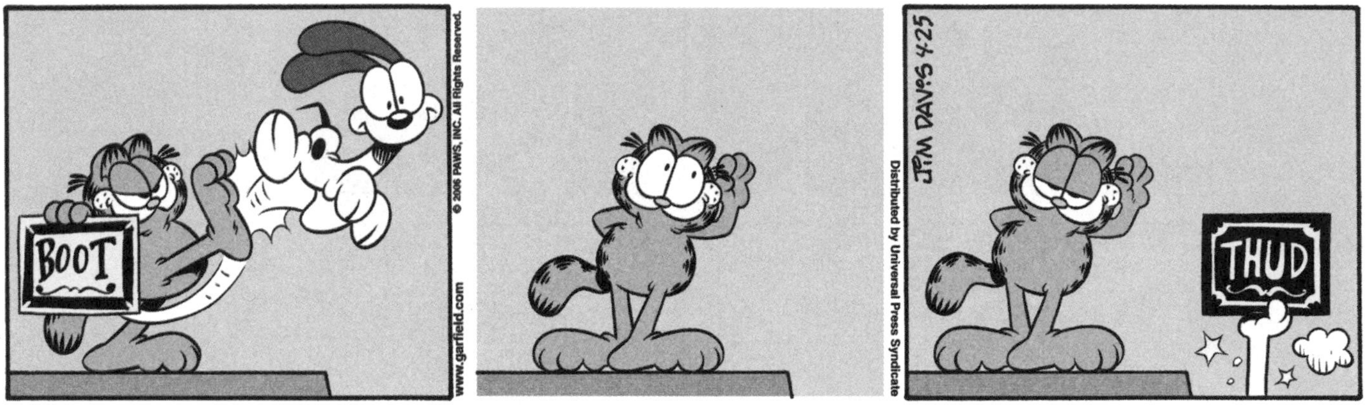
BOOT
© 2006 PAWS, INC. All Rights Reserved.
www.garfield.com
Distributed by Universal Press Syndicate
JPM DAVIS 4-25
THUD

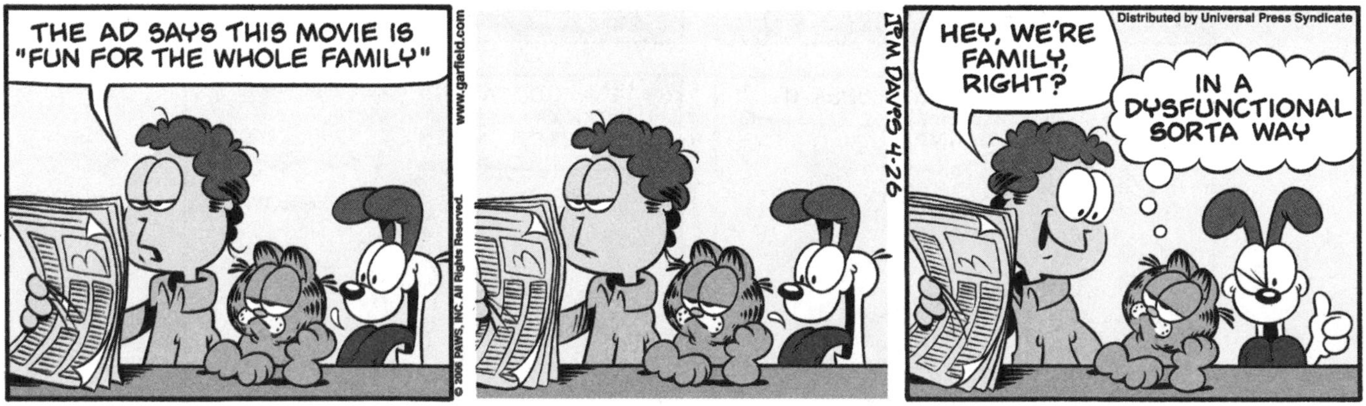
THE AD SAYS THIS MOVIE IS "FUN FOR THE WHOLE FAMILY"
www.garfield.com
© 2006 PAWS, INC. All Rights Reserved.
JPM DAVIS 4-26
Distributed by Universal Press Syndicate
HEY, WE'RE FAMILY, RIGHT?
IN A DYSFUNCTIONAL SORTA WAY

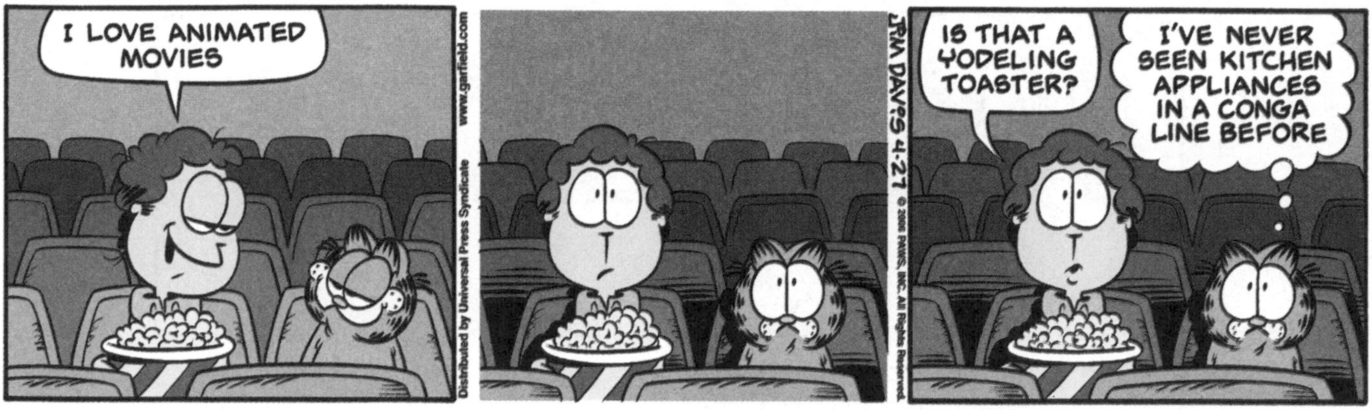
I LOVE ANIMATED MOVIES
Distributed by Universal Press Syndicate www.garfield.com
JIM DAVIS 4-27 © 2006 PAWS, INC. All Rights Reserved.
IS THAT A YODELING TOASTER?
I'VE NEVER SEEN KITCHEN APPLIANCES IN A CONGA LINE BEFORE

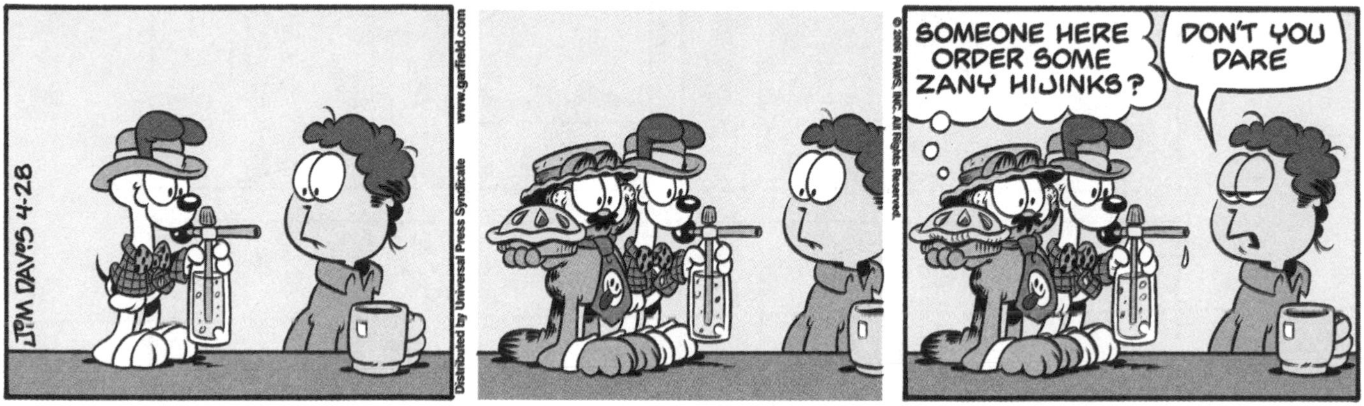
JIM DAVIS 4-28
Distributed by Universal Press Syndicate www.garfield.com
© 2006 PAWS, INC. All Rights Reserved.
SOMEONE HERE ORDER SOME ZANY HIJINKS?
DON'T YOU DARE

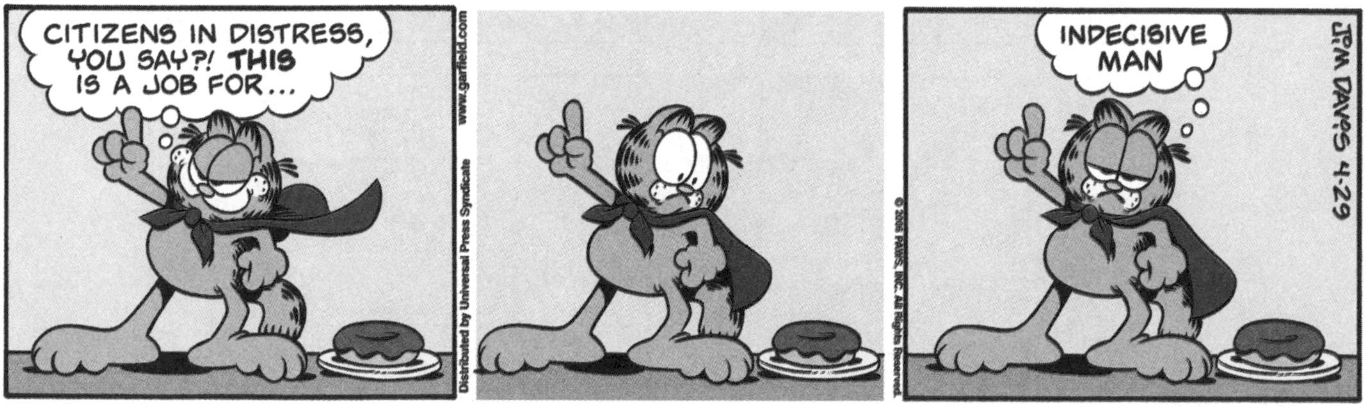
CITIZENS IN DISTRESS, YOU SAY?! THIS IS A JOB FOR...
Distributed by Universal Press Syndicate www.garfield.com
© 2006 PAWS, INC. All Rights Reserved.
INDECISIVE MAN
JIM DAVIS 4-29

GARFIELD
© 2006 PAWS, INC. All Rights Reserved.
RATTLE
RATTLE
RATTLE
RATTLE
RATTLE
CLICK
JIM DAVIS 4-30
www.garfield.com
Distributed by Universal Press Syndicate
TOO GOOD FOR THE PET DOOR?
IT'S A DIGNITY THING

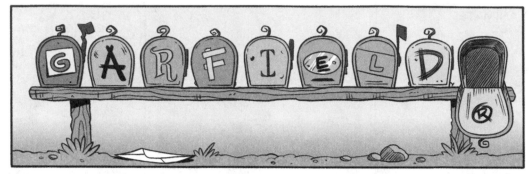

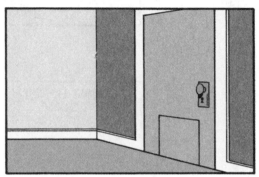

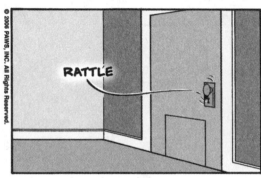

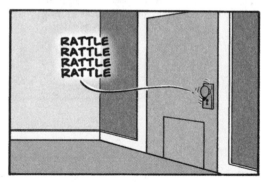

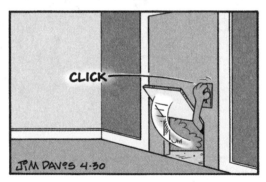

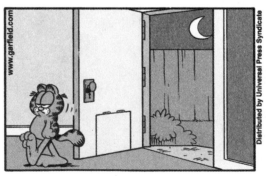

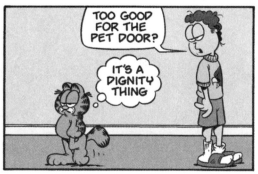

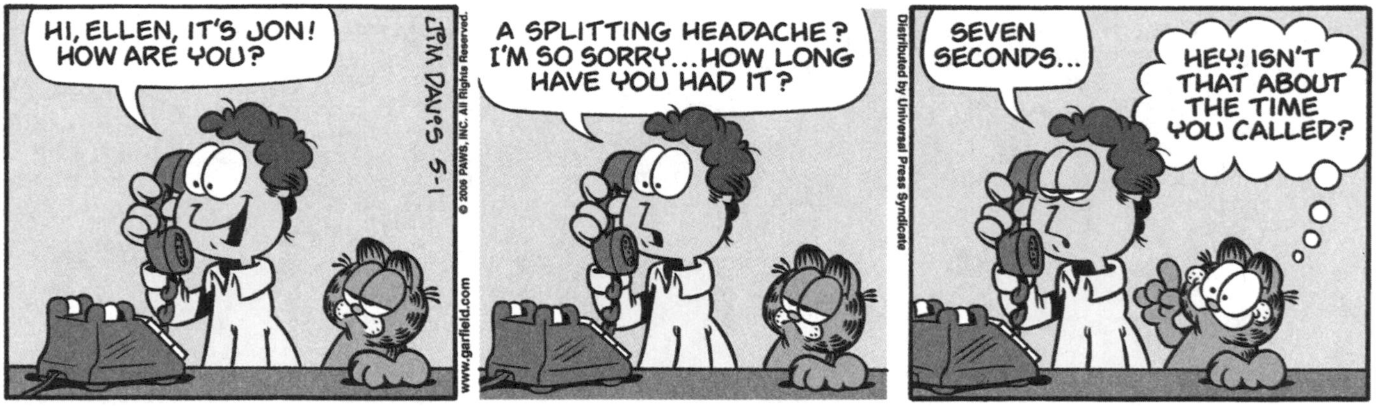
HI, ELLEN, IT'S JON! HOW ARE YOU?
JIM DAVIS 5-1
© 2006 PAWS, INC. All Rights Reserved.
www.garfield.com
A SPLITTING HEADACHE? I'M SO SORRY... HOW LONG HAVE YOU HAD IT?
Distributed by Universal Press Syndicate
SEVEN SECONDS...
HEY! ISN'T THAT ABOUT THE TIME YOU CALLED?

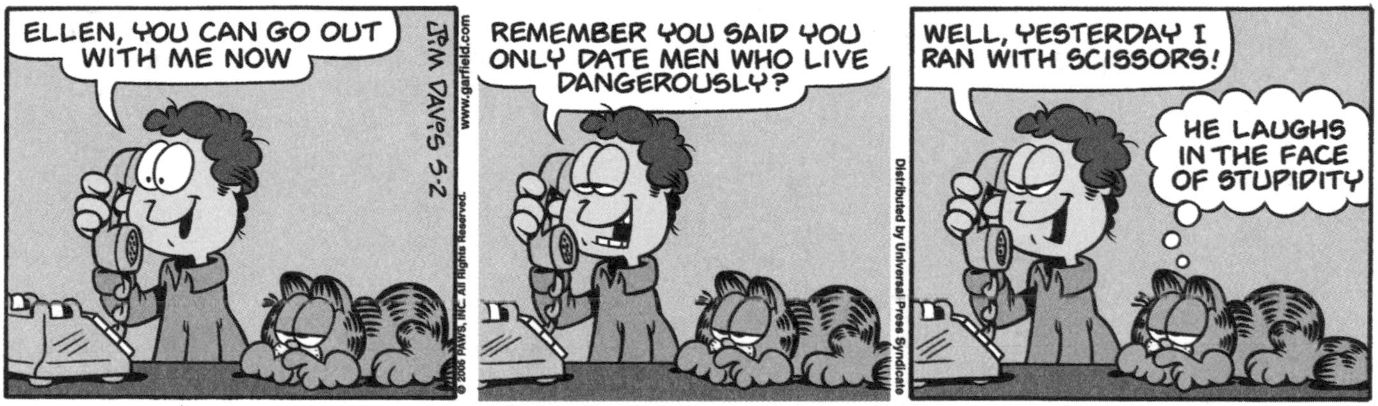
ELLEN, YOU CAN GO OUT WITH ME NOW
JIM DAVIS 5-2
www.garfield.com
© 2006 PAWS, INC. All Rights Reserved.
REMEMBER YOU SAID YOU ONLY DATE MEN WHO LIVE DANGEROUSLY?
Distributed by Universal Press Syndicate
WELL, YESTERDAY I RAN WITH SCISSORS!
HE LAUGHS IN THE FACE OF STUPIDITY

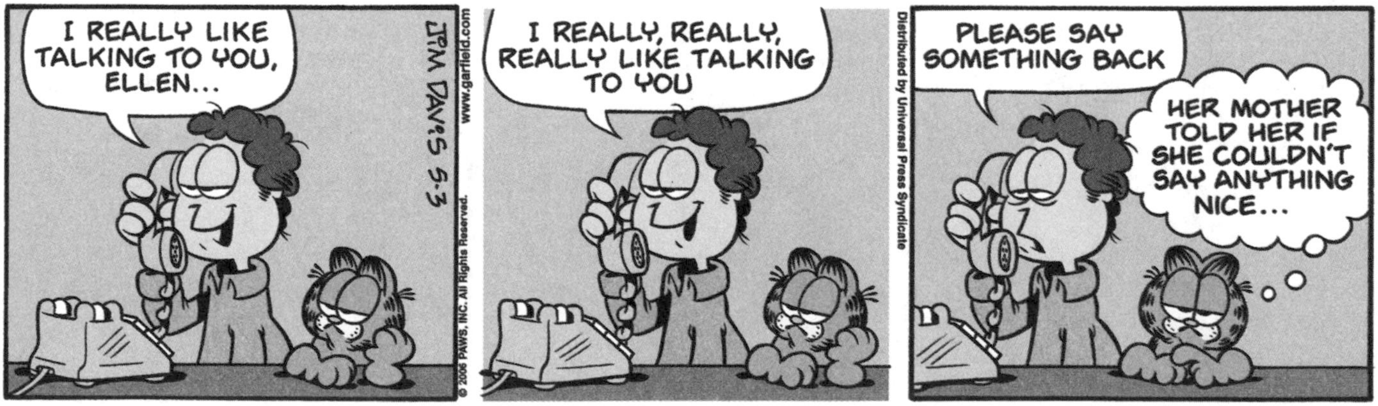
I REALLY LIKE TALKING TO YOU, ELLEN...
JIM DAVIS 5-3
www.garfield.com
© 2006 PAWS, INC. All Rights Reserved.
I REALLY, REALLY, REALLY LIKE TALKING TO YOU
Distributed by Universal Press Syndicate
PLEASE SAY SOMETHING BACK
HER MOTHER TOLD HER IF SHE COULDN'T SAY ANYTHING NICE...

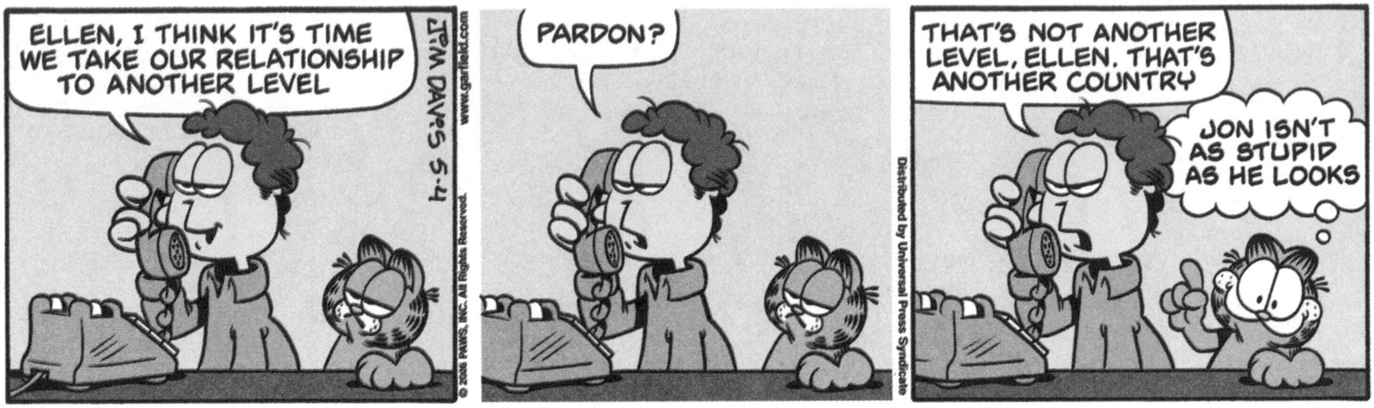
ELLEN, I THINK IT'S TIME WE TAKE OUR RELATIONSHIP TO ANOTHER LEVEL
JIM DAVIS 5-4
PARDON?
THAT'S NOT ANOTHER LEVEL, ELLEN. THAT'S ANOTHER COUNTRY
JON ISN'T AS STUPID AS HE LOOKS
www.garfield.com
© 2006 PAWS, INC. All Rights Reserved.
Distributed by Universal Press Syndicate

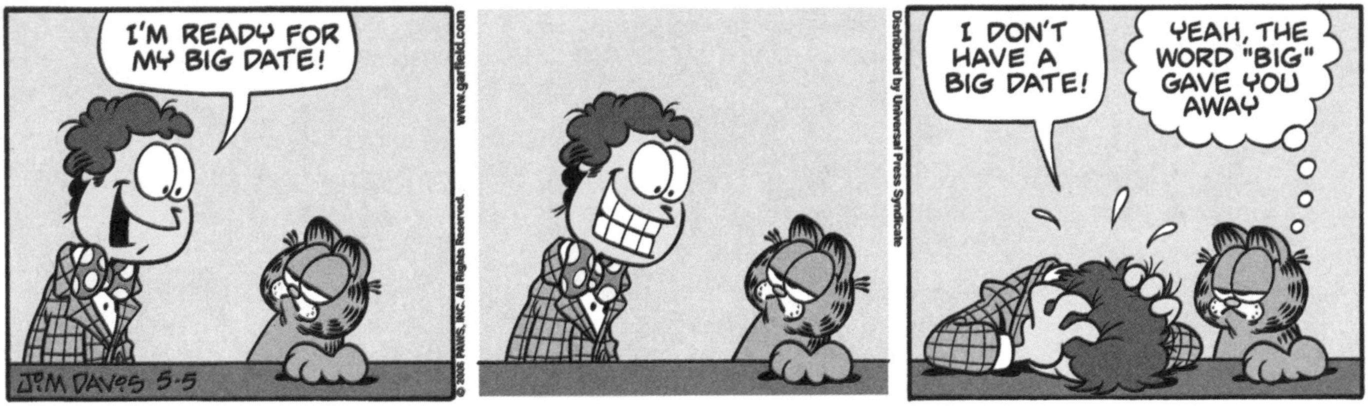
I'M READY FOR MY BIG DATE!
JIM DAVIS 5-5
I DON'T HAVE A BIG DATE!
YEAH, THE WORD "BIG" GAVE YOU AWAY
www.garfield.com
© 2006 PAWS, INC. All Rights Reserved.
Distributed by Universal Press Syndicate

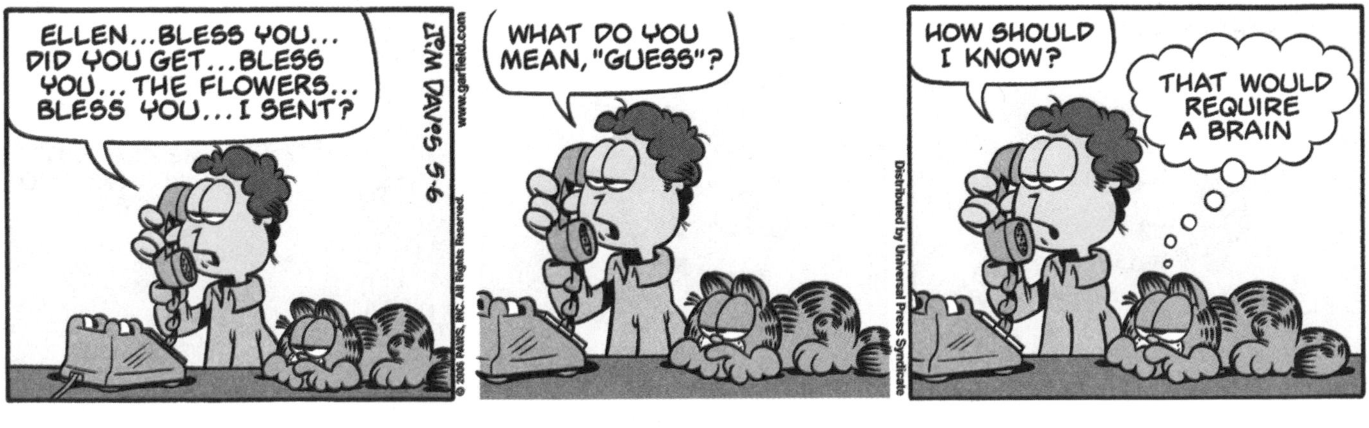
ELLEN...BLESS YOU... DID YOU GET...BLESS YOU... THE FLOWERS... BLESS YOU...I SENT?
JIM DAVIS 5-6
WHAT DO YOU MEAN, "GUESS"?
HOW SHOULD I KNOW?
THAT WOULD REQUIRE A BRAIN
www.garfield.com
© 2006 PAWS, INC. All Rights Reserved.
Distributed by Universal Press Syndicate

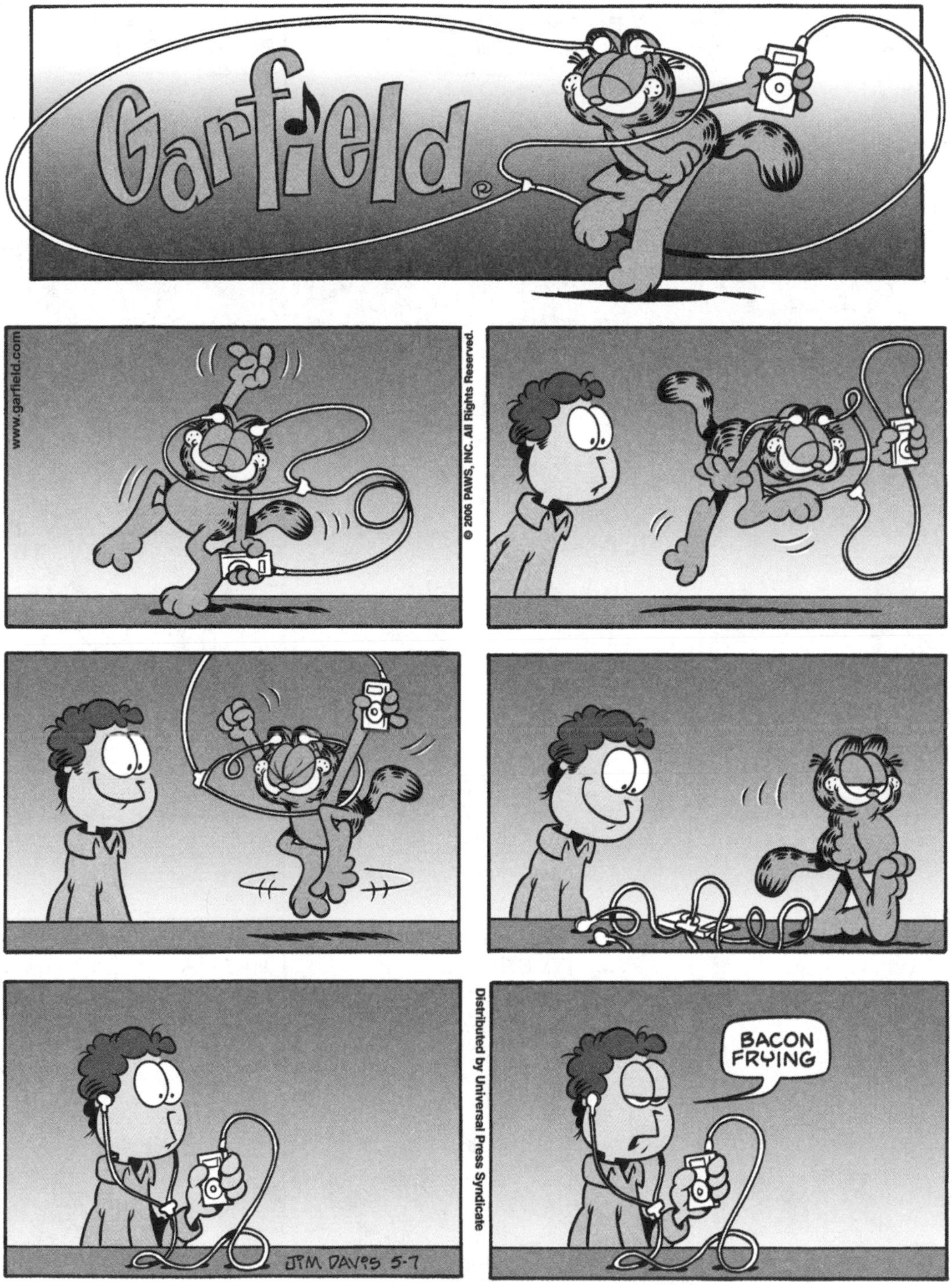
Garfield
www.garfield.com
© 2006 PAWS, INC. All Rights Reserved.
Distributed by Universal Press Syndicate
JIM DAVIS 5-7
BACON FRYING

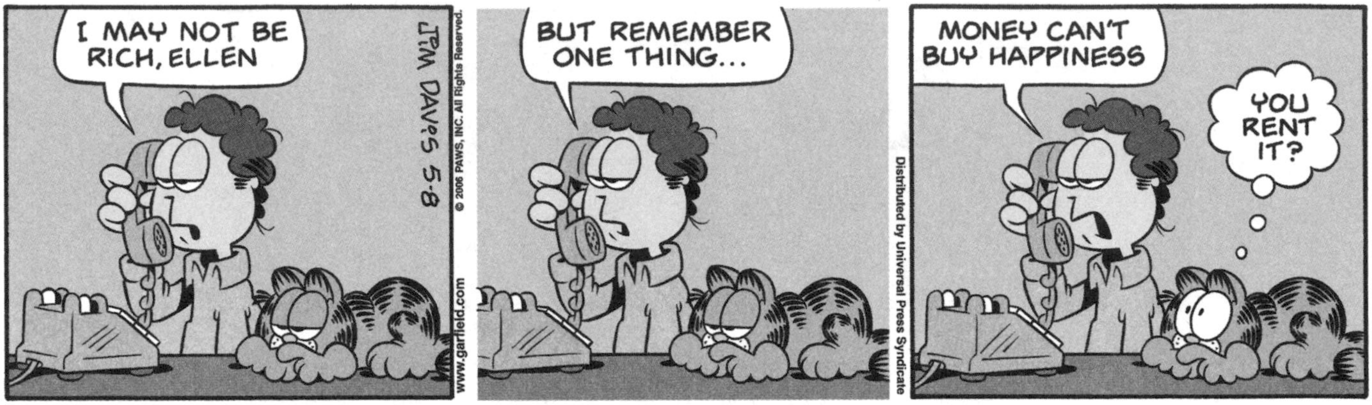
I MAY NOT BE RICH, ELLEN
JIM DAVIS 5-8
© 2006 PAWS, INC. All Rights Reserved.
www.garfield.com
BUT REMEMBER ONE THING...
Distributed by Universal Press Syndicate
MONEY CAN'T BUY HAPPINESS
YOU RENT IT?

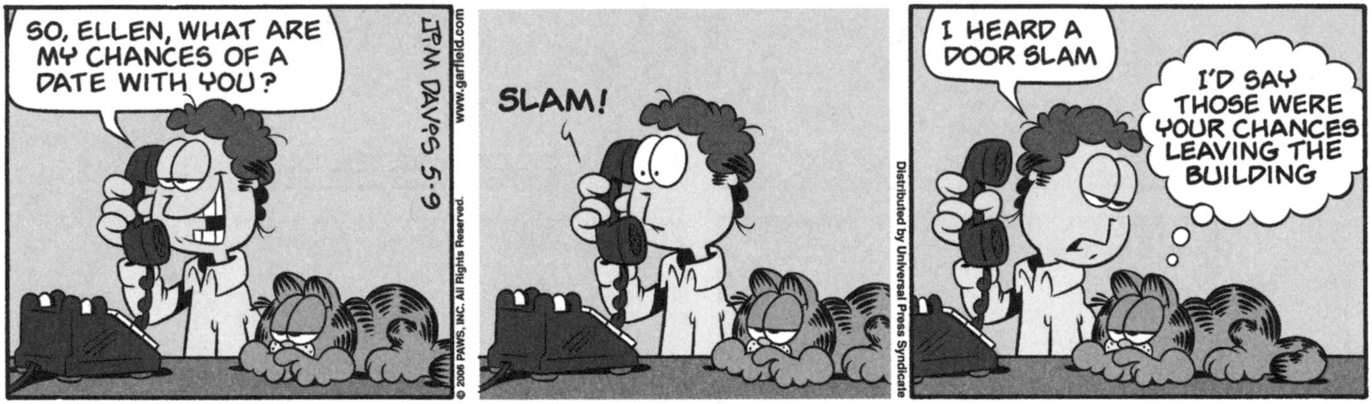
SO, ELLEN, WHAT ARE MY CHANCES OF A DATE WITH YOU?
JIM DAVIS 5-9
www.garfield.com
© 2006 PAWS, INC. All Rights Reserved.
SLAM!
Distributed by Universal Press Syndicate
I HEARD A DOOR SLAM
I'D SAY THOSE WERE YOUR CHANCES LEAVING THE BUILDING

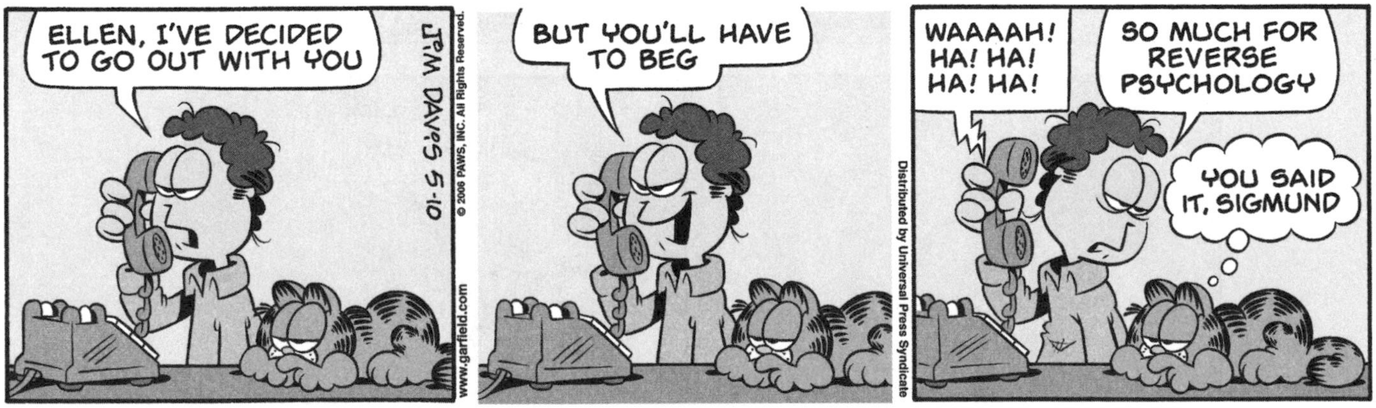
ELLEN, I'VE DECIDED TO GO OUT WITH YOU
JIM DAVIS 5-10
© 2006 PAWS, INC. All Rights Reserved.
www.garfield.com
BUT YOU'LL HAVE TO BEG
Distributed by Universal Press Syndicate
WAAAAH! HA! HA! HA! HA!
SO MUCH FOR REVERSE PSYCHOLOGY
YOU SAID IT, SIGMUND

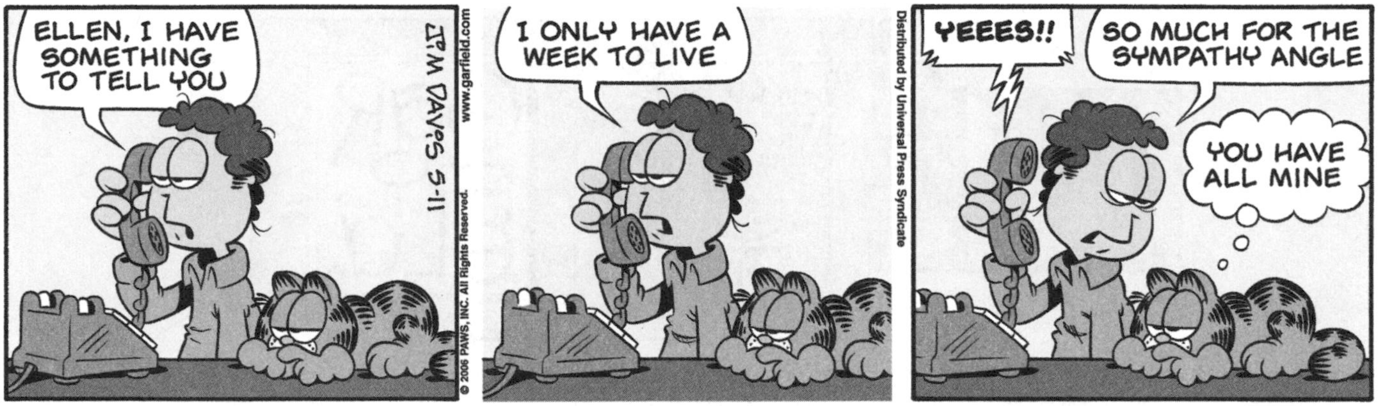
ELLEN, I HAVE SOMETHING TO TELL YOU
JIM DAVIS 5-11
www.garfield.com
© 2006 PAWS, INC. All Rights Reserved.
I ONLY HAVE A WEEK TO LIVE
Distributed by Universal Press Syndicate
YEEES!!
SO MUCH FOR THE SYMPATHY ANGLE
YOU HAVE ALL MINE

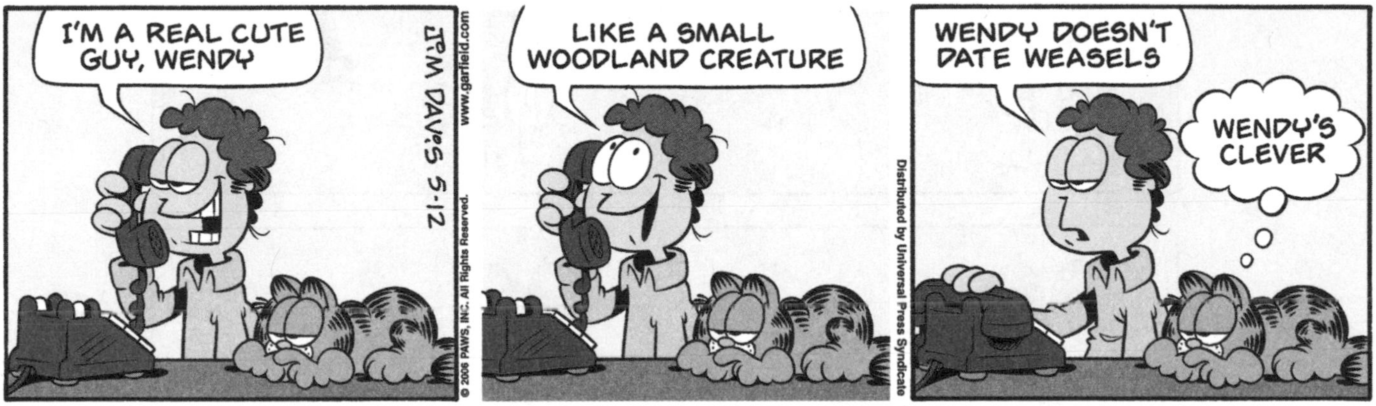
I'M A REAL CUTE GUY, WENDY
JIM DAVIS 5-12
www.garfield.com
© 2006 PAWS, INC. All Rights Reserved.
LIKE A SMALL WOODLAND CREATURE
Distributed by Universal Press Syndicate
WENDY DOESN'T DATE WEASELS
WENDY'S CLEVER

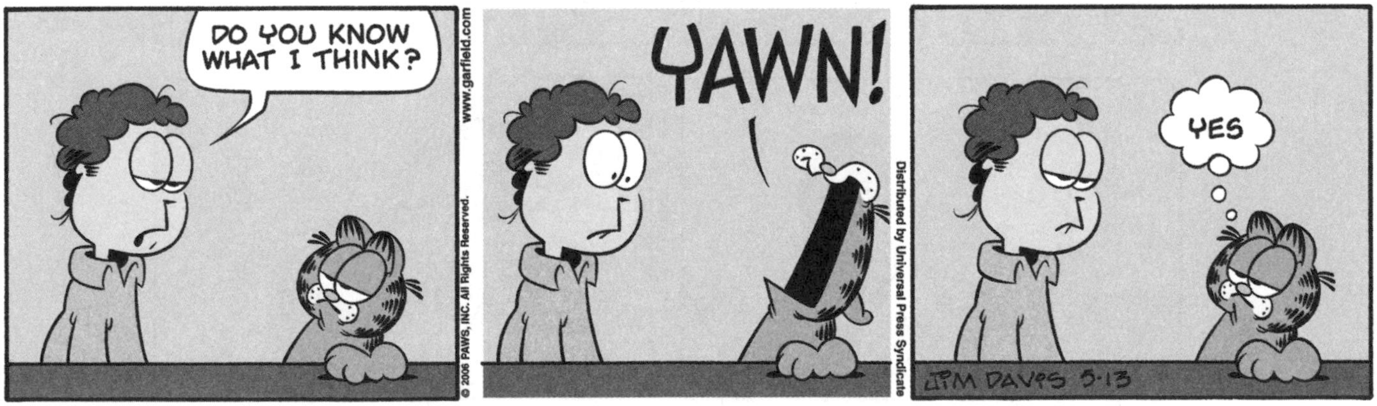
DO YOU KNOW WHAT I THINK?
www.garfield.com
© 2006 PAWS, INC. All Rights Reserved.
YAWN!
Distributed by Universal Press Syndicate
YES
JIM DAVIS 5-13

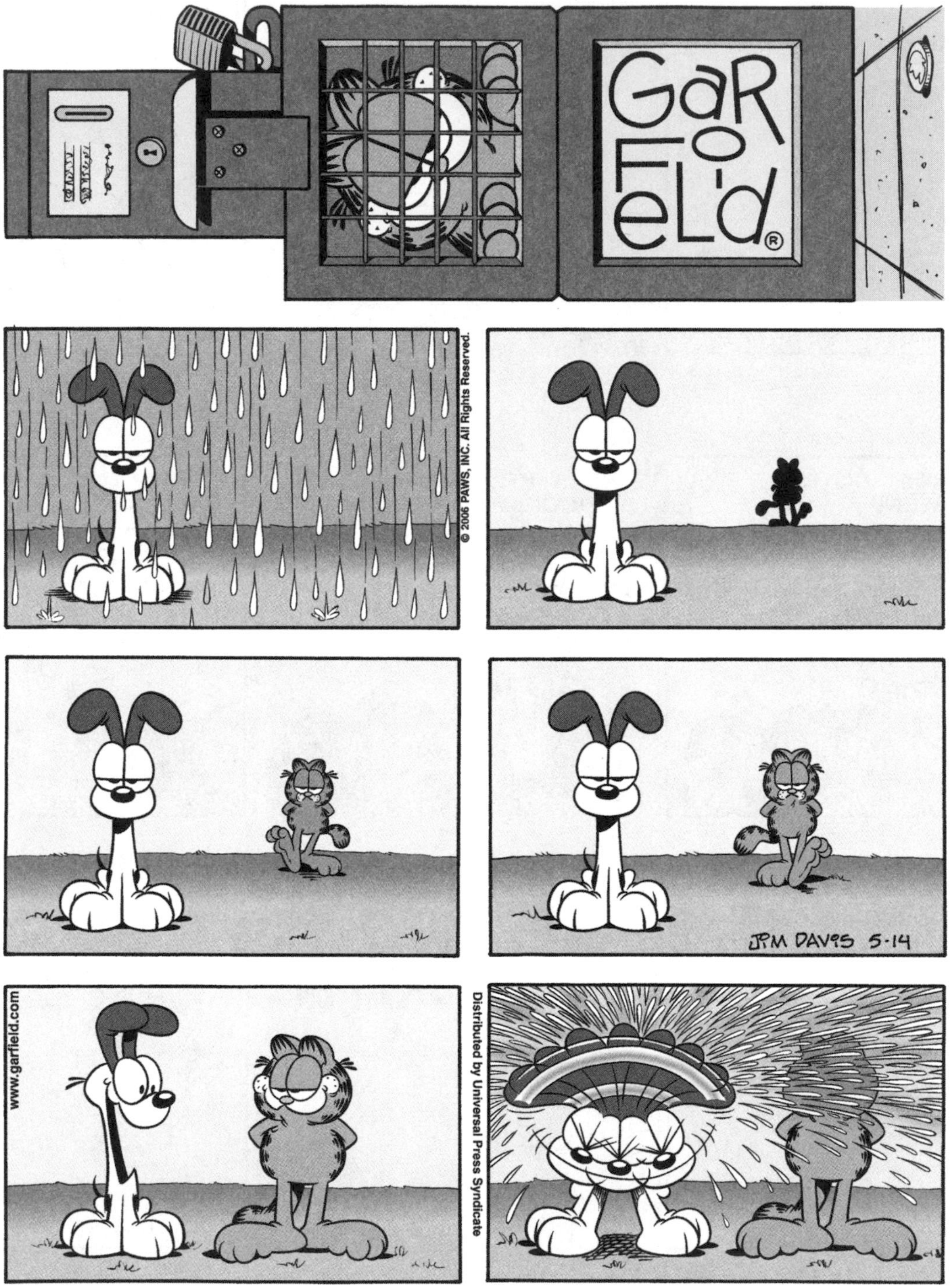
© 2006 PAWS, INC. All Rights Reserved.
JIM DAVIS 5-14
www.garfield.com
Distributed by Universal Press Syndicate

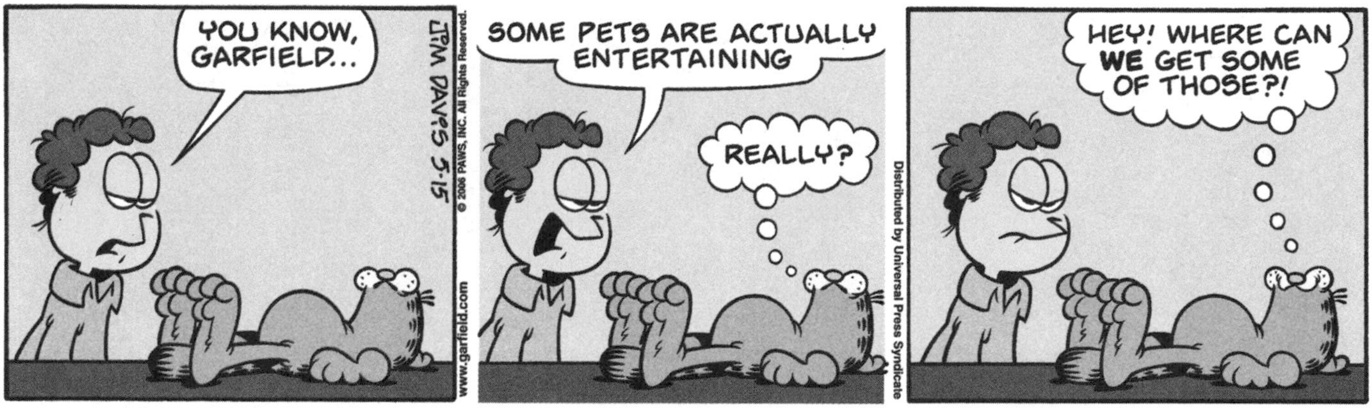
YOU KNOW, GARFIELD...
JIM DAVIS 5-15
© 2006 PAWS, INC. All Rights Reserved.
www.garfield.com
SOME PETS ARE ACTUALLY ENTERTAINING
REALLY?
Distributed by Universal Press Syndicate
HEY! WHERE CAN **WE** GET SOME OF THOSE?!

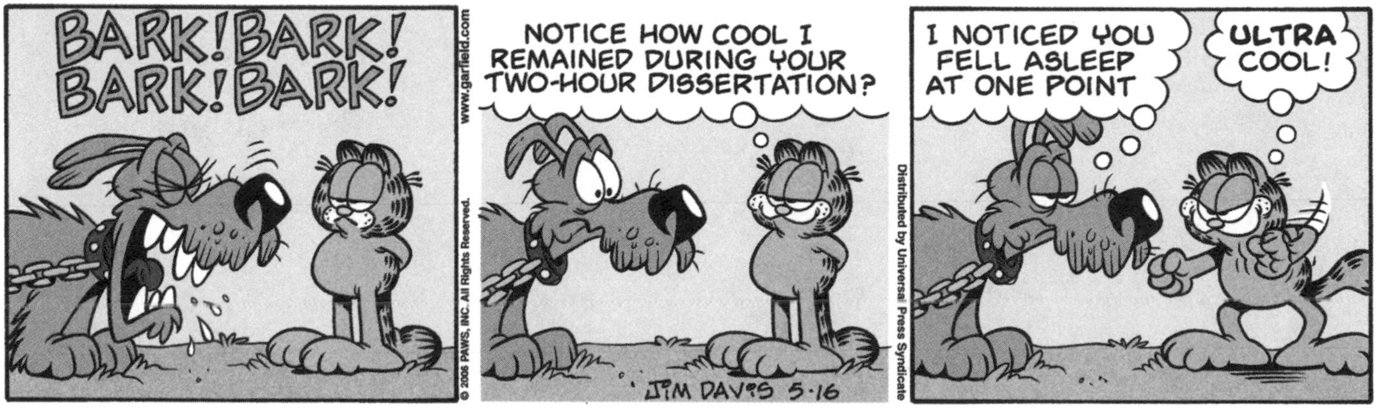
BARK! BARK! BARK! BARK!
www.garfield.com
© 2006 PAWS, INC. All Rights Reserved.
NOTICE HOW COOL I REMAINED DURING YOUR TWO-HOUR DISSERTATION?
JIM DAVIS 5-16
Distributed by Universal Press Syndicate
I NOTICED YOU FELL ASLEEP AT ONE POINT
ULTRA COOL!

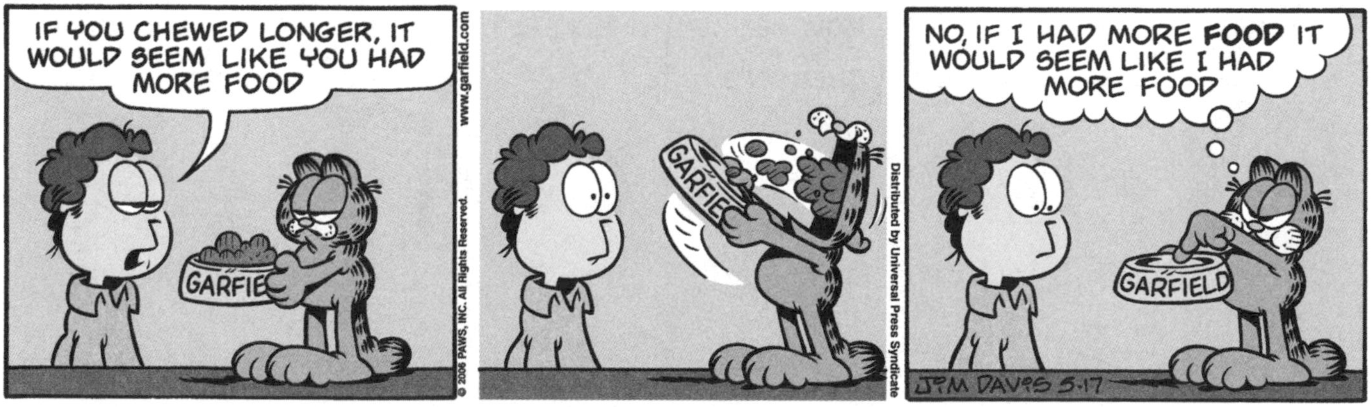
IF YOU CHEWED LONGER, IT WOULD SEEM LIKE YOU HAD MORE FOOD
GARFIE
www.garfield.com
© 2006 PAWS, INC. All Rights Reserved.
GARFIE
Distributed by Universal Press Syndicate
NO, IF I HAD MORE **FOOD** IT WOULD SEEM LIKE I HAD MORE FOOD
GARFIELD
JIM DAVIS 5-17

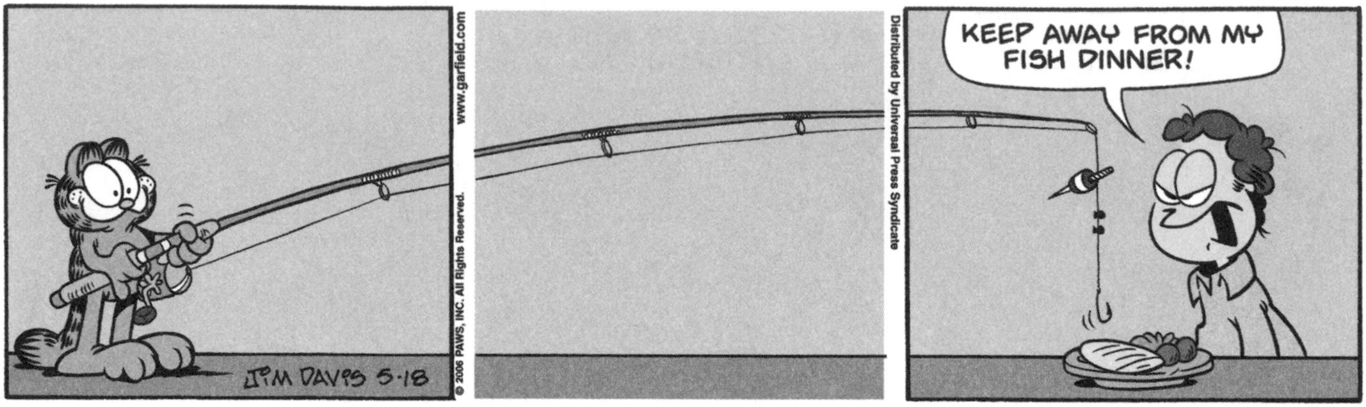
JIM DAVIS 5·18
© 2006 PAWS, INC. All Rights Reserved. www.garfield.com
Distributed by Universal Press Syndicate
KEEP AWAY FROM MY FISH DINNER!

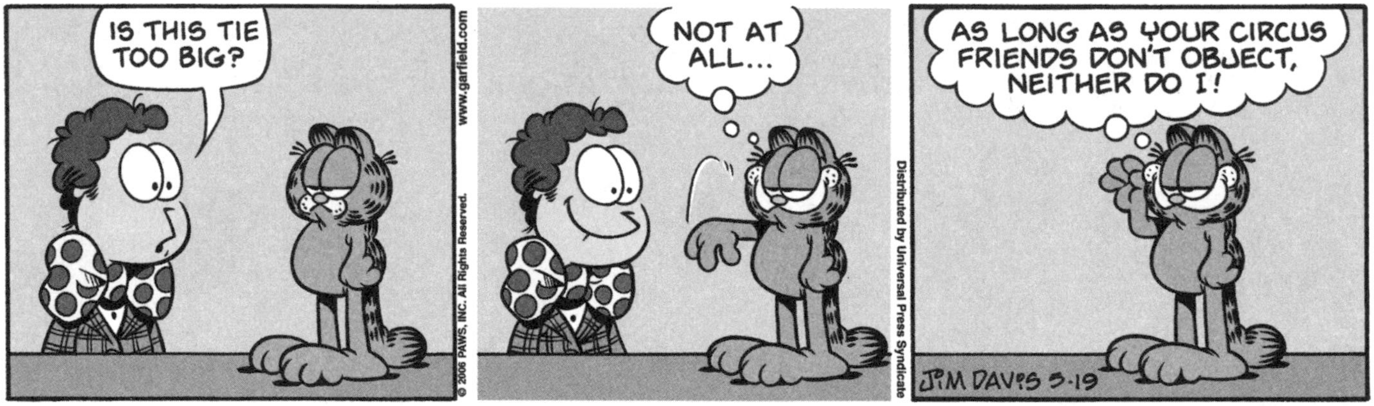
IS THIS TIE TOO BIG?
© 2006 PAWS, INC. All Rights Reserved. www.garfield.com
NOT AT ALL...
Distributed by Universal Press Syndicate
AS LONG AS YOUR CIRCUS FRIENDS DON'T OBJECT, NEITHER DO I!
JIM DAVIS 5·19

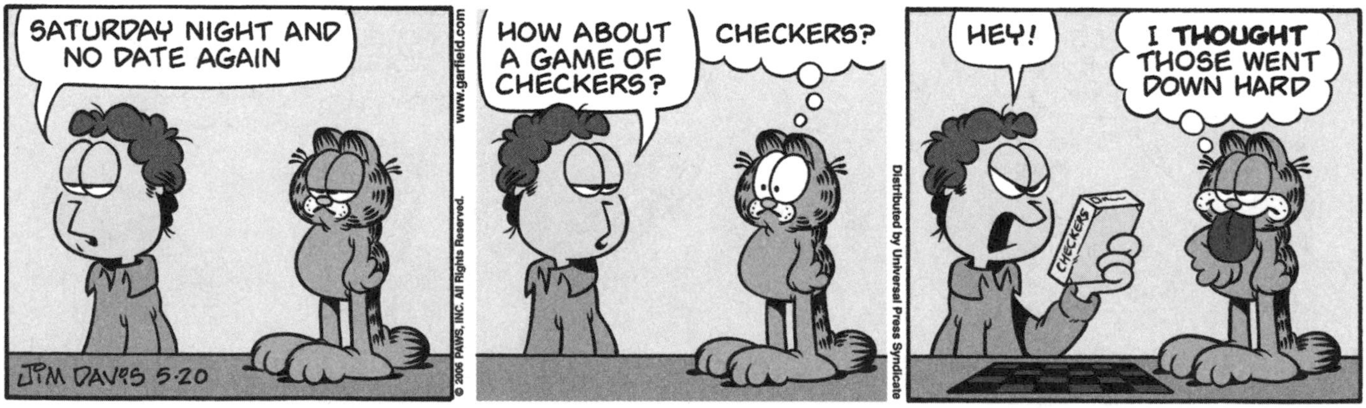
SATURDAY NIGHT AND NO DATE AGAIN
JIM DAVIS 5·20
© 2006 PAWS, INC. All Rights Reserved. www.garfield.com
HOW ABOUT A GAME OF CHECKERS?
CHECKERS?
Distributed by Universal Press Syndicate
HEY!
I **THOUGHT** THOSE WENT DOWN HARD
CHECKERS

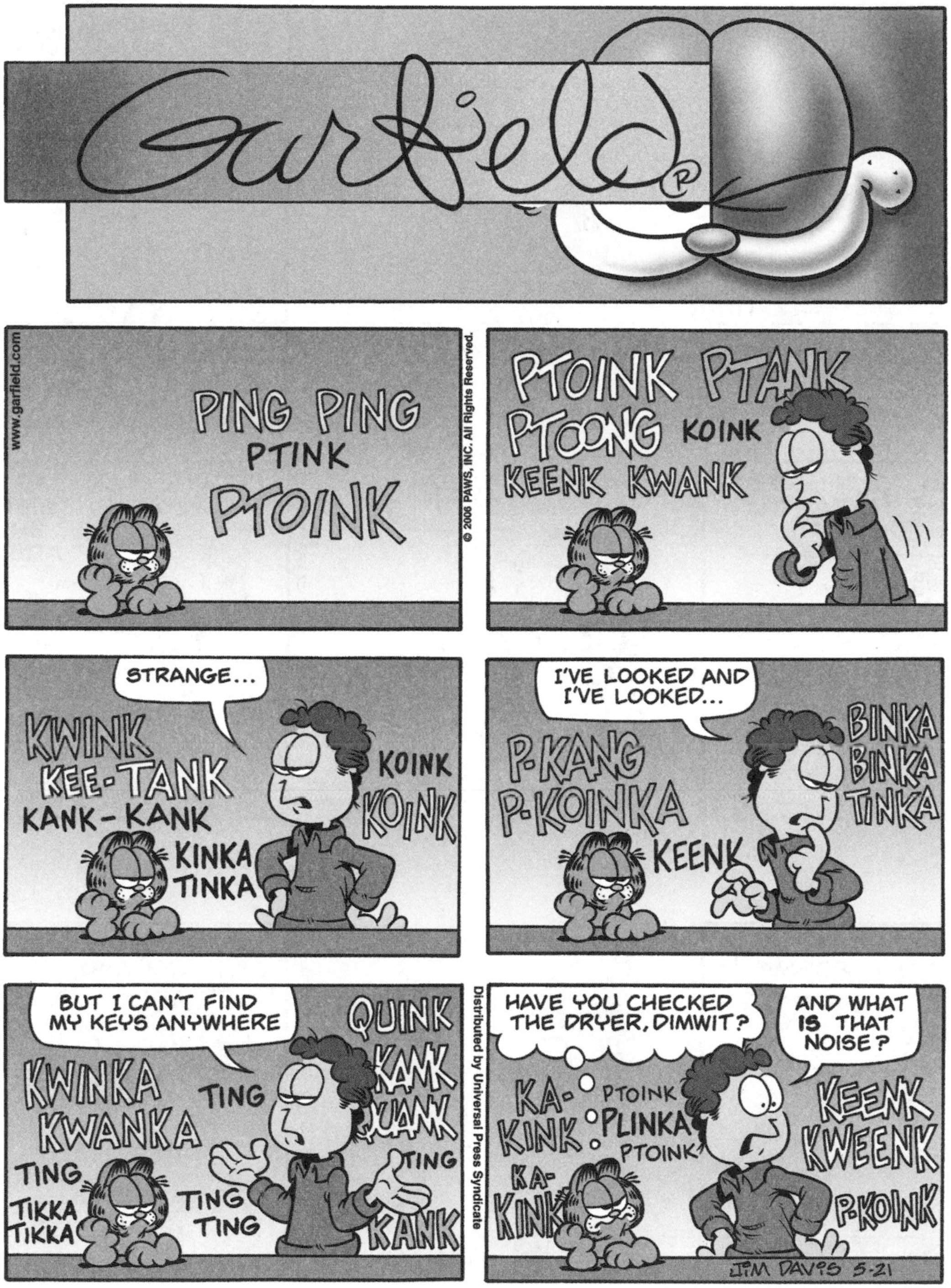
Garfield
www.garfield.com
© 2006 PAWS, INC. All Rights Reserved.
PING PING
PTINK
PTOINK
PTOINK PTANK
PTOONG KOINK
KEENK KWANK
STRANGE...
KWINK
KEE-TANK
KANK-KANK
KINKA
TINKA
KOINK
KOINK
I'VE LOOKED AND I'VE LOOKED...
P-KANG
P-KOINKA
KEENK
BINKA
BINKA
TINKA
BUT I CAN'T FIND MY KEYS ANYWHERE
KWINKA
KWANKA
TING
TING
TIKKA
TIKKA
TING
TING
QUINK
KANK
QUANK
TING
KANK
Distributed by Universal Press Syndicate
HAVE YOU CHECKED THE DRYER, DIMWIT?
AND WHAT IS THAT NOISE?
KA-
KINK
PTOINK
PLINKA
PTOINK
KA-
KINK
KEENK
KWEENK
P-KOINK
JIM DAVIS 5-21

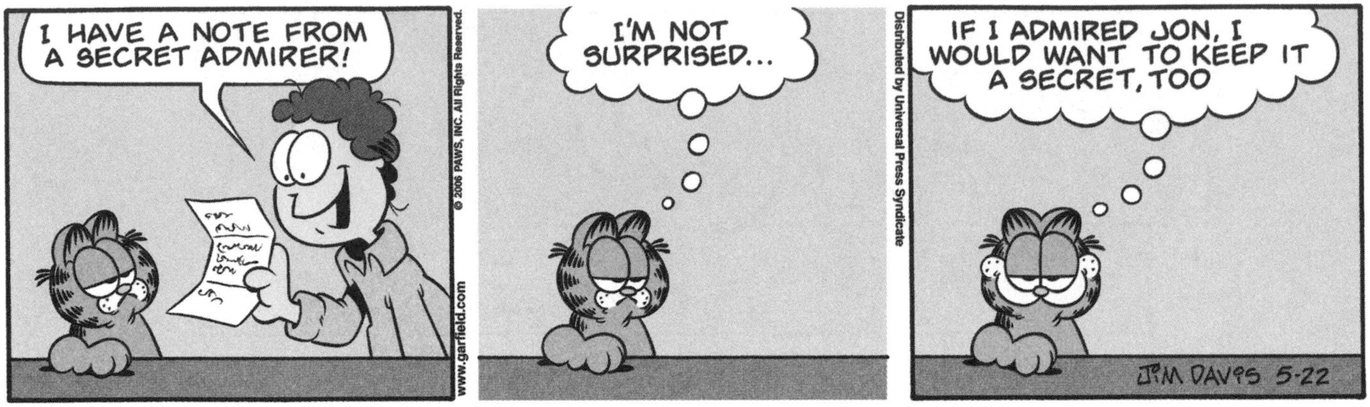
I HAVE A NOTE FROM A SECRET ADMIRER!
© 2006 PAWS, INC. All Rights Reserved.
www.garfield.com
I'M NOT SURPRISED...
Distributed by Universal Press Syndicate
IF I ADMIRED JON, I WOULD WANT TO KEEP IT A SECRET, TOO
JIM DAVIS 5-22

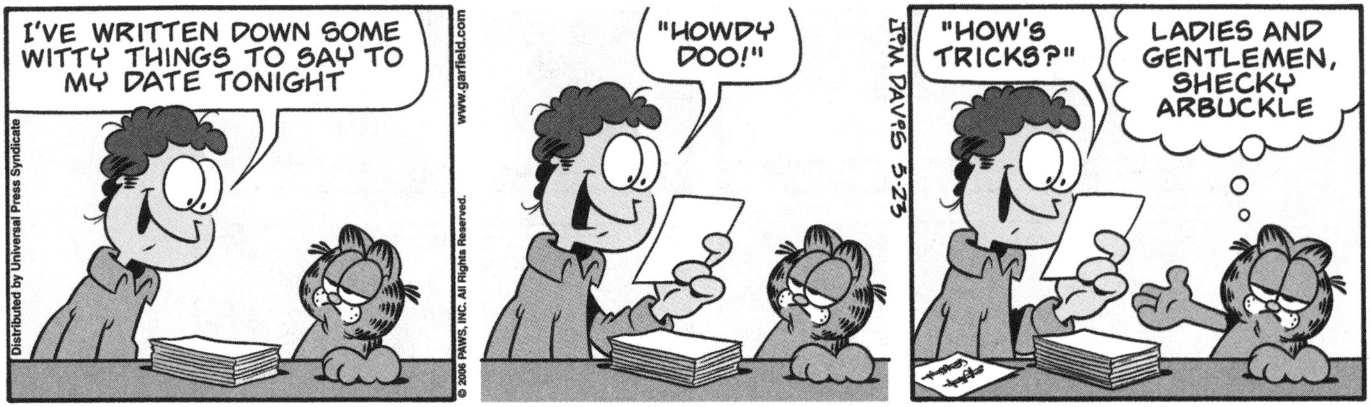
Distributed by Universal Press Syndicate
I'VE WRITTEN DOWN SOME WITTY THINGS TO SAY TO MY DATE TONIGHT
www.garfield.com
© 2006 PAWS, INC. All Rights Reserved.
"HOWDY DOO!"
JIM DAVIS 5-23
"HOW'S TRICKS?"
LADIES AND GENTLEMEN, SHECKY ARBUCKLE

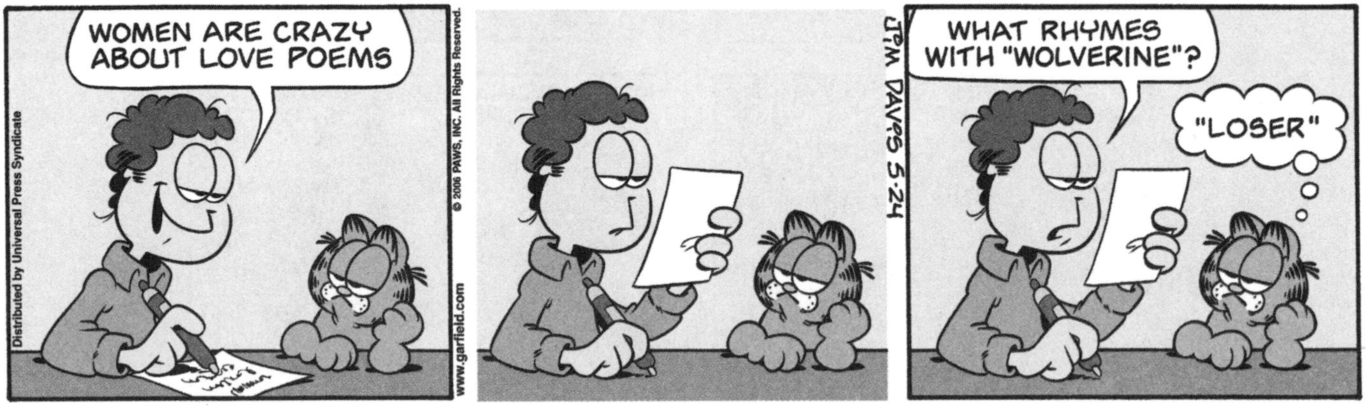
Distributed by Universal Press Syndicate
WOMEN ARE CRAZY ABOUT LOVE POEMS
© 2006 PAWS, INC. All Rights Reserved.
www.garfield.com
JIM DAVIS 5-24
WHAT RHYMES WITH "WOLVERINE"?
"LOSER"

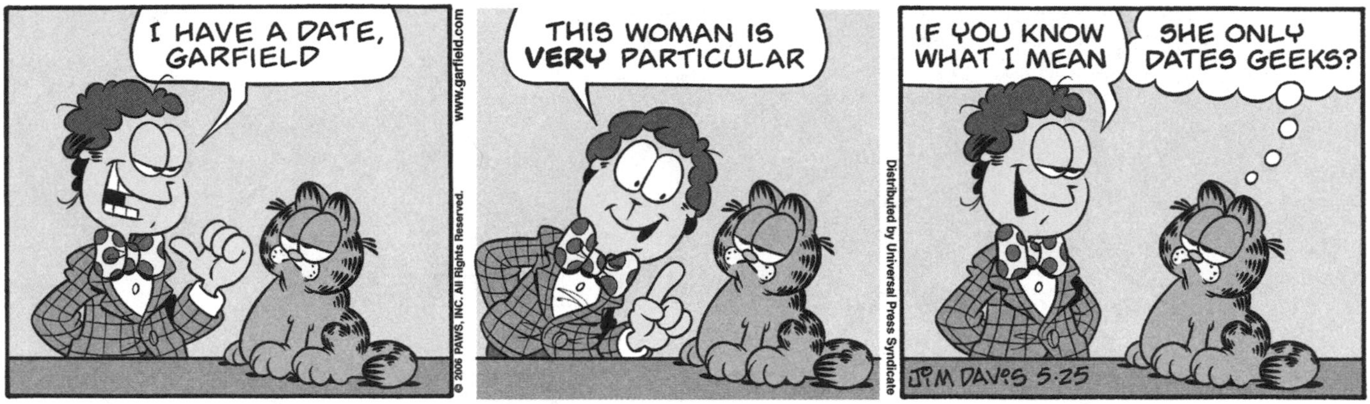
I HAVE A DATE, GARFIELD
THIS WOMAN IS **VERY** PARTICULAR
IF YOU KNOW WHAT I MEAN
SHE ONLY DATES GEEKS?
© 2006 PAWS, INC. All Rights Reserved. www.garfield.com
Distributed by Universal Press Syndicate
JIM DAVIS 5-25

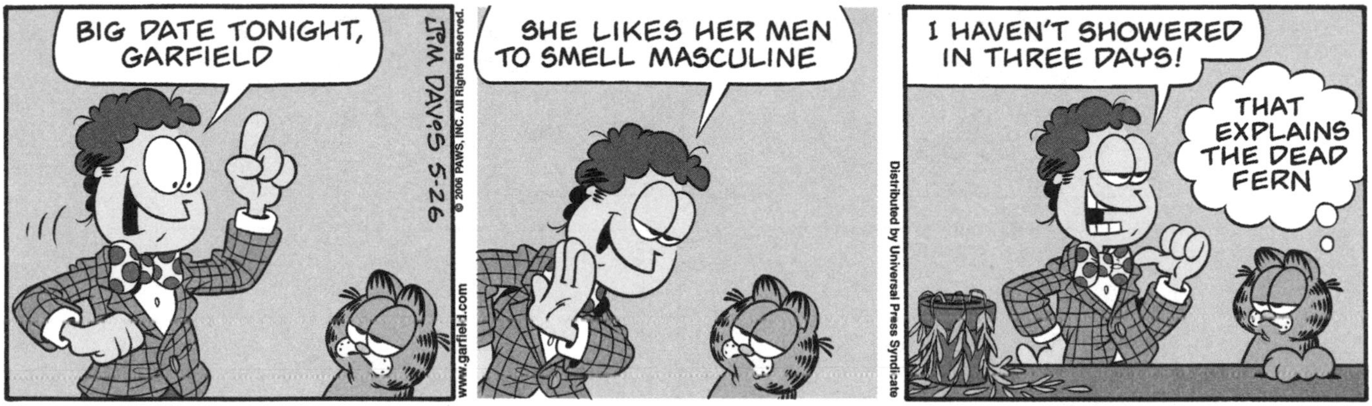
BIG DATE TONIGHT, GARFIELD
SHE LIKES HER MEN TO SMELL MASCULINE
I HAVEN'T SHOWERED IN THREE DAYS!
THAT EXPLAINS THE DEAD FERN
JIM DAVIS 5-26
© 2006 PAWS, INC. All Rights Reserved. www.garfield.com
Distributed by Universal Press Syndicate

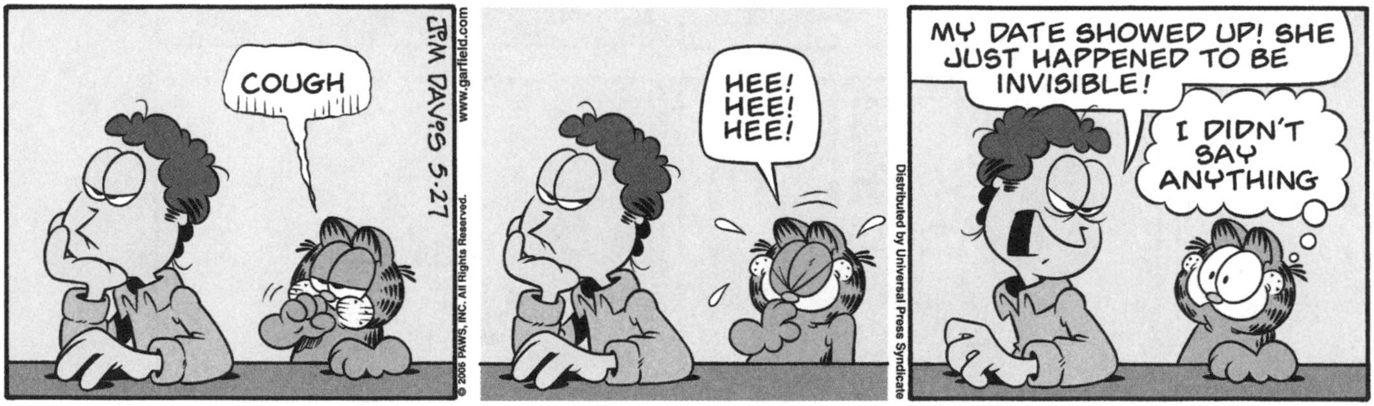
COUGH
HEE! HEE! HEE!
MY DATE SHOWED UP! SHE JUST HAPPENED TO BE INVISIBLE!
I DIDN'T SAY ANYTHING
JIM DAVIS 5-27
© 2006 PAWS, INC. All Rights Reserved. www.garfield.com
Distributed by Universal Press Syndicate

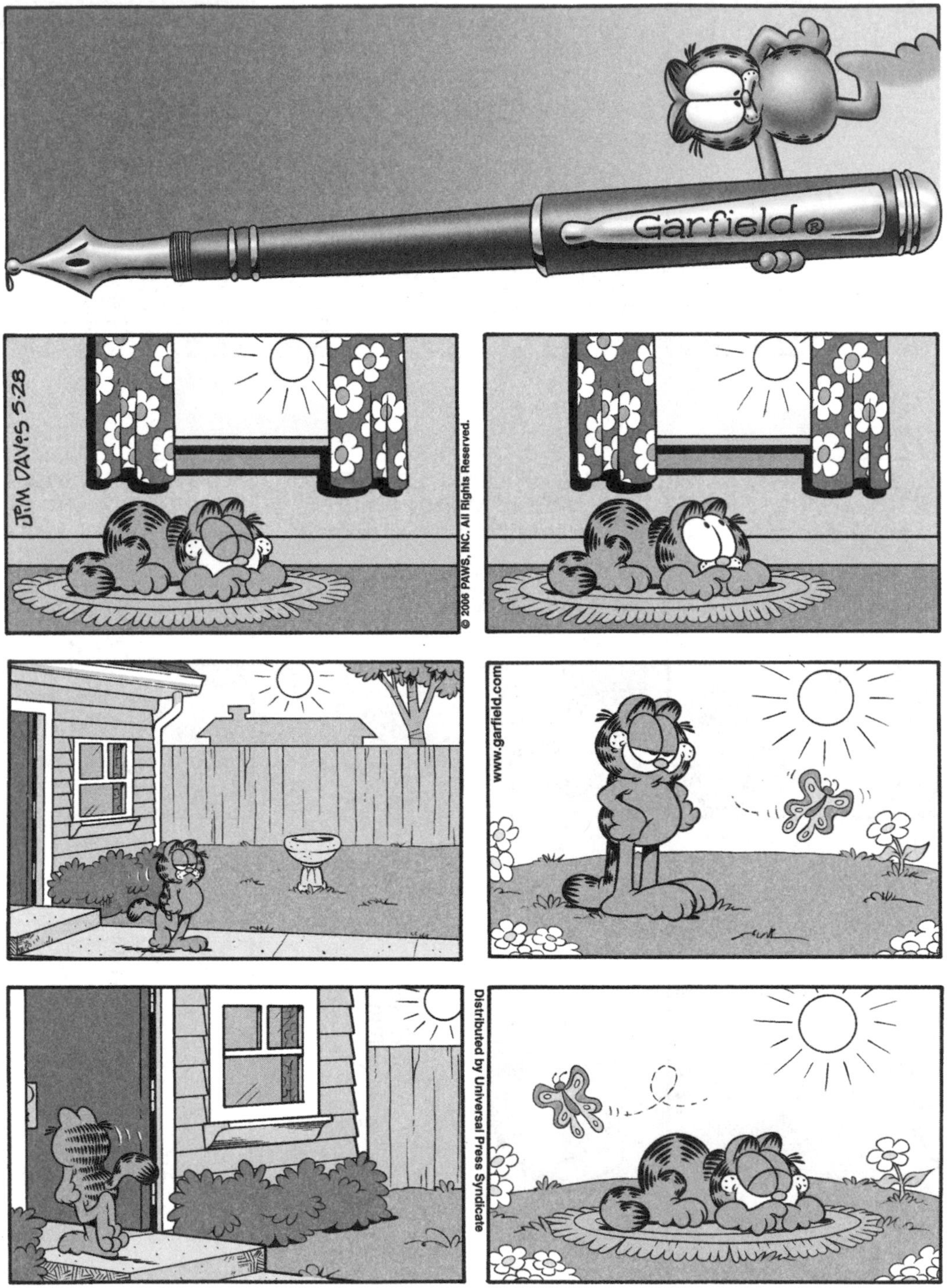
Garfield®
JIM DAVIS 5-28
© 2006 PAWS, INC. All Rights Reserved.
www.garfield.com
Distributed by Universal Press Syndicate

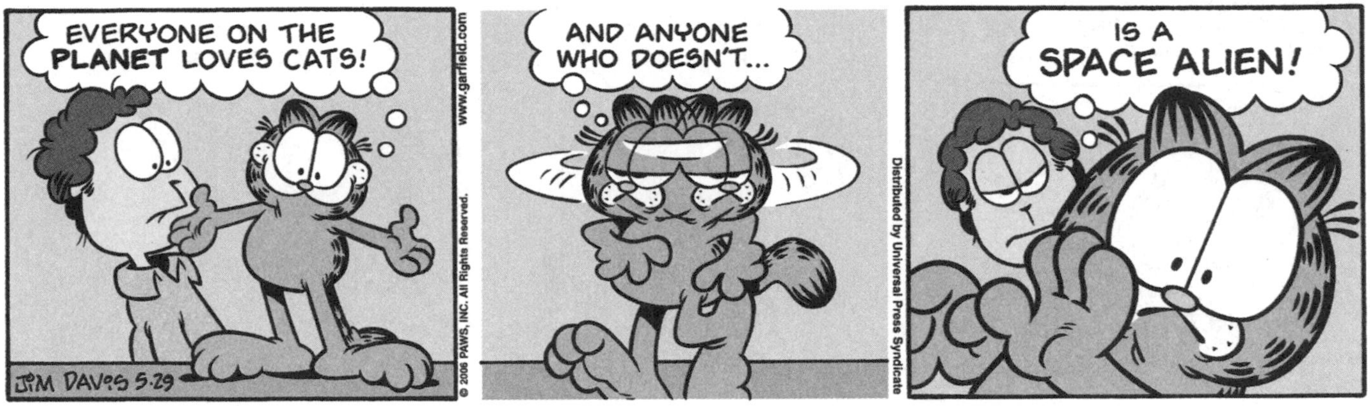
EVERYONE ON THE **PLANET** LOVES CATS!
JIM DAVIS 5-29
www.garfield.com
© 2006 PAWS, INC. All Rights Reserved.
AND ANYONE WHO DOESN'T...
Distributed by Universal Press Syndicate
IS A SPACE ALIEN!

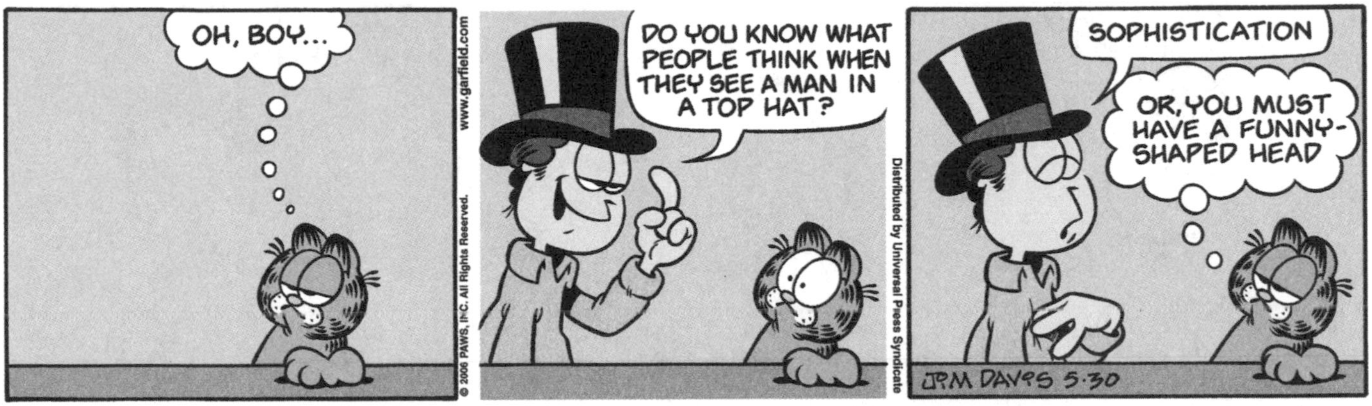
OH, BOY...
www.garfield.com
© 2006 PAWS, INC. All Rights Reserved.
DO YOU KNOW WHAT PEOPLE THINK WHEN THEY SEE A MAN IN A TOP HAT?
Distributed by Universal Press Syndicate
SOPHISTICATION
OR, YOU MUST HAVE A FUNNY-SHAPED HEAD
JIM DAVIS 5-30

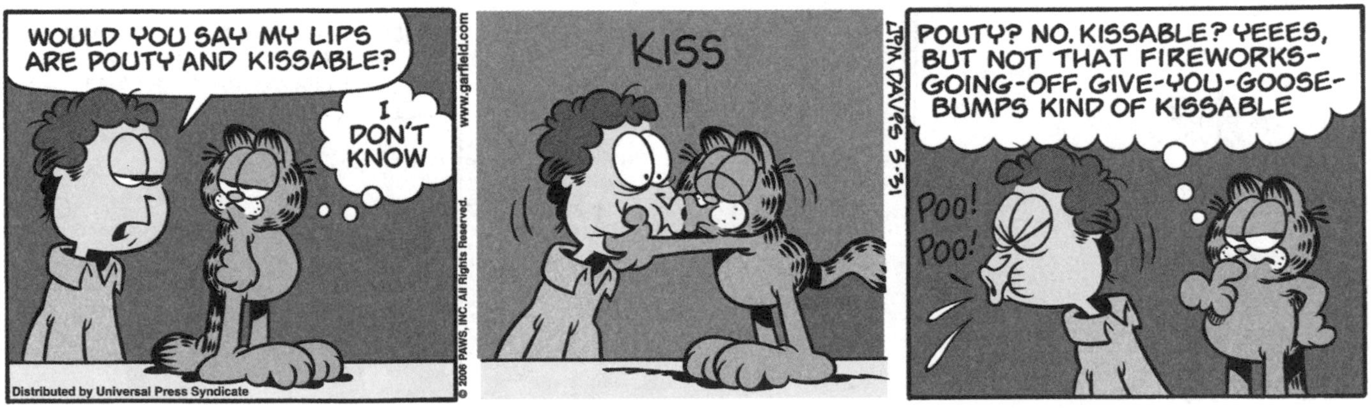
WOULD YOU SAY MY LIPS ARE POUTY AND KISSABLE?
I DON'T KNOW
Distributed by Universal Press Syndicate
www.garfield.com
© 2006 PAWS, INC. All Rights Reserved.
KISS
JIM DAVIS 5-31
POUTY? NO. KISSABLE? YEEES, BUT NOT THAT FIREWORKS-GOING-OFF, GIVE-YOU-GOOSE-BUMPS KIND OF KISSABLE
Poo! Poo!

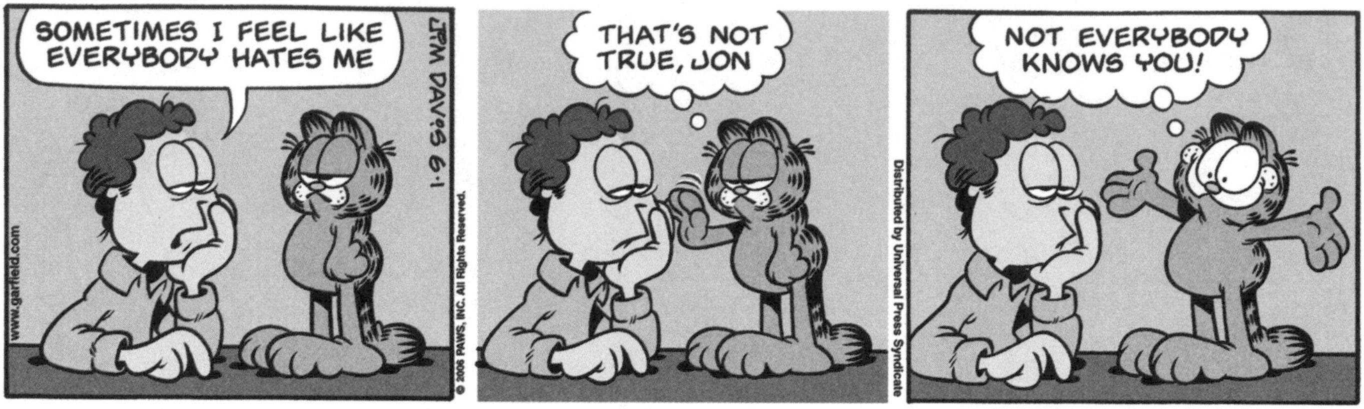
SOMETIMES I FEEL LIKE EVERYBODY HATES ME
JIM DAVIS 6-1
www.garfield.com
© 2006 PAWS, INC. All Rights Reserved.
THAT'S NOT TRUE, JON
Distributed by Universal Press Syndicate
NOT EVERYBODY KNOWS YOU!

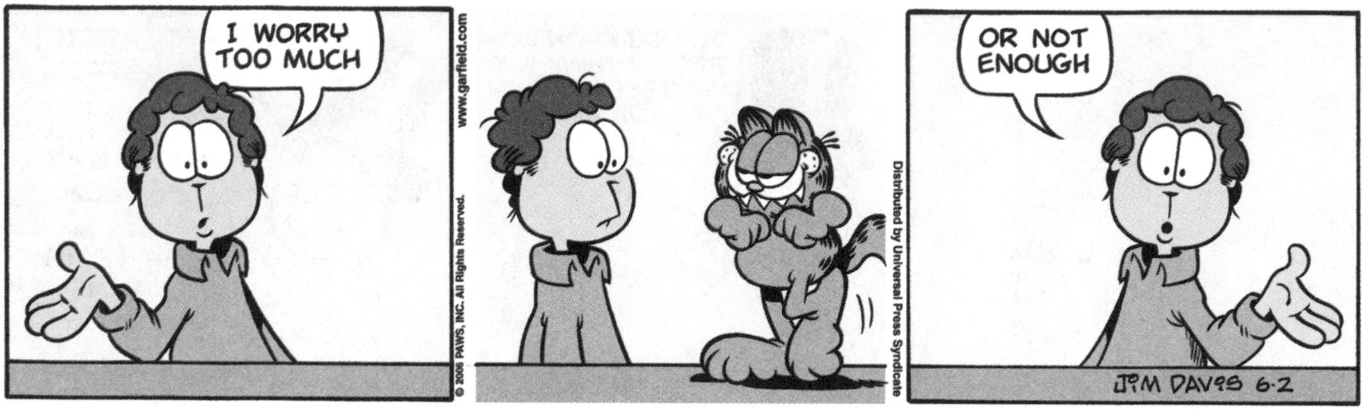
I WORRY TOO MUCH
www.garfield.com
© 2006 PAWS, INC. All Rights Reserved.
Distributed by Universal Press Syndicate
OR NOT ENOUGH
JIM DAVIS 6-2

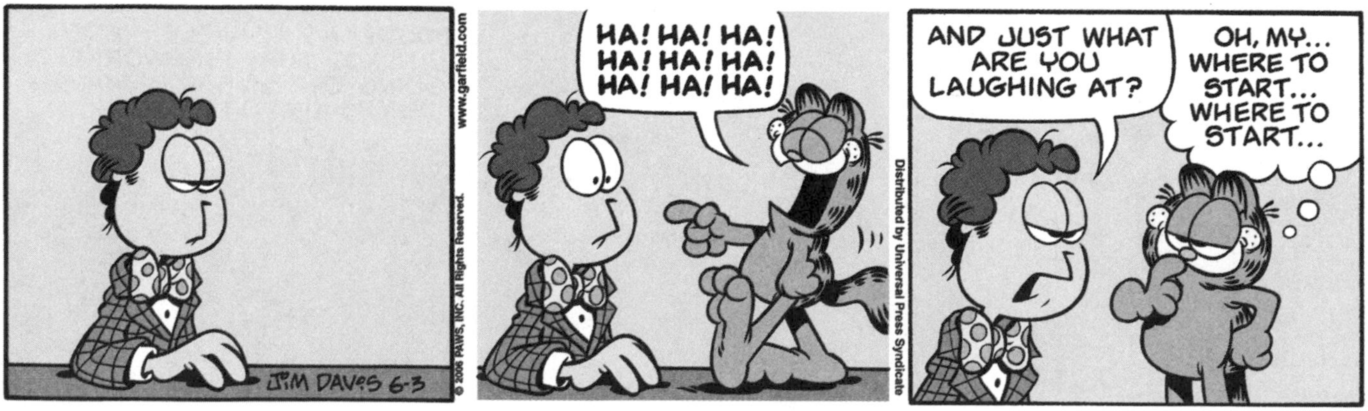
JIM DAVIS 6-3
www.garfield.com
© 2006 PAWS, INC. All Rights Reserved.
HA! HA! HA! HA! HA! HA! HA! HA! HA!
Distributed by Universal Press Syndicate
AND JUST WHAT ARE YOU LAUGHING AT?
OH, MY... WHERE TO START... WHERE TO START...

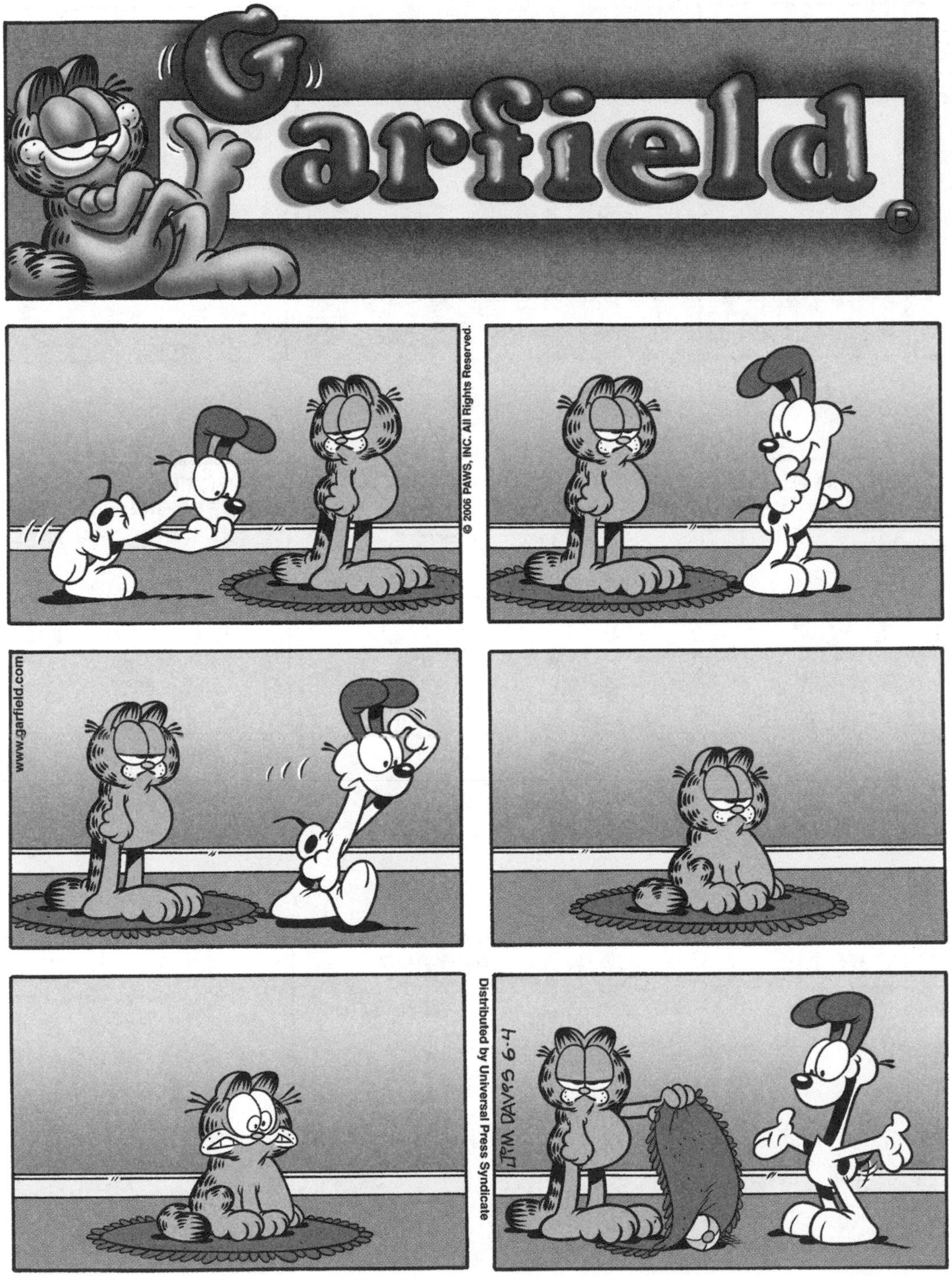
Garfield
© 2006 PAWS, INC. All Rights Reserved.
www.garfield.com
Distributed by Universal Press Syndicate
JPM DAVIS 6-4

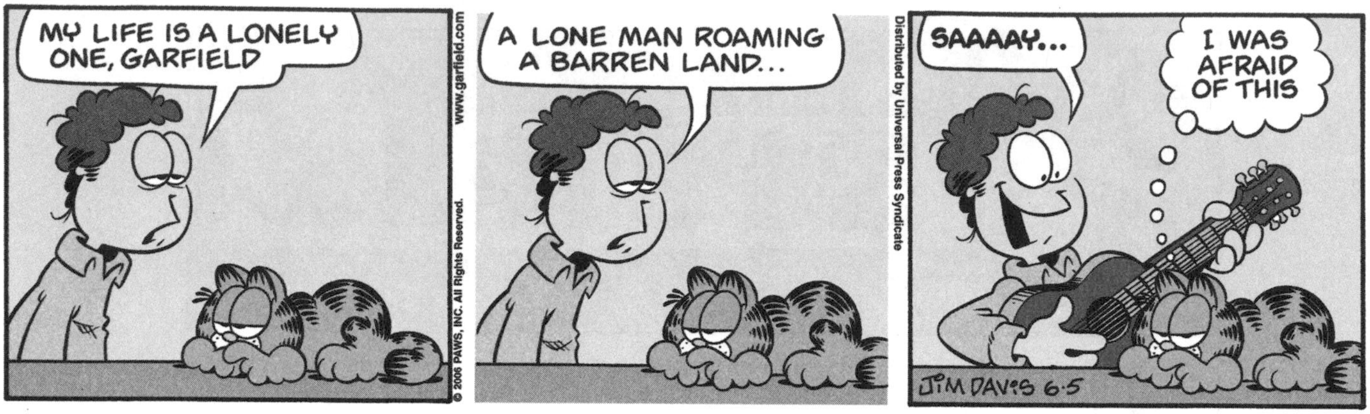
MY LIFE IS A LONELY ONE, GARFIELD
© 2006 PAWS, INC. All Rights Reserved. www.garfield.com
A LONE MAN ROAMING A BARREN LAND...
Distributed by Universal Press Syndicate
SAAAAY...
I WAS AFRAID OF THIS
JIM DAVIS 6-5

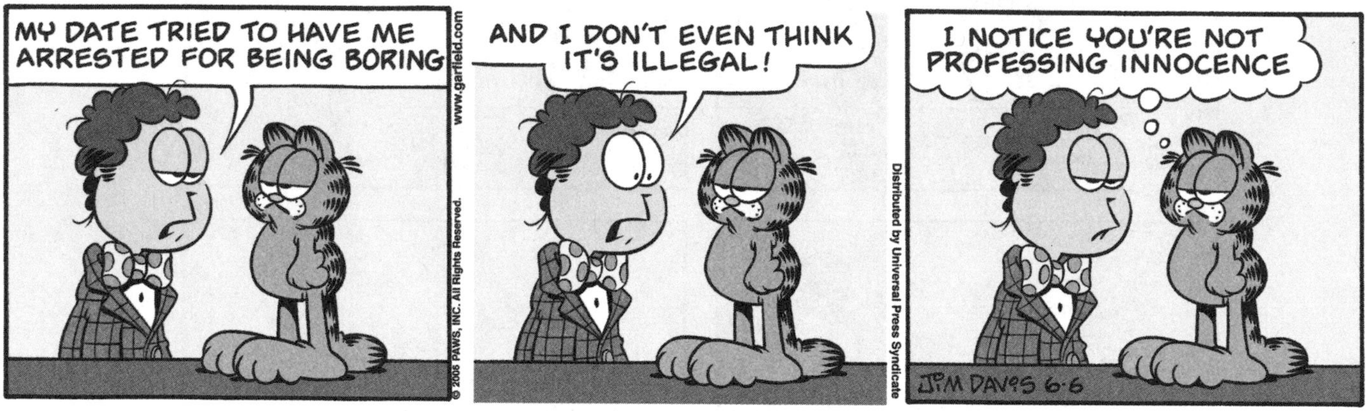
MY DATE TRIED TO HAVE ME ARRESTED FOR BEING BORING
© 2006 PAWS, INC. All Rights Reserved. www.garfield.com
AND I DON'T EVEN THINK IT'S ILLEGAL!
Distributed by Universal Press Syndicate
I NOTICE YOU'RE NOT PROFESSING INNOCENCE
JIM DAVIS 6-6

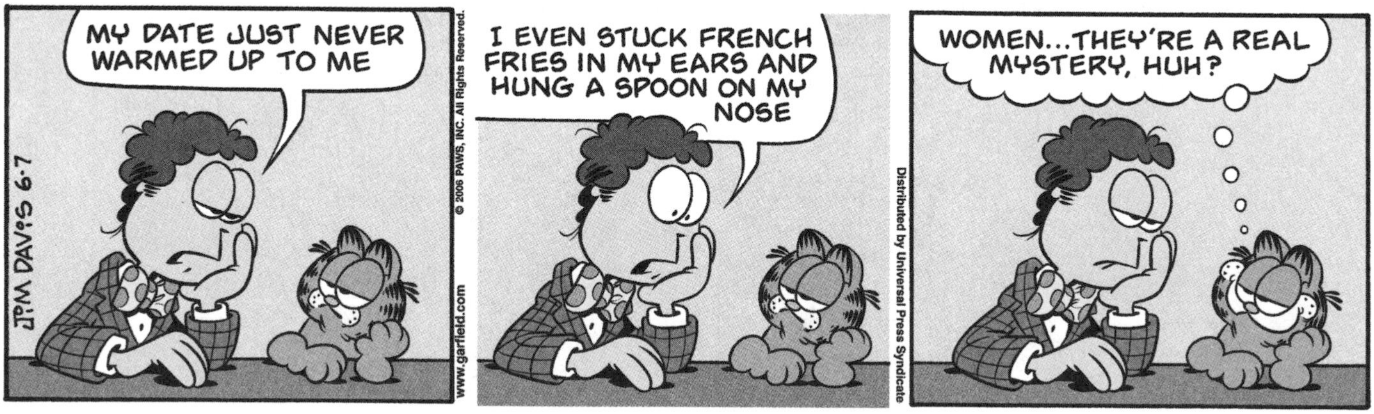
MY DATE JUST NEVER WARMED UP TO ME
JIM DAVIS 6-7
© 2006 PAWS, INC. All Rights Reserved. www.garfield.com
I EVEN STUCK FRENCH FRIES IN MY EARS AND HUNG A SPOON ON MY NOSE
Distributed by Universal Press Syndicate
WOMEN...THEY'RE A REAL MYSTERY, HUH?

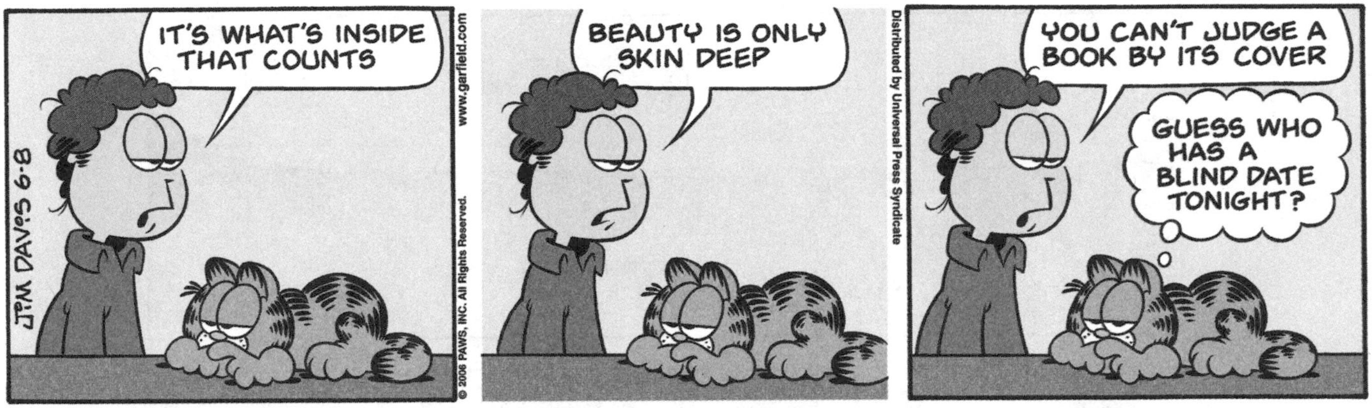
JIM DAVIS 6-8
IT'S WHAT'S INSIDE THAT COUNTS
© 2006 PAWS, INC. All Rights Reserved. www.garfield.com
BEAUTY IS ONLY SKIN DEEP
Distributed by Universal Press Syndicate
YOU CAN'T JUDGE A BOOK BY ITS COVER
GUESS WHO HAS A BLIND DATE TONIGHT?

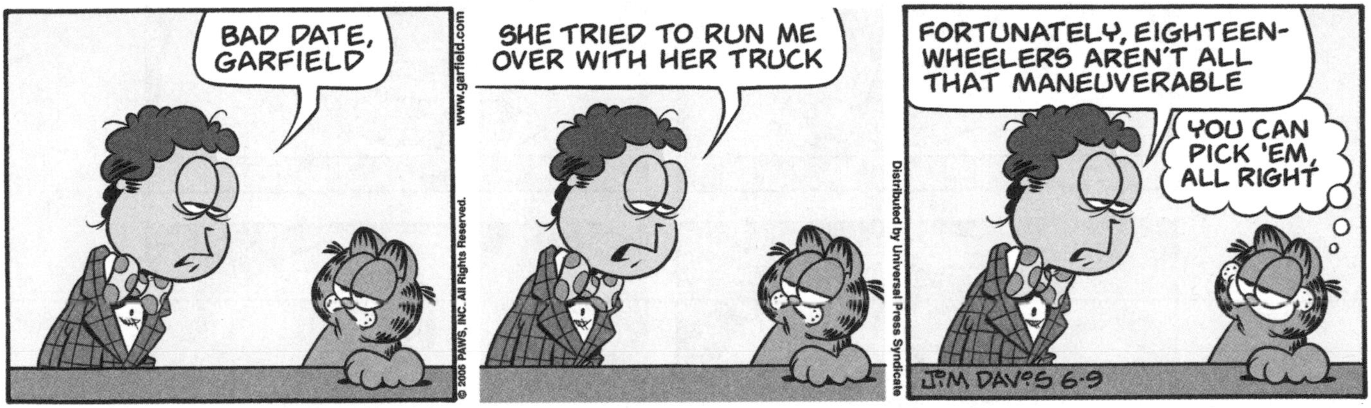
BAD DATE, GARFIELD
© 2006 PAWS, INC. All Rights Reserved. www.garfield.com
SHE TRIED TO RUN ME OVER WITH HER TRUCK
Distributed by Universal Press Syndicate
FORTUNATELY, EIGHTEEN-WHEELERS AREN'T ALL THAT MANEUVERABLE
YOU CAN PICK 'EM, ALL RIGHT
JIM DAVIS 6-9

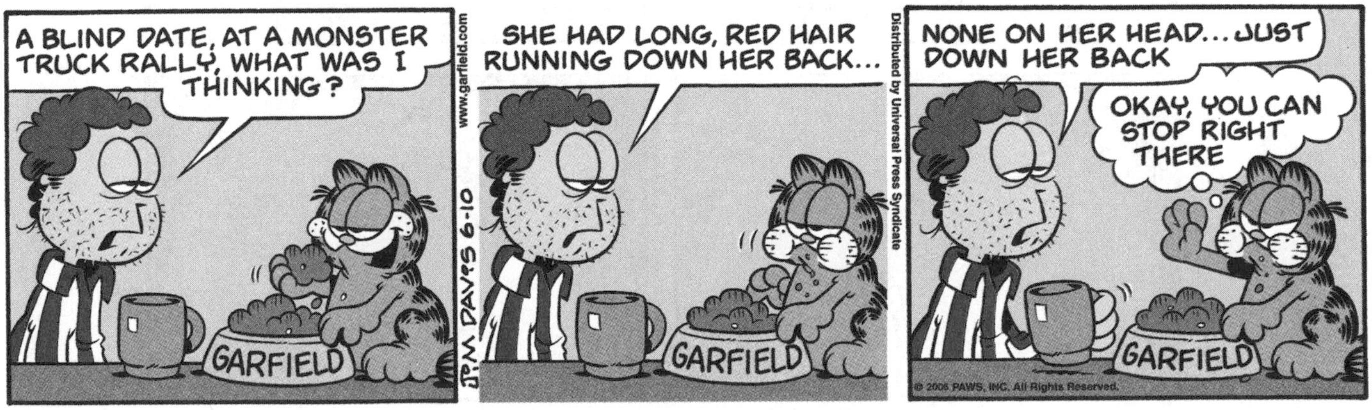
A BLIND DATE, AT A MONSTER TRUCK RALLY, WHAT WAS I THINKING?
GARFIELD
www.garfield.com
JIM DAVIS 6-10
SHE HAD LONG, RED HAIR RUNNING DOWN HER BACK...
GARFIELD
Distributed by Universal Press Syndicate
NONE ON HER HEAD...JUST DOWN HER BACK
OKAY, YOU CAN STOP RIGHT THERE
GARFIELD
© 2006 PAWS, INC. All Rights Reserved.

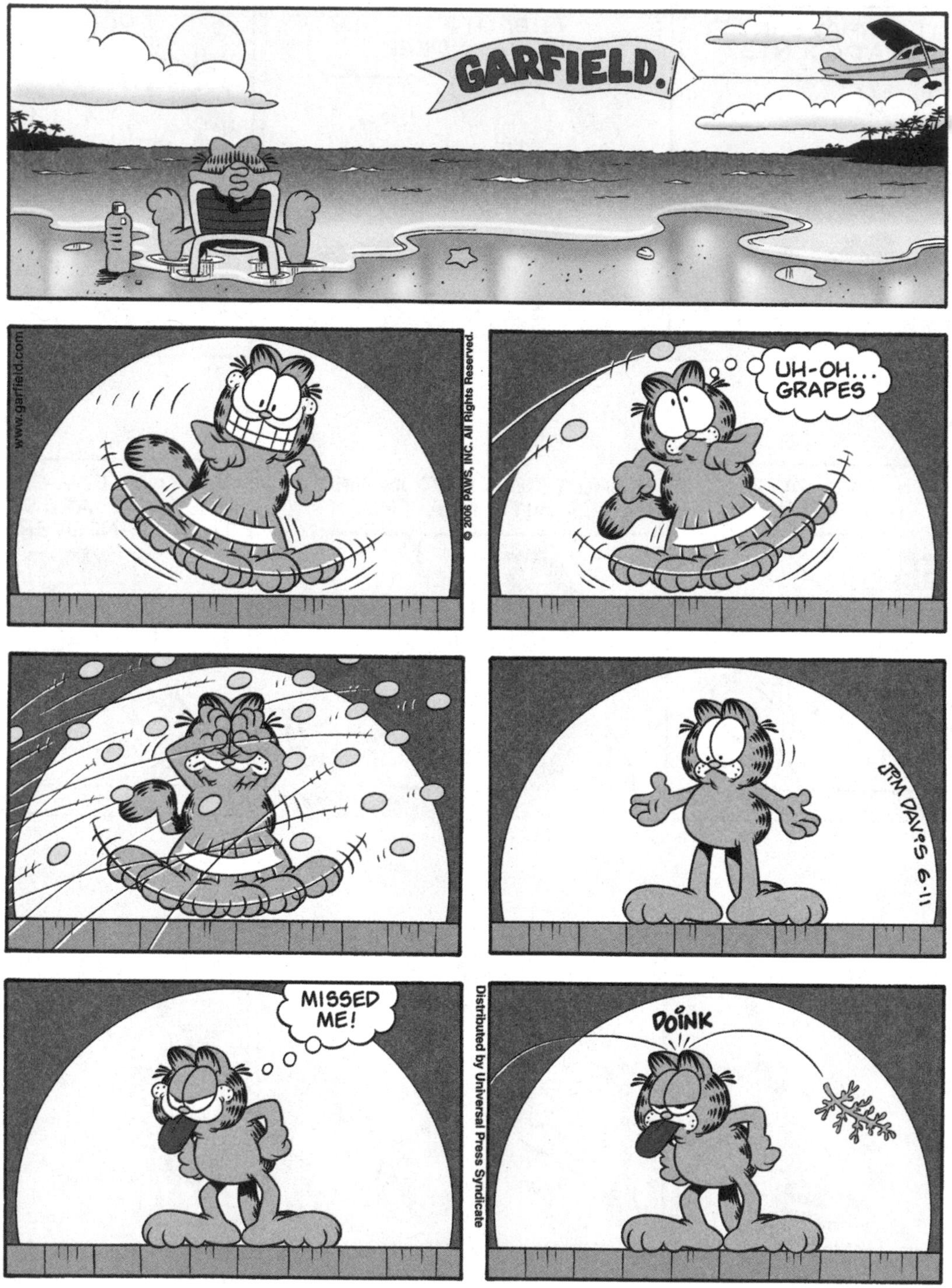
GARFIELD.
www.garfield.com
© 2006 PAWS, INC. All Rights Reserved.
UH-OH... GRAPES
JIM DAVIS 6-11
MISSED ME!
Distributed by Universal Press Syndicate
DOINK

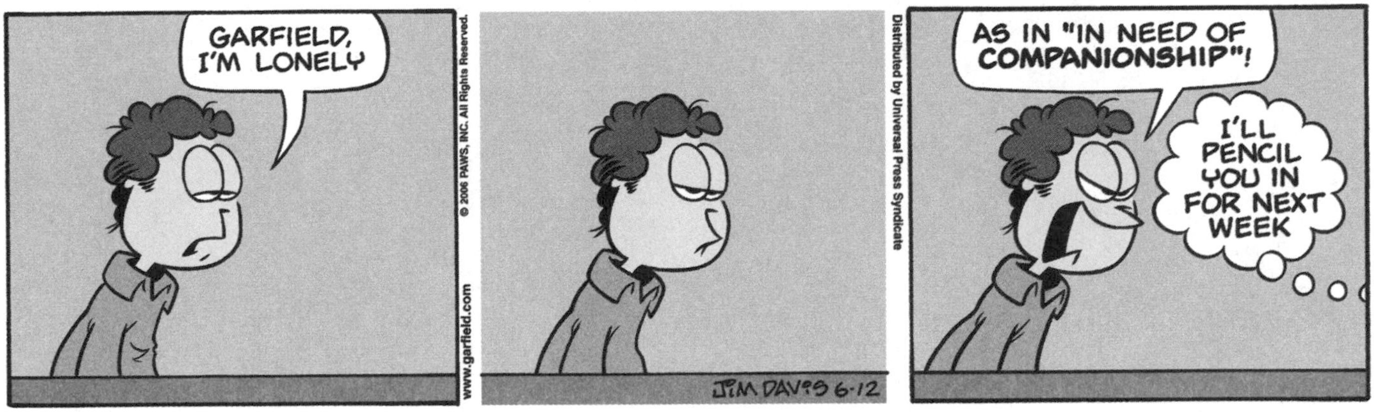
GARFIELD, I'M LONELY
© 2006 PAWS, INC. All Rights Reserved.
www.garfield.com
JIM DAVIS 6-12
Distributed by Universal Press Syndicate
AS IN "IN NEED OF COMPANIONSHIP"!
I'LL PENCIL YOU IN FOR NEXT WEEK

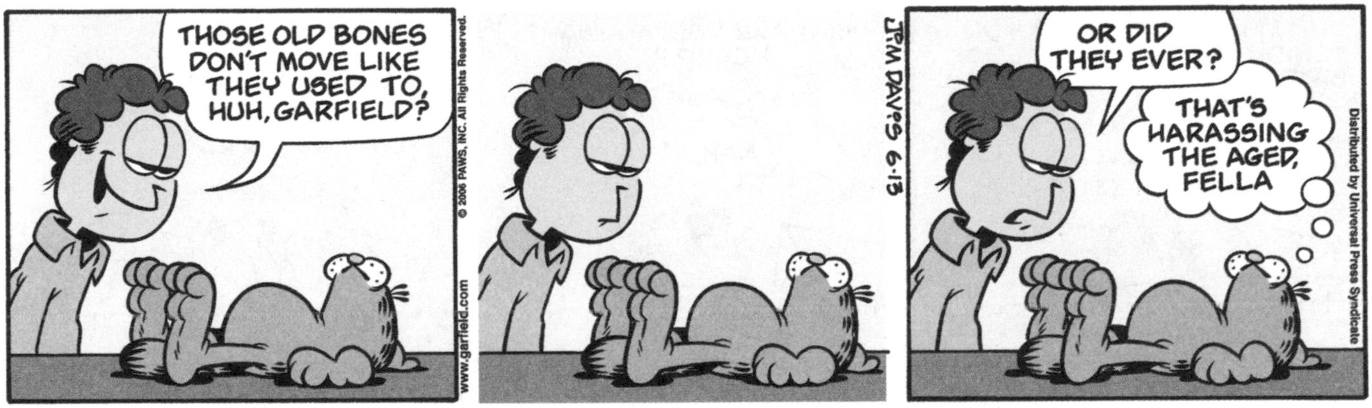
THOSE OLD BONES DON'T MOVE LIKE THEY USED TO, HUH, GARFIELD?
© 2006 PAWS, INC. All Rights Reserved.
www.garfield.com
JIM DAVIS 6-13
OR DID THEY EVER?
THAT'S HARASSING THE AGED, FELLA
Distributed by Universal Press Syndicate

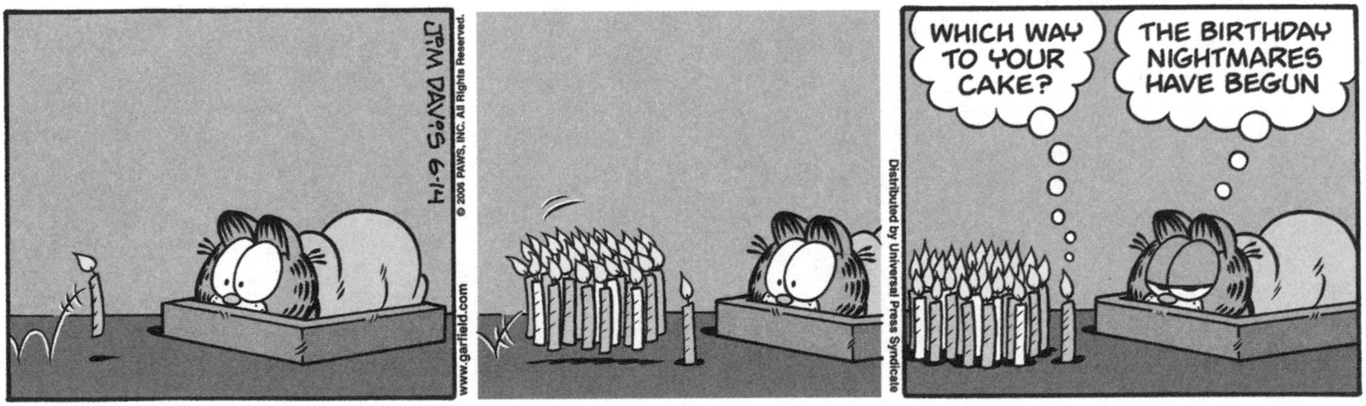
JIM DAVIS 6-14
© 2006 PAWS, INC. All Rights Reserved.
www.garfield.com
Distributed by Universal Press Syndicate
WHICH WAY TO YOUR CAKE?
THE BIRTHDAY NIGHTMARES HAVE BEGUN

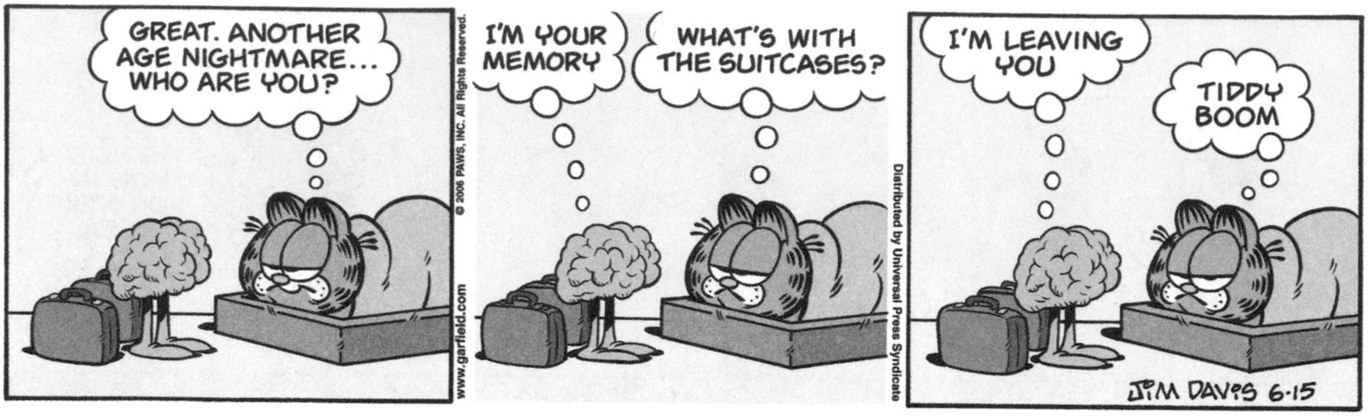
GREAT. ANOTHER AGE NIGHTMARE... WHO ARE YOU?
I'M YOUR MEMORY
WHAT'S WITH THE SUITCASES?
I'M LEAVING YOU
TIDDY BOOM
JIM DAVIS 6-15
© 2006 PAWS, INC. All Rights Reserved.
www.garfield.com
Distributed by Universal Press Syndicate

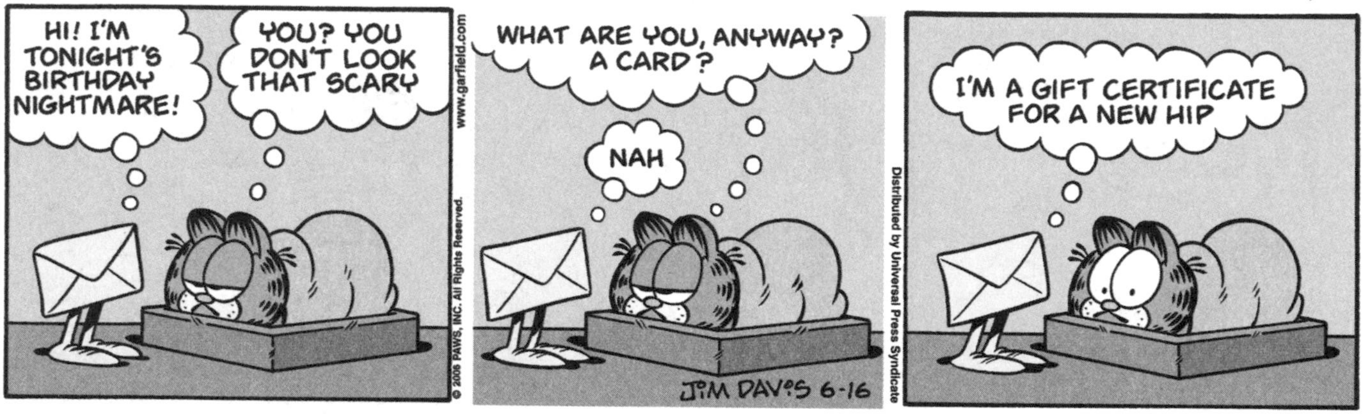
HI! I'M TONIGHT'S BIRTHDAY NIGHTMARE!
YOU? YOU DON'T LOOK THAT SCARY
WHAT ARE YOU, ANYWAY? A CARD?
NAH
I'M A GIFT CERTIFICATE FOR A NEW HIP
JIM DAVIS 6-16
© 2006 PAWS, INC. All Rights Reserved.
www.garfield.com
Distributed by Universal Press Syndicate

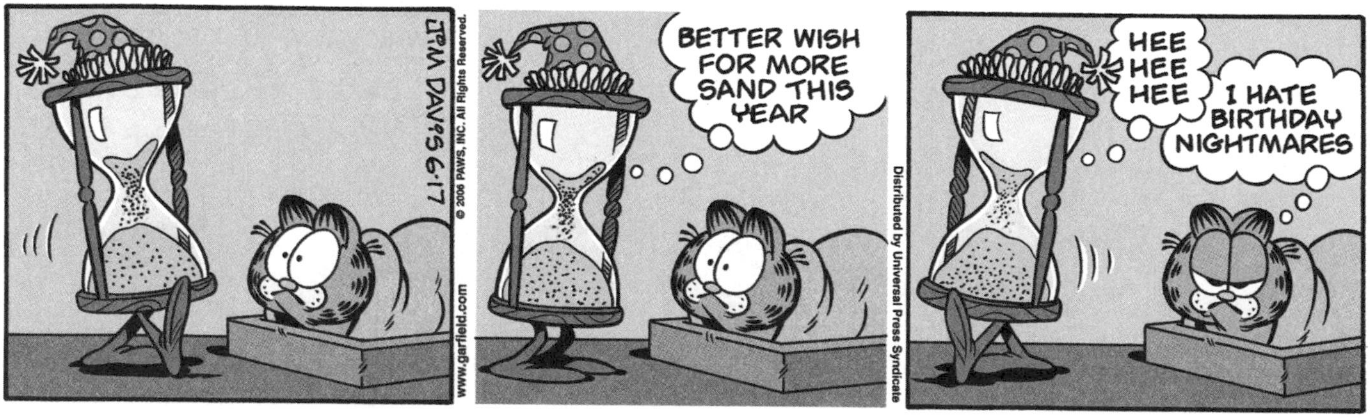
JIM DAVIS 6-17
BETTER WISH FOR MORE SAND THIS YEAR
HEE HEE HEE
I HATE BIRTHDAY NIGHTMARES
© 2006 PAWS, INC. All Rights Reserved.
www.garfield.com
Distributed by Universal Press Syndicate

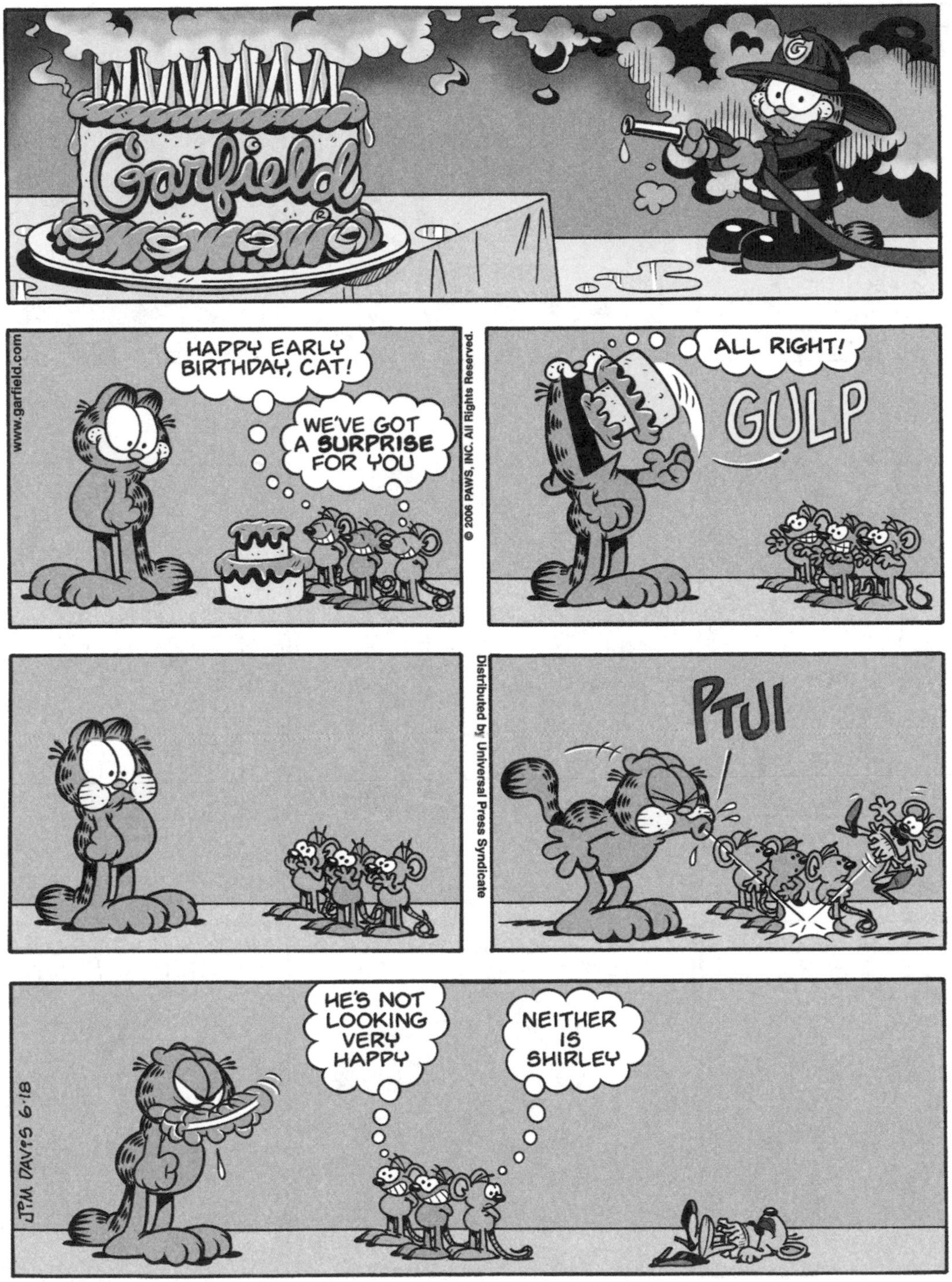
Garfield
www.garfield.com
HAPPY EARLY BIRTHDAY, CAT!
WE'VE GOT A **SURPRISE** FOR YOU
© 2006 PAWS, INC. All Rights Reserved.
ALL RIGHT!
GULP
Distributed by Universal Press Syndicate
PTUI
JPM DAVIS 6-18
HE'S NOT LOOKING VERY HAPPY
NEITHER IS SHIRLEY

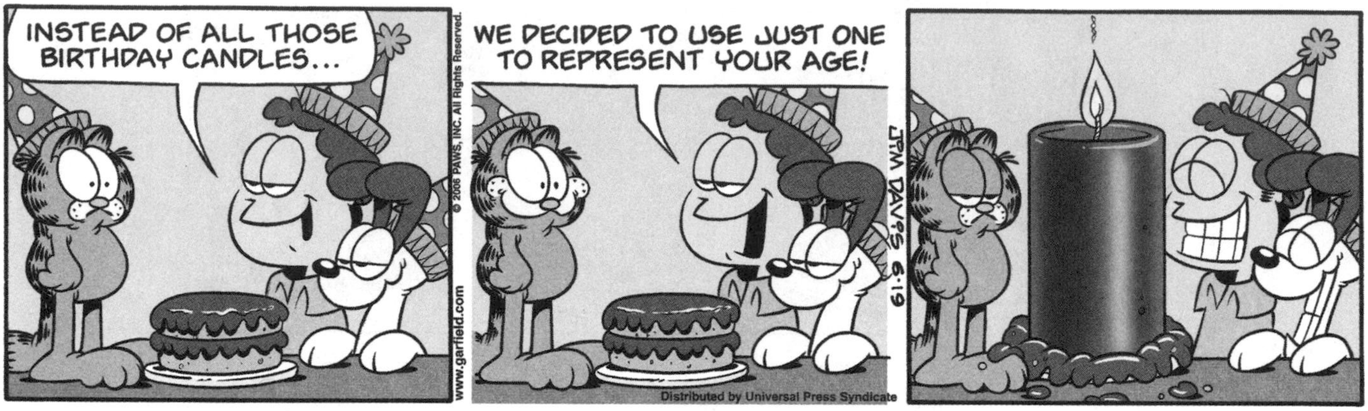
INSTEAD OF ALL THOSE BIRTHDAY CANDLES...
WE DECIDED TO USE JUST ONE TO REPRESENT YOUR AGE!
© 2006 PAWS, INC. All Rights Reserved.
www.garfield.com
JIM DAVIS 6-19
Distributed by Universal Press Syndicate

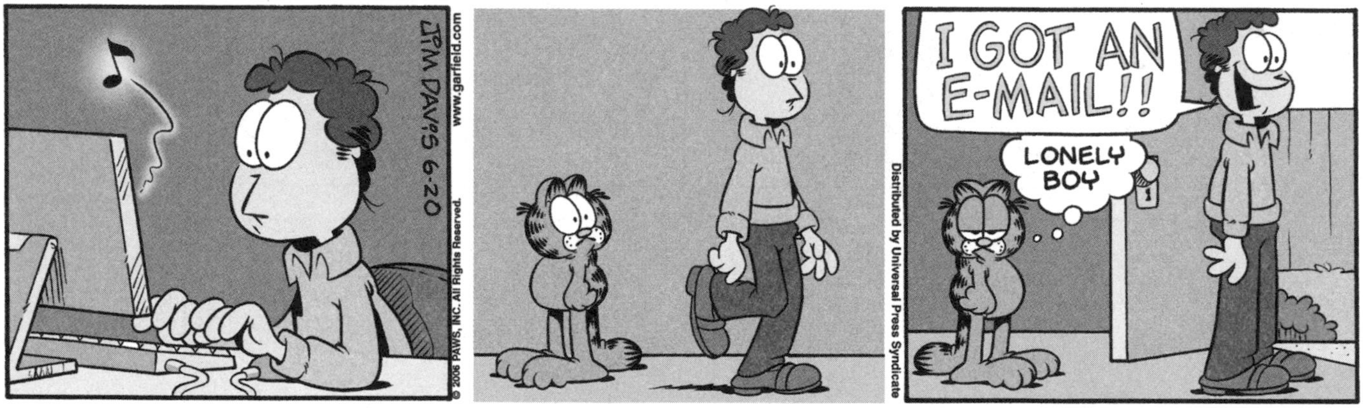
JIM DAVIS 6-20
www.garfield.com
© 2006 PAWS, INC. All Rights Reserved.
Distributed by Universal Press Syndicate
I GOT AN E-MAIL!!
LONELY BOY

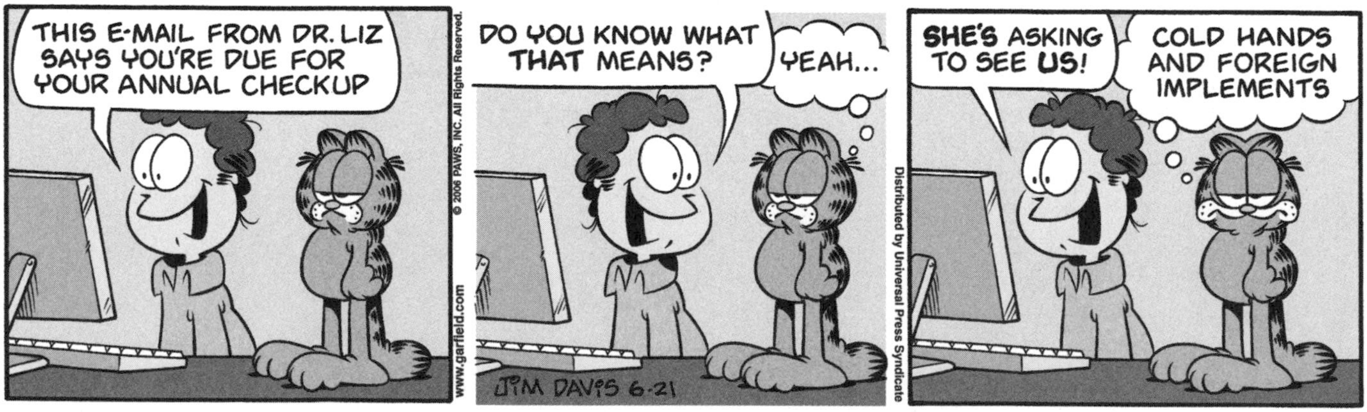
THIS E-MAIL FROM DR. LIZ SAYS YOU'RE DUE FOR YOUR ANNUAL CHECKUP
© 2006 PAWS, INC. All Rights Reserved.
www.garfield.com
DO YOU KNOW WHAT THAT MEANS?
YEAH...
JIM DAVIS 6-21
Distributed by Universal Press Syndicate
SHE'S ASKING TO SEE US!
COLD HANDS AND FOREIGN IMPLEMENTS

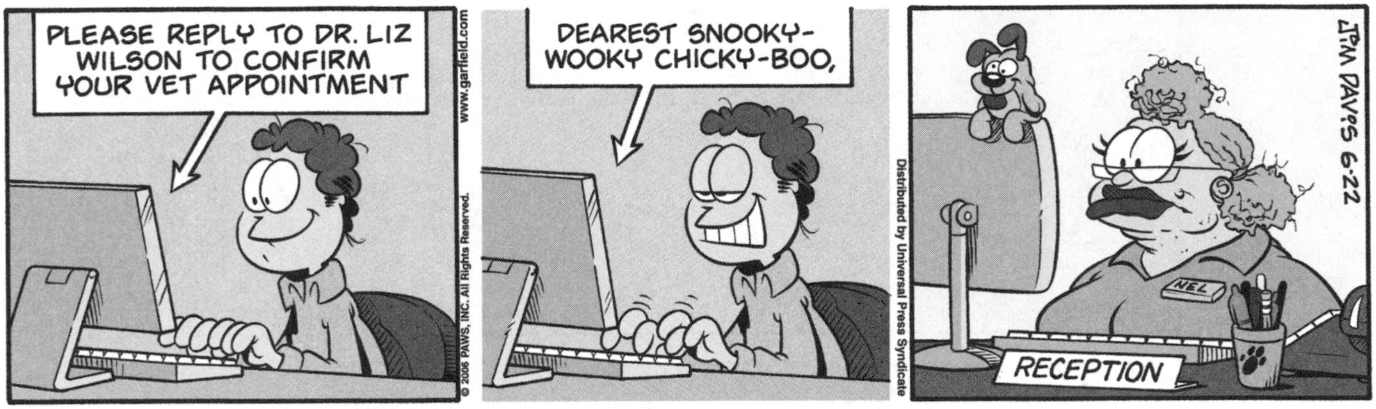
PLEASE REPLY TO DR. LIZ WILSON TO CONFIRM YOUR VET APPOINTMENT
© 2006 PAWS, INC. All Rights Reserved.
www.garfield.com
DEAREST SNOOKY-WOOKY CHICKY-BOO,
Distributed by Universal Press Syndicate
NEL
RECEPTION
JIM DAVIS 6-22

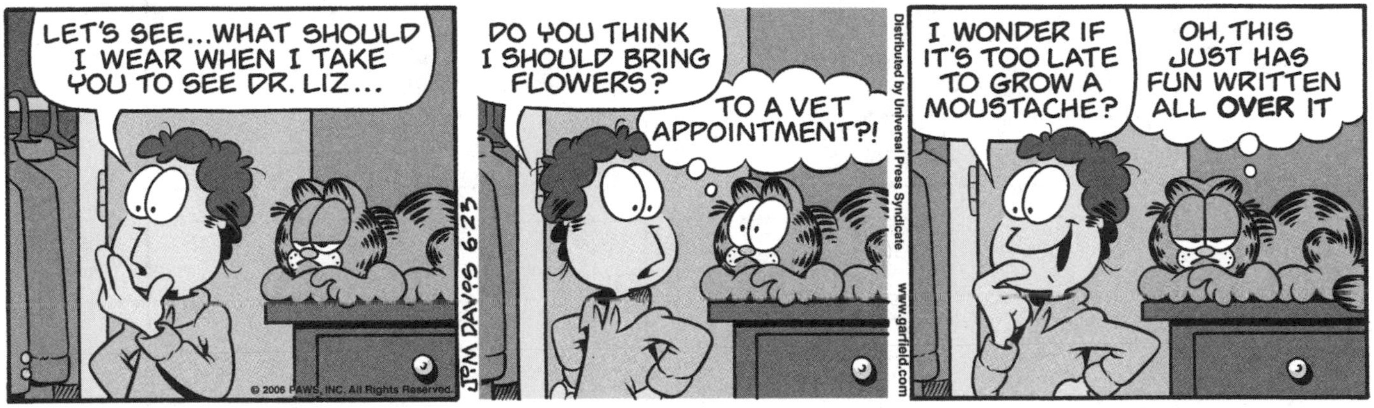
LET'S SEE...WHAT SHOULD I WEAR WHEN I TAKE YOU TO SEE DR. LIZ...
© 2006 PAWS, INC. All Rights Reserved.
JIM DAVIS 6-23
DO YOU THINK I SHOULD BRING FLOWERS?
TO A VET APPOINTMENT?!
Distributed by Universal Press Syndicate
www.garfield.com
I WONDER IF IT'S TOO LATE TO GROW A MOUSTACHE?
OH, THIS JUST HAS FUN WRITTEN ALL **OVER** IT

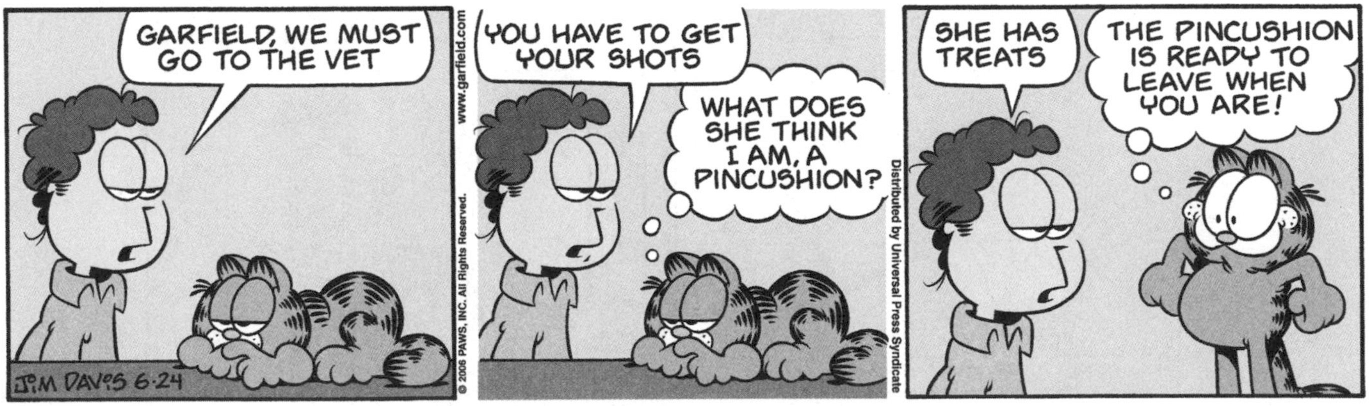
GARFIELD, WE MUST GO TO THE VET
JIM DAVIS 6-24
© 2006 PAWS, INC. All Rights Reserved.
www.garfield.com
YOU HAVE TO GET YOUR SHOTS
WHAT DOES SHE THINK I AM, A PINCUSHION?
Distributed by Universal Press Syndicate
SHE HAS TREATS
THE PINCUSHION IS READY TO LEAVE WHEN YOU ARE!

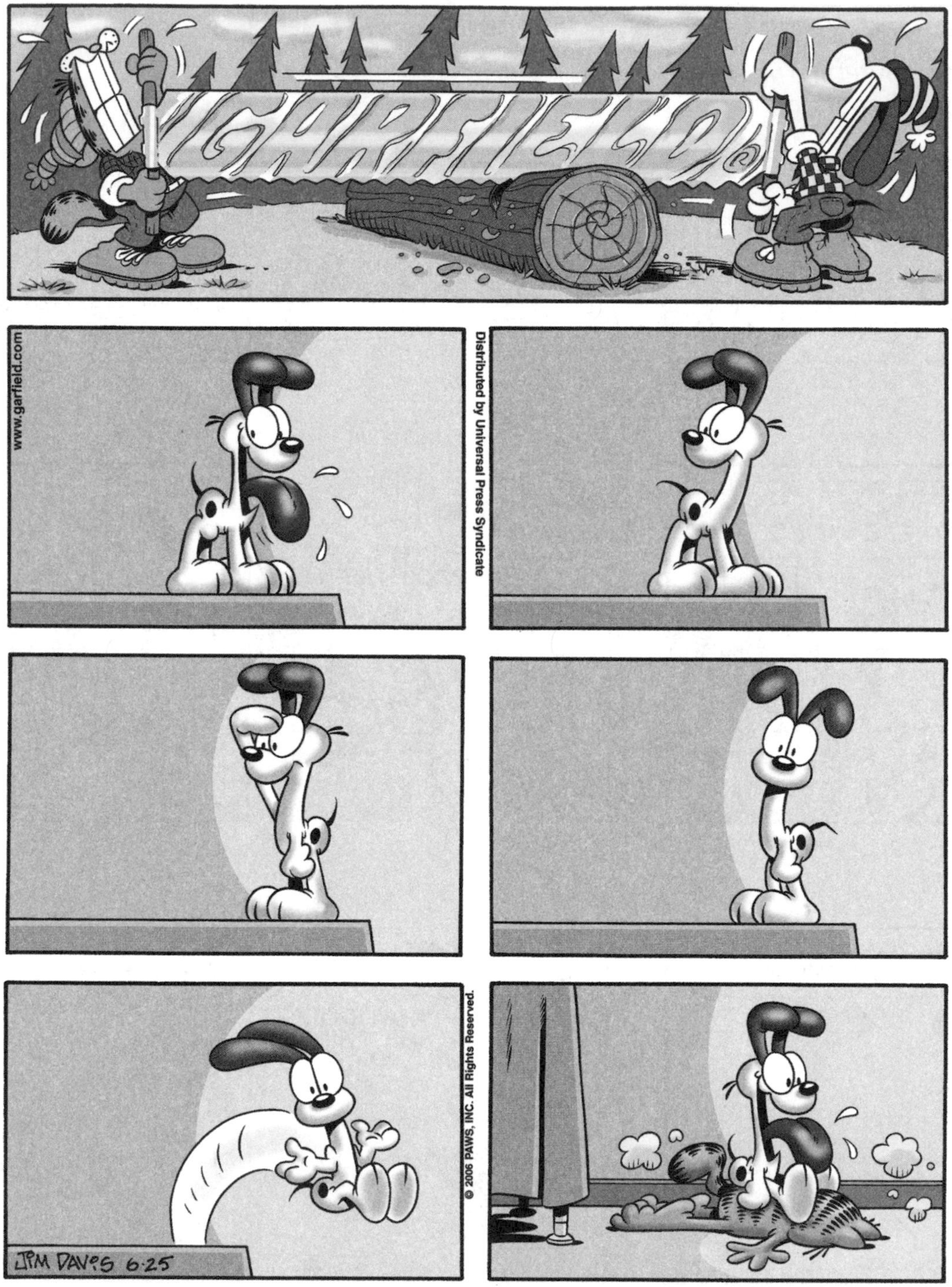
GARFIELD
www.garfield.com
Distributed by Universal Press Syndicate
© 2006 PAWS, INC. All Rights Reserved.
JIM DAVIS 6-25

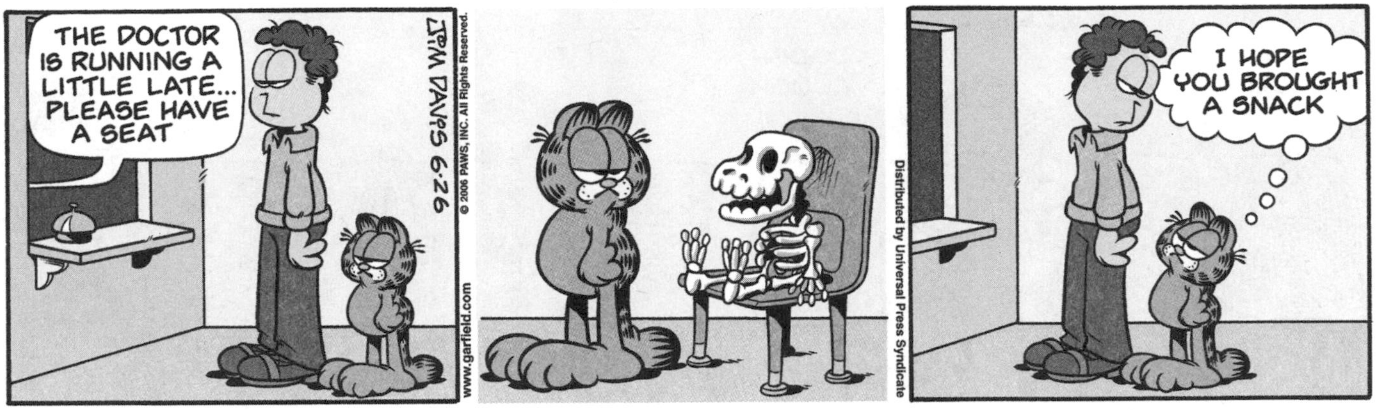
THE DOCTOR IS RUNNING A LITTLE LATE... PLEASE HAVE A SEAT
JIM DAVIS 6·26
© 2006 PAWS, INC. All Rights Reserved.
www.garfield.com
Distributed by Universal Press Syndicate
I HOPE YOU BROUGHT A SNACK

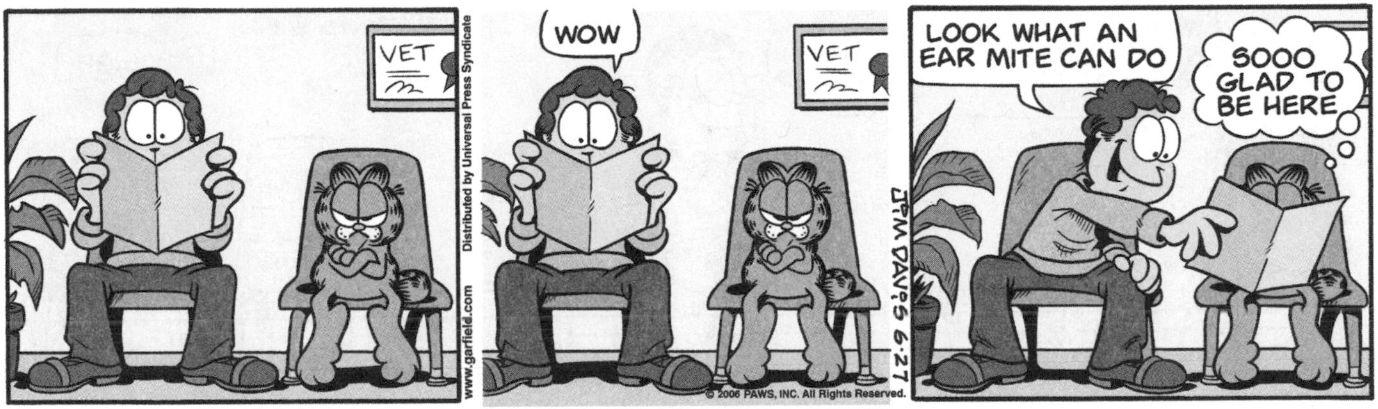
VET
Distributed by Universal Press Syndicate
www.garfield.com
WOW
JIM DAVIS 6·27
© 2006 PAWS, INC. All Rights Reserved.
LOOK WHAT AN EAR MITE CAN DO
SOOO GLAD TO BE HERE

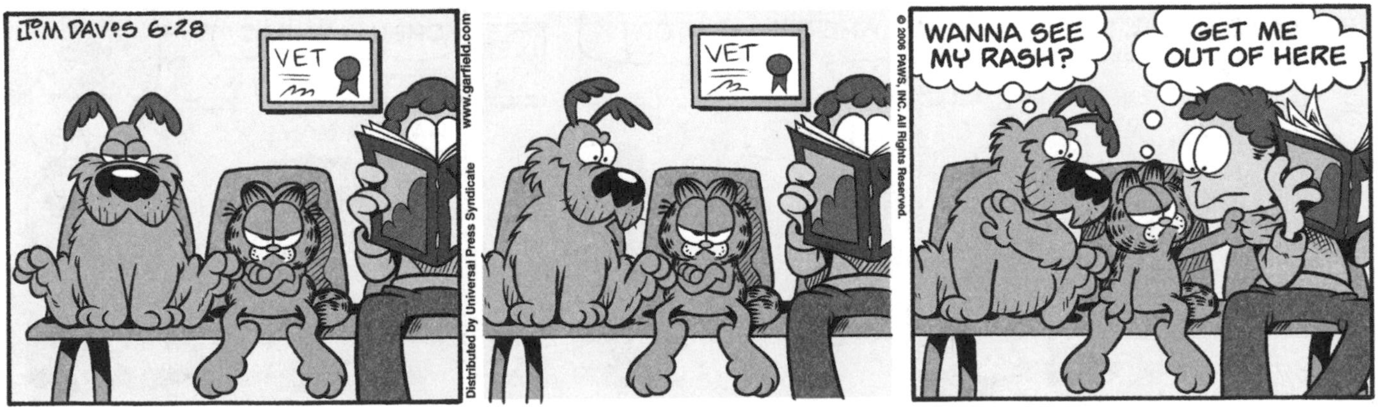
JIM DAVIS 6·28
VET
www.garfield.com
Distributed by Universal Press Syndicate
© 2006 PAWS, INC. All Rights Reserved.
WANNA SEE MY RASH?
GET ME OUT OF HERE

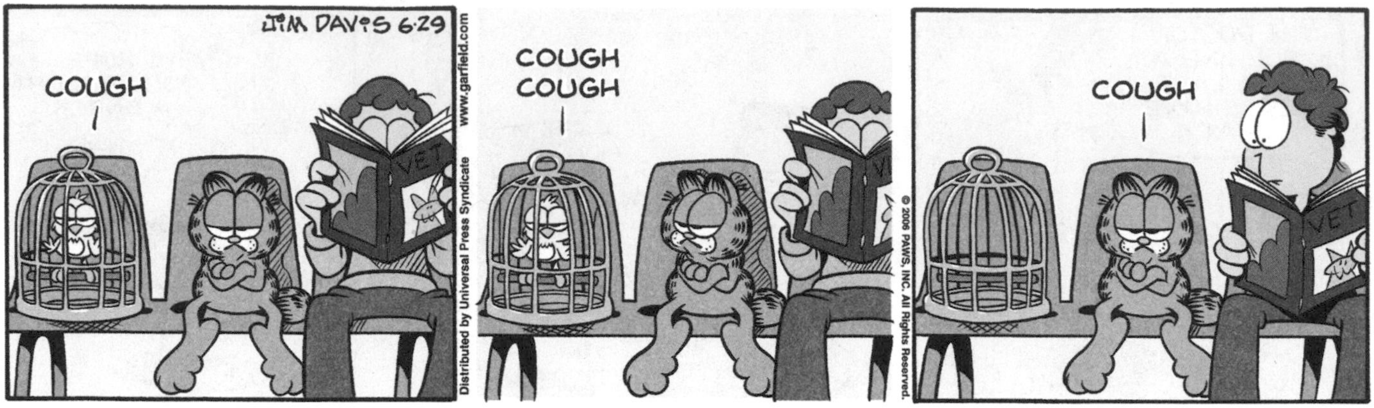
JIM DAVIS 6-29
COUGH
Distributed by Universal Press Syndicate www.garfield.com
COUGH COUGH
© 2006 PAWS, INC. All Rights Reserved.
COUGH

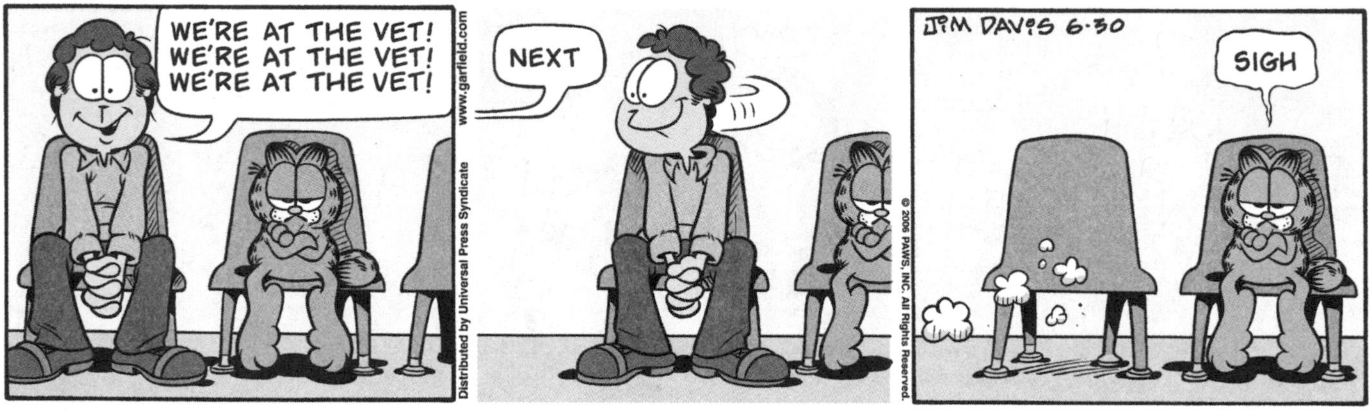
WE'RE AT THE VET! WE'RE AT THE VET! WE'RE AT THE VET!
Distributed by Universal Press Syndicate www.garfield.com
NEXT
© 2006 PAWS, INC. All Rights Reserved.
JIM DAVIS 6-30
SIGH

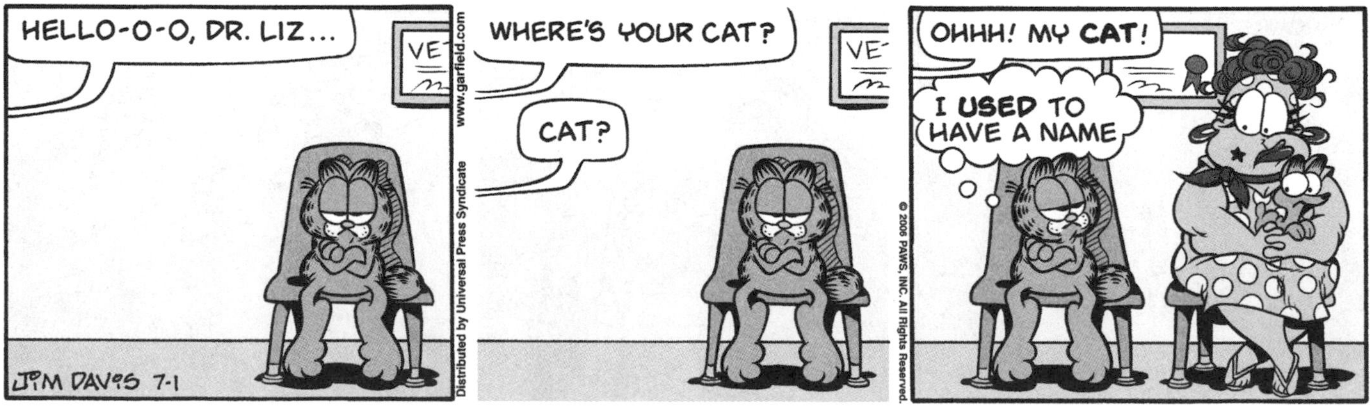
HELLO-O-O, DR. LIZ...
JIM DAVIS 7-1
Distributed by Universal Press Syndicate www.garfield.com
WHERE'S YOUR CAT?
CAT?
© 2006 PAWS, INC. All Rights Reserved.
OHHH! MY CAT!
I USED TO HAVE A NAME

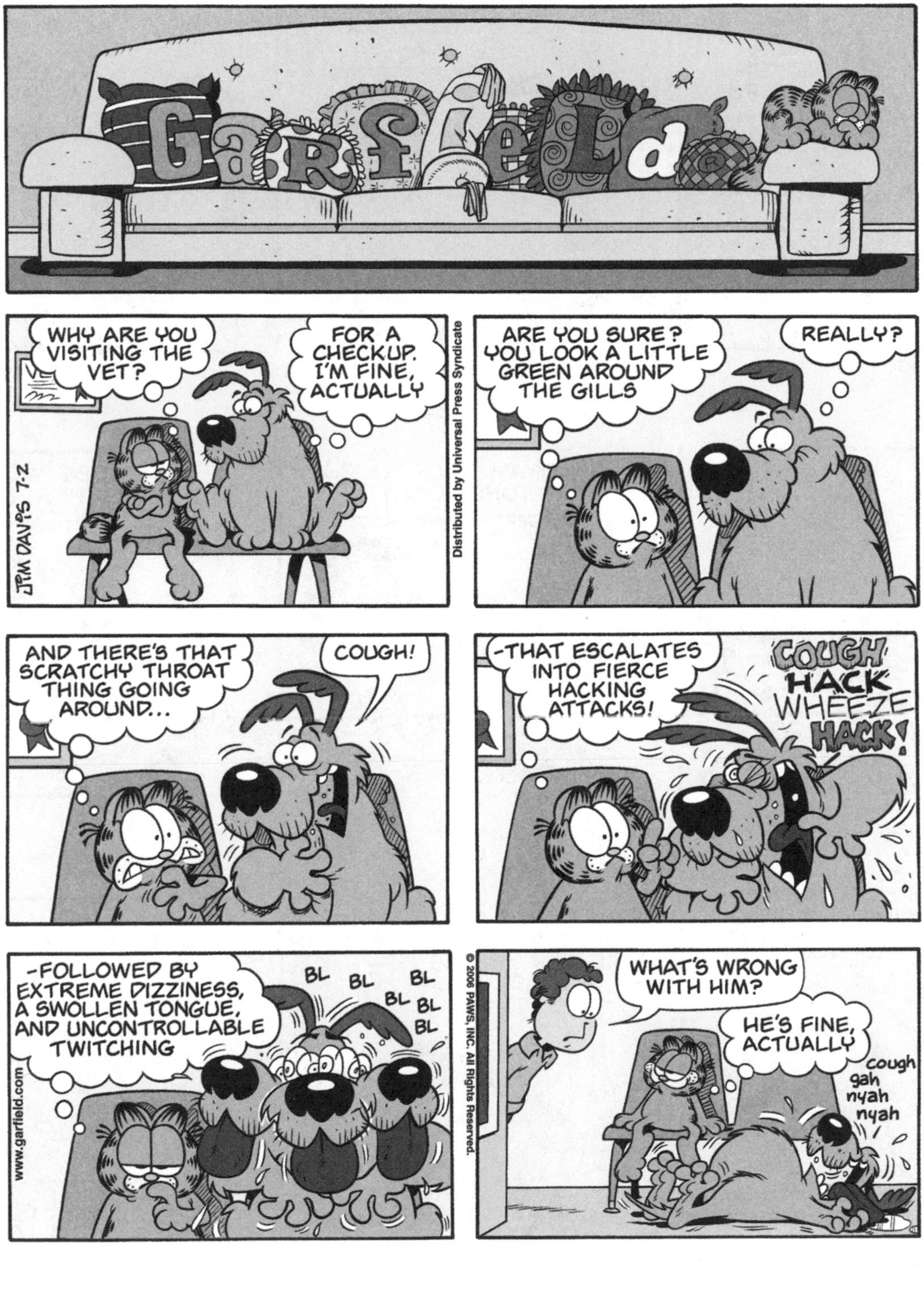
Garfield
JIM DAVIS 7-2
WHY ARE YOU VISITING THE VET?
FOR A CHECKUP. I'M FINE, ACTUALLY
Distributed by Universal Press Syndicate
ARE YOU SURE? YOU LOOK A LITTLE GREEN AROUND THE GILLS
REALLY?
AND THERE'S THAT SCRATCHY THROAT THING GOING AROUND...
COUGH!
-THAT ESCALATES INTO FIERCE HACKING ATTACKS!
COUGH HACK WHEEZE HACK!
-FOLLOWED BY EXTREME DIZZINESS, A SWOLLEN TONGUE, AND UNCONTROLLABLE TWITCHING
BL BL BL BL BL BL
www.garfield.com
© 2006 PAWS, INC. All Rights Reserved.
WHAT'S WRONG WITH HIM?
HE'S FINE, ACTUALLY
cough gah nyah nyah

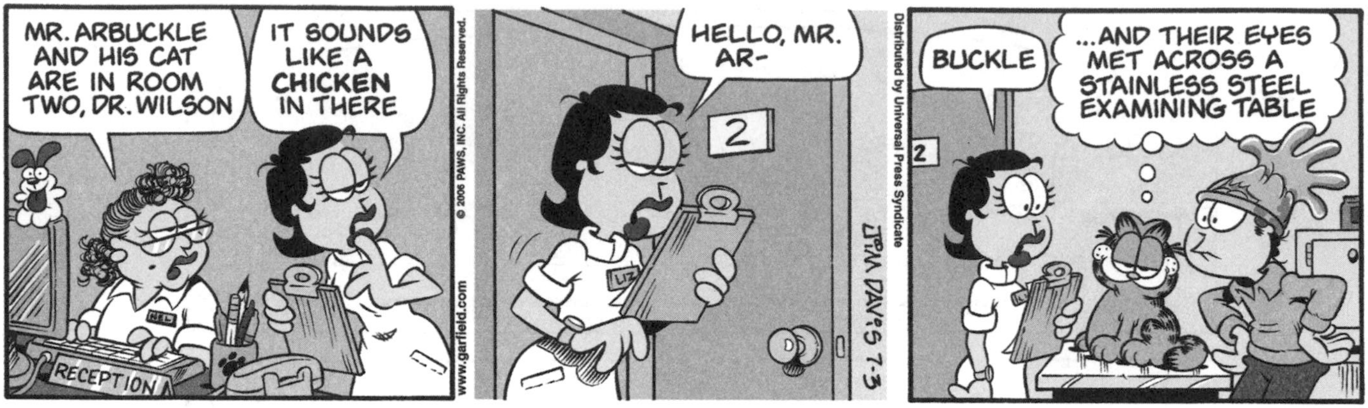
MR. ARBUCKLE AND HIS CAT ARE IN ROOM TWO, DR. WILSON
IT SOUNDS LIKE A **CHICKEN** IN THERE
RECEPTION
© 2006 PAWS, INC. All Rights Reserved.
www.garfield.com
HELLO, MR. AR-
2
JIM DAVIS 7-3
Distributed by Universal Press Syndicate
BUCKLE
...AND THEIR EYES MET ACROSS A STAINLESS STEEL EXAMINING TABLE

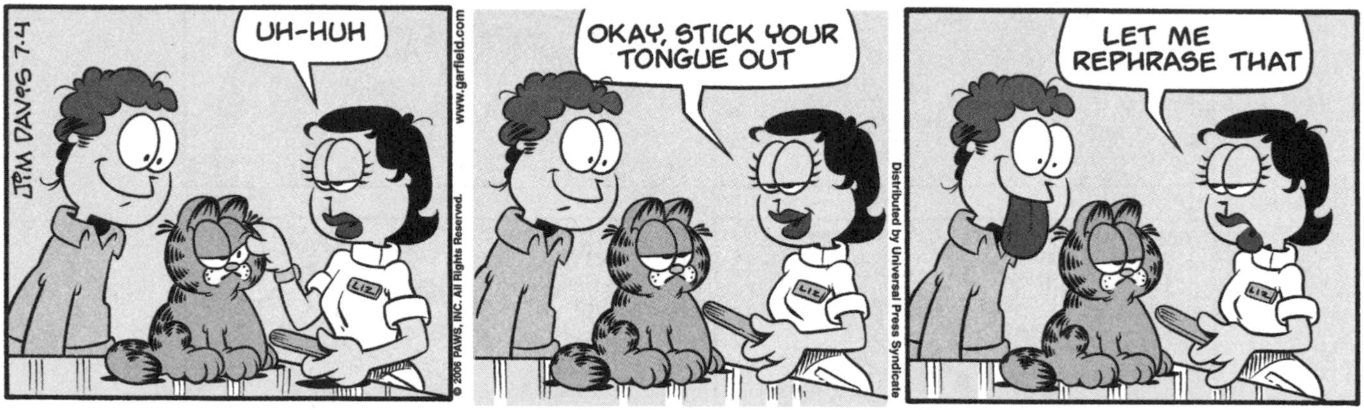
JIM DAVIS 7-4
UH-HUH
© 2006 PAWS, INC. All Rights Reserved.
www.garfield.com
OKAY, STICK YOUR TONGUE OUT
Distributed by Universal Press Syndicate
LET ME REPHRASE THAT

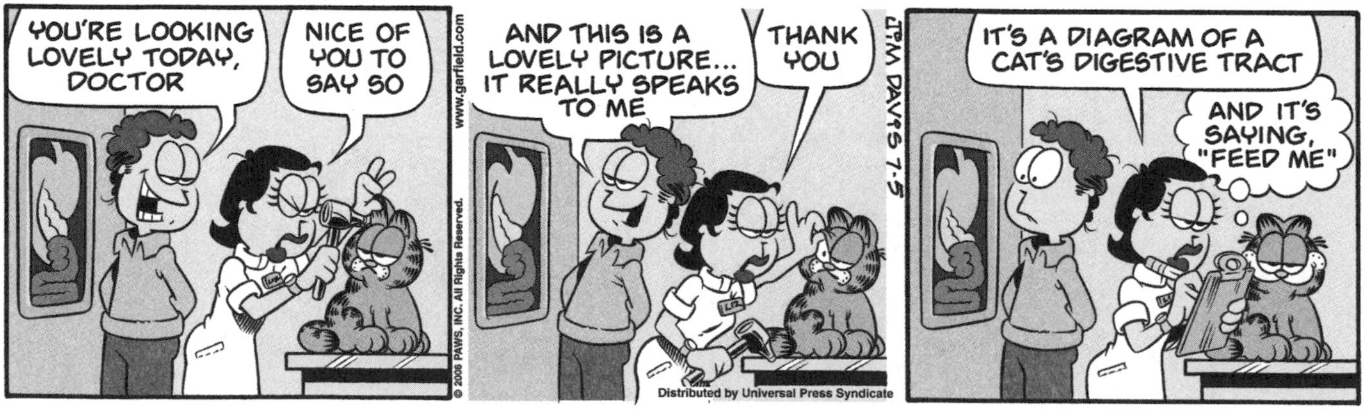
YOU'RE LOOKING LOVELY TODAY, DOCTOR
NICE OF YOU TO SAY SO
© 2006 PAWS, INC. All Rights Reserved.
www.garfield.com
AND THIS IS A LOVELY PICTURE... IT REALLY SPEAKS TO ME
THANK YOU
JIM DAVIS 7-5
Distributed by Universal Press Syndicate
IT'S A DIAGRAM OF A CAT'S DIGESTIVE TRACT
AND IT'S SAYING, "FEED ME"

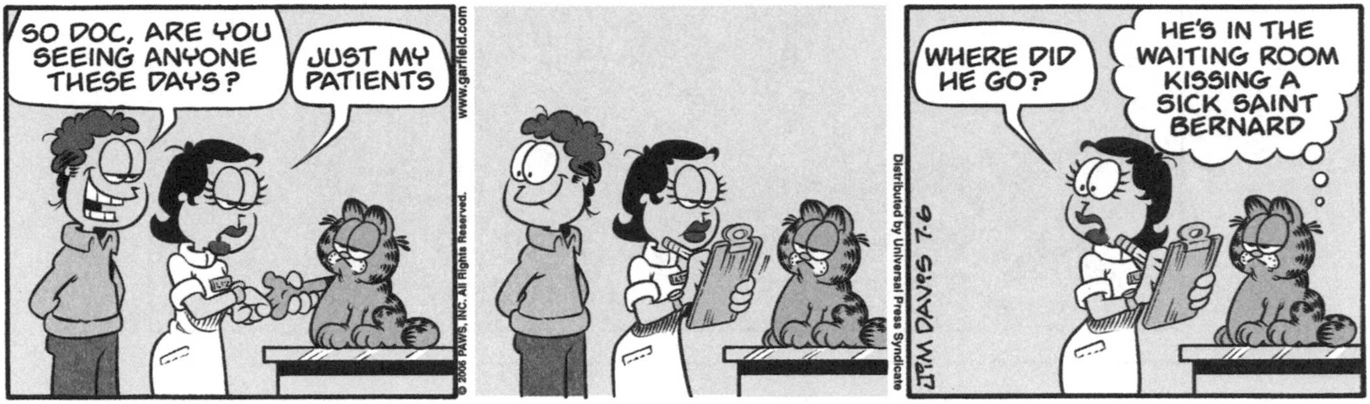
SO DOC, ARE YOU SEEING ANYONE THESE DAYS?
JUST MY PATIENTS
WHERE DID HE GO?
HE'S IN THE WAITING ROOM KISSING A SICK SAINT BERNARD
www.garfield.com
© 2006 PAWS, INC. All Rights Reserved.
Distributed by Universal Press Syndicate
JIM DAVIS 7.6

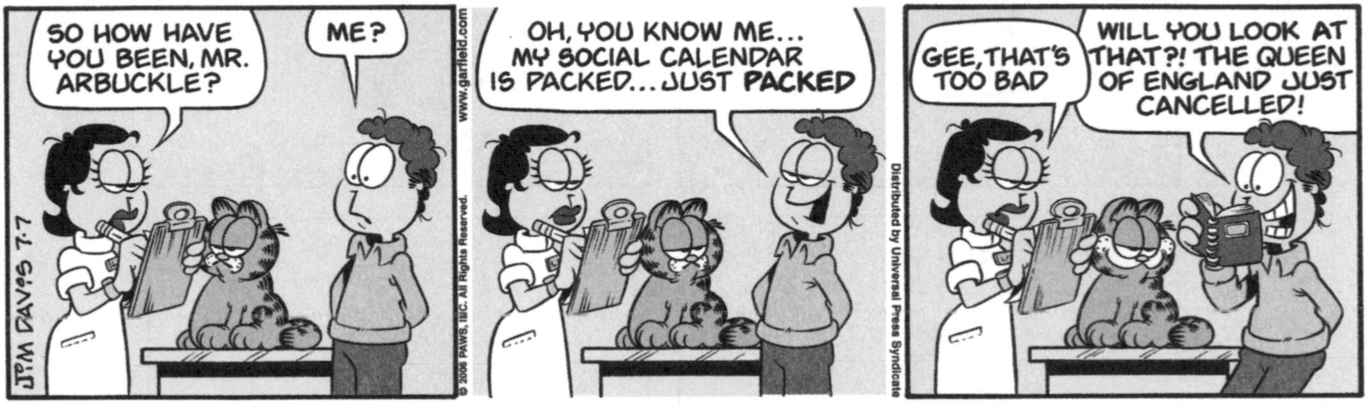
SO HOW HAVE YOU BEEN, MR. ARBUCKLE?
ME?
OH, YOU KNOW ME... MY SOCIAL CALENDAR IS PACKED... JUST PACKED
GEE, THAT'S TOO BAD
WILL YOU LOOK AT THAT?! THE QUEEN OF ENGLAND JUST CANCELLED!
JIM DAVIS 7.7
www.garfield.com
© 2006 PAWS, INC. All Rights Reserved.
Distributed by Universal Press Syndicate

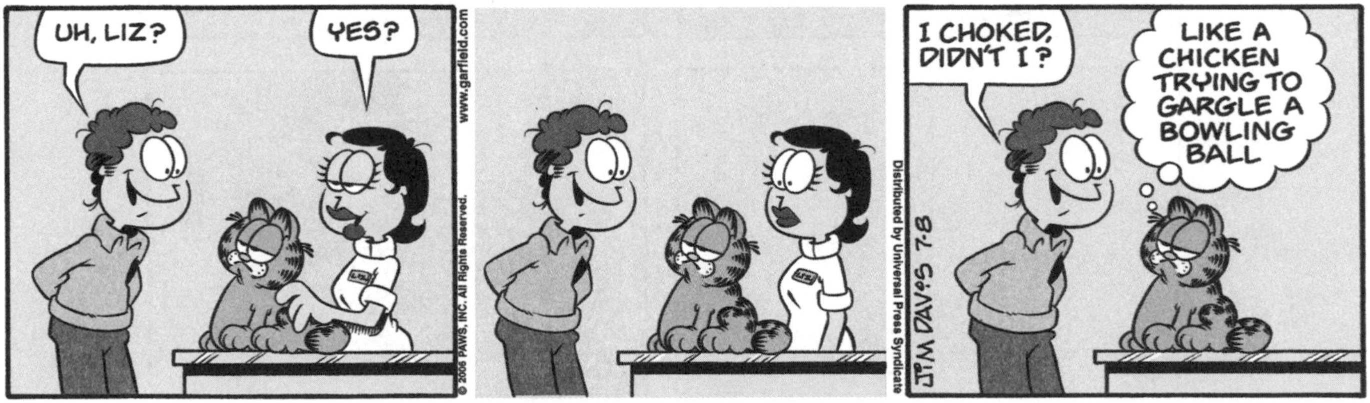
UH, LIZ?
YES?
I CHOKED, DIDN'T I?
LIKE A CHICKEN TRYING TO GARGLE A BOWLING BALL
www.garfield.com
© 2006 PAWS, INC. All Rights Reserved.
Distributed by Universal Press Syndicate
JIM DAVIS 7.8

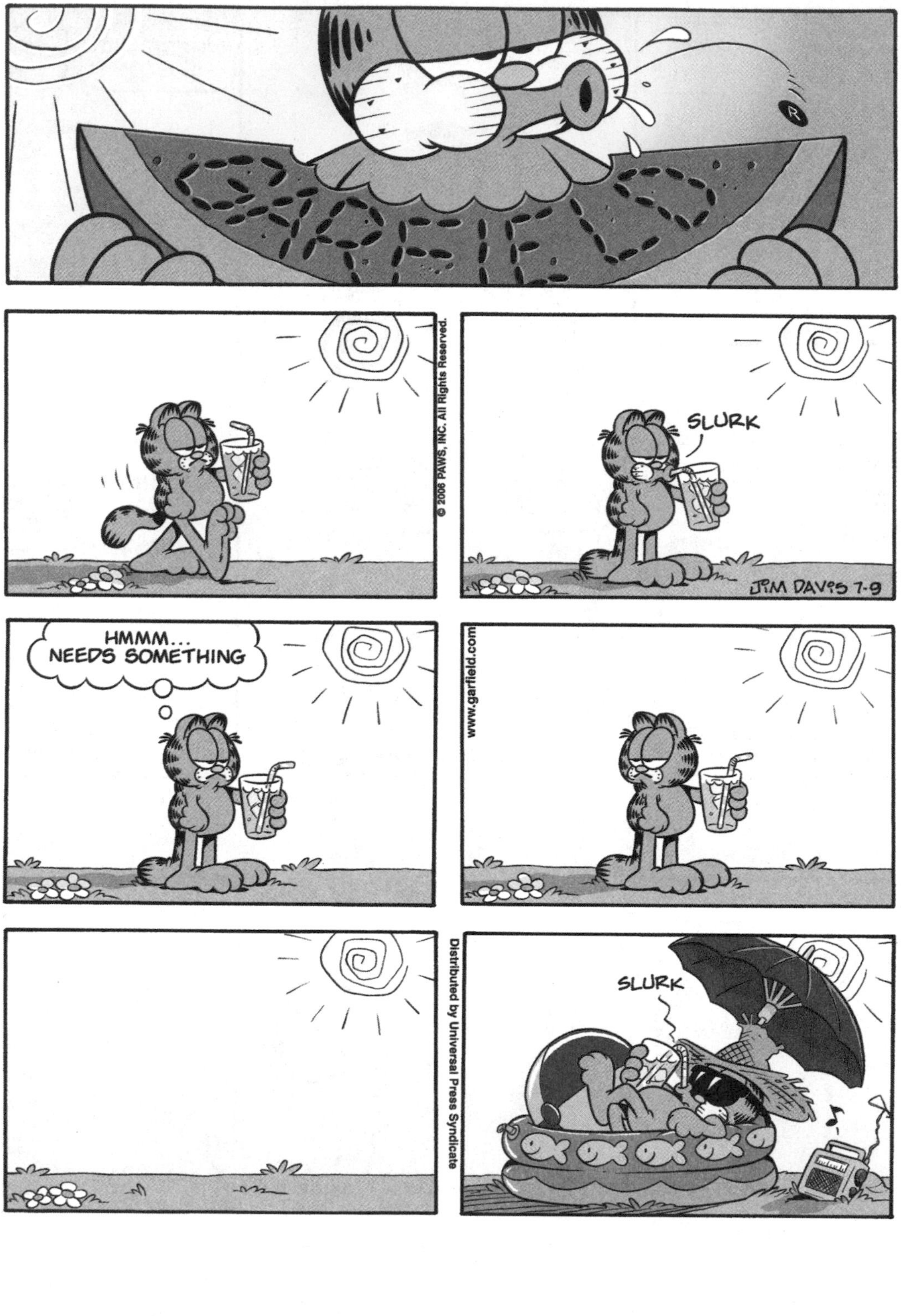
GARFIELD
© 2008 PAWS, INC. All Rights Reserved.
SLURK
JIM DAVIS 7-9
HMMM...
NEEDS SOMETHING
www.garfield.com
Distributed by Universal Press Syndicate
SLURK

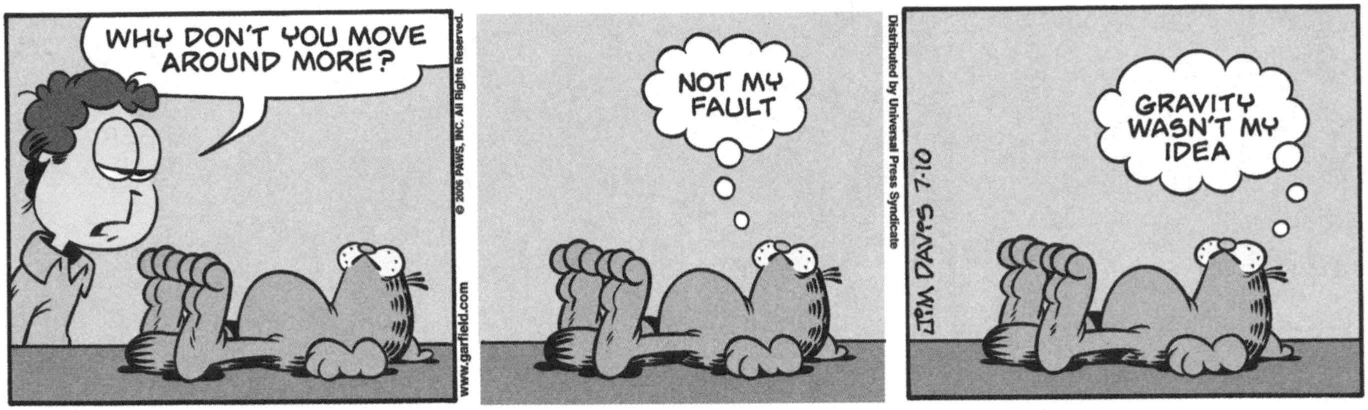
WHY DON'T YOU MOVE AROUND MORE?
NOT MY FAULT
GRAVITY WASN'T MY IDEA
JIM DAVIS 7·10
© 2006 PAWS, INC. All Rights Reserved.
www.garfield.com
Distributed by Universal Press Syndicate

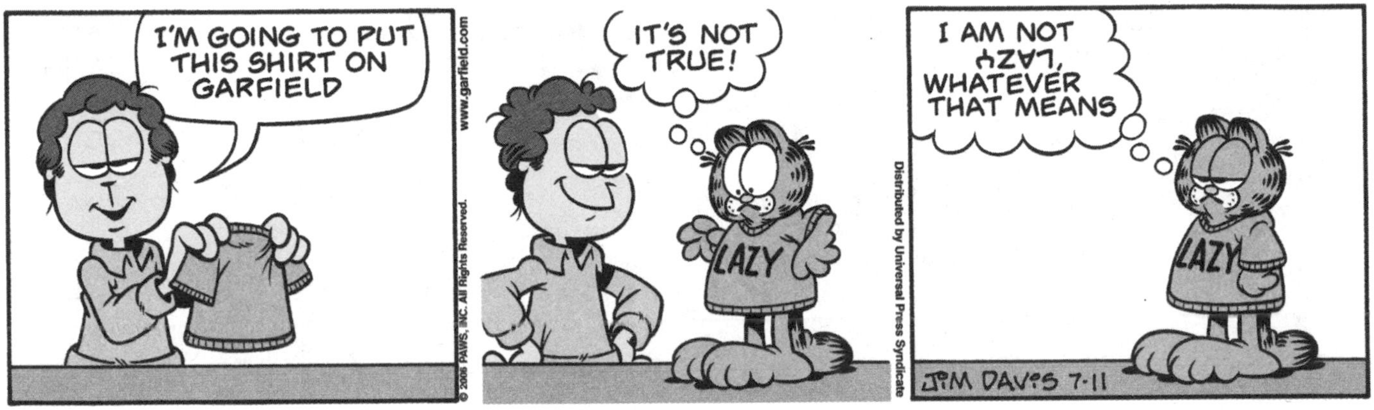
I'M GOING TO PUT THIS SHIRT ON GARFIELD
IT'S NOT TRUE!
LAZY
I AM NOT ʎZⱯ˥, WHATEVER THAT MEANS
LAZY
JIM DAVIS 7·11
© 2006 PAWS, INC. All Rights Reserved.
www.garfield.com
Distributed by Universal Press Syndicate

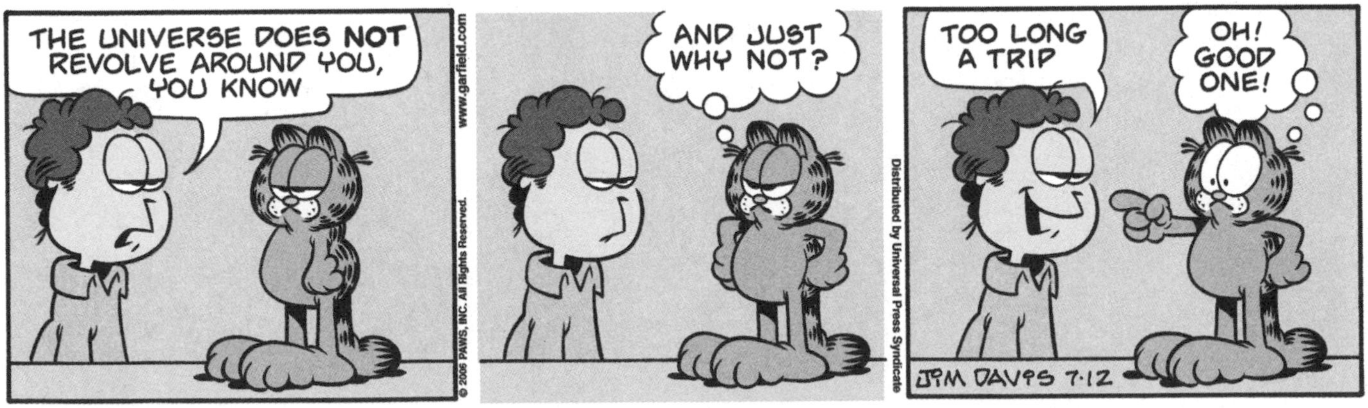
THE UNIVERSE DOES **NOT** REVOLVE AROUND YOU, YOU KNOW
AND JUST WHY NOT?
TOO LONG A TRIP
OH! GOOD ONE!
JIM DAVIS 7·12
© 2006 PAWS, INC. All Rights Reserved.
www.garfield.com
Distributed by Universal Press Syndicate

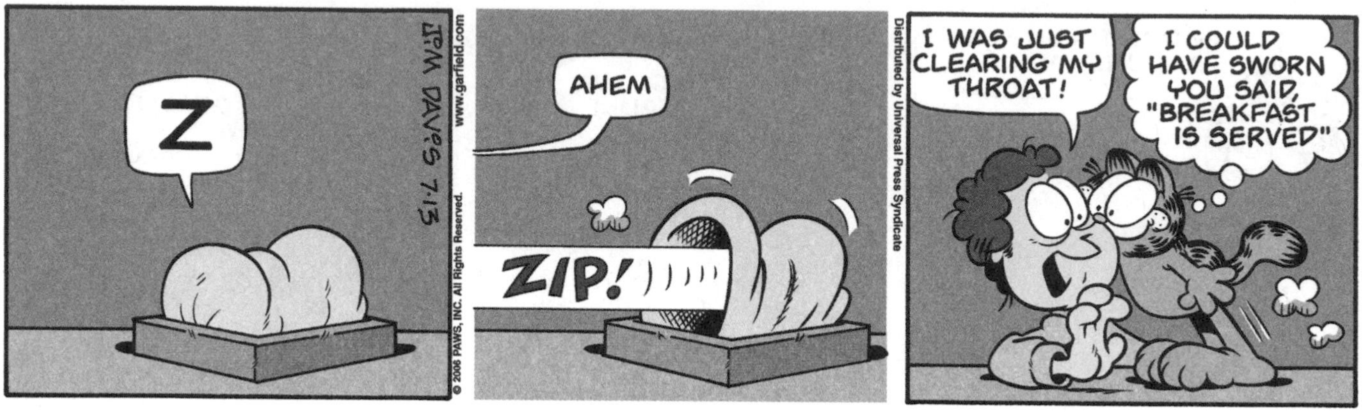
Z
JIM DAVIS 7-13
© 2006 PAWS, INC. All Rights Reserved. www.garfield.com
AHEM
ZIP!
Distributed by Universal Press Syndicate
I WAS JUST CLEARING MY THROAT!
I COULD HAVE SWORN YOU SAID, "BREAKFAST IS SERVED"

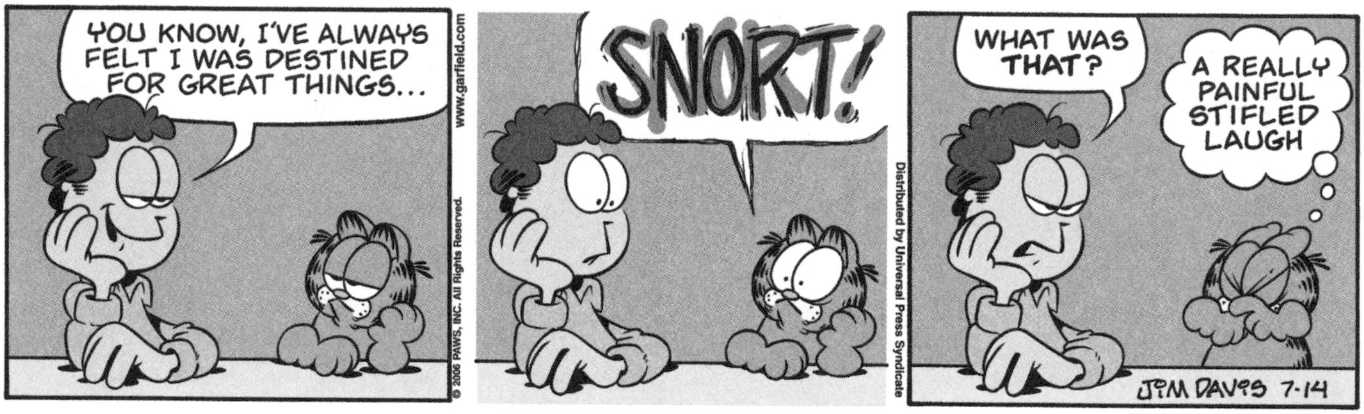
YOU KNOW, I'VE ALWAYS FELT I WAS DESTINED FOR GREAT THINGS...
© 2006 PAWS, INC. All Rights Reserved. www.garfield.com
SNORT!
Distributed by Universal Press Syndicate
WHAT WAS THAT?
A REALLY PAINFUL STIFLED LAUGH
JIM DAVIS 7-14

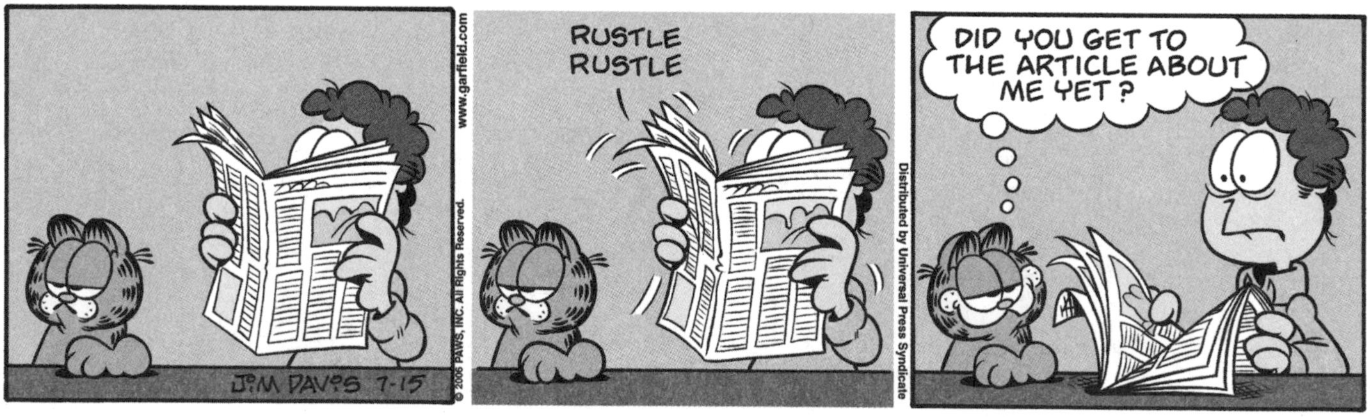
JIM DAVIS 7-15
© 2006 PAWS, INC. All Rights Reserved. www.garfield.com
RUSTLE RUSTLE
Distributed by Universal Press Syndicate
DID YOU GET TO THE ARTICLE ABOUT ME YET?

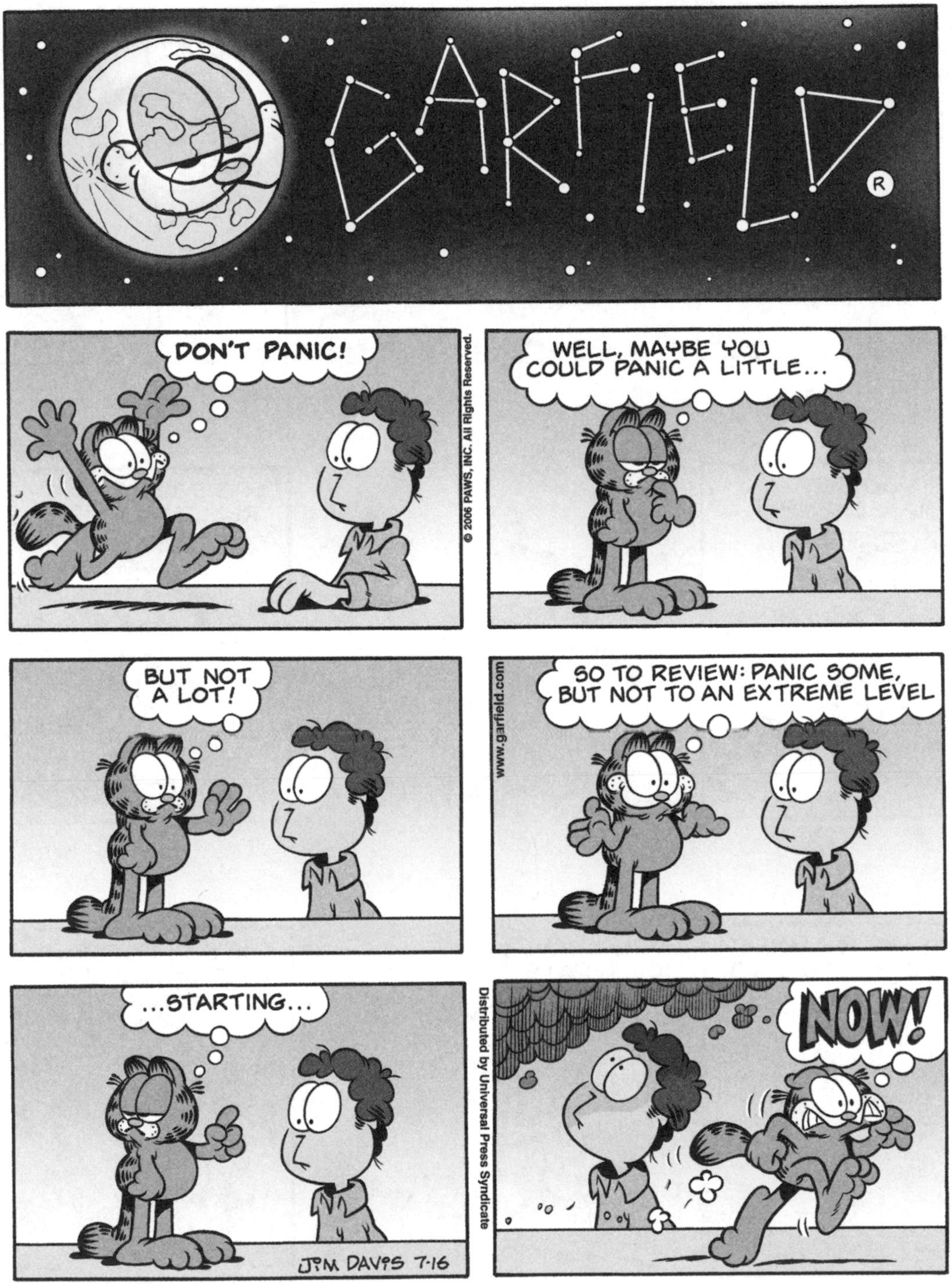
GARFIELD®
DON'T PANIC!
© 2006 PAWS, INC. All Rights Reserved.
WELL, MAYBE YOU COULD PANIC A LITTLE...
BUT NOT A LOT!
www.garfield.com
SO TO REVIEW: PANIC SOME, BUT NOT TO AN EXTREME LEVEL
...STARTING...
JIM DAVIS 7-16
Distributed by Universal Press Syndicate
NOW!

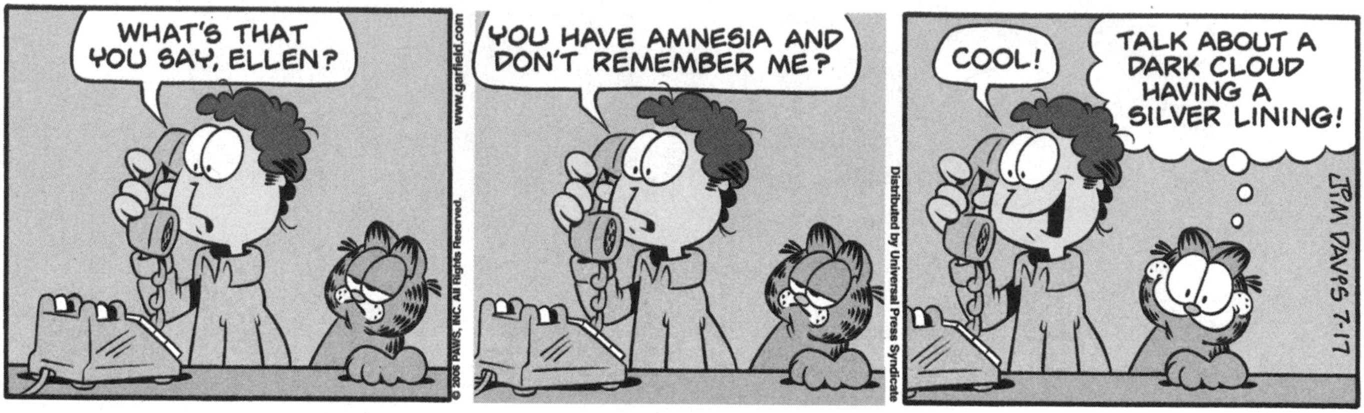
WHAT'S THAT YOU SAY, ELLEN?
YOU HAVE AMNESIA AND DON'T REMEMBER ME?
COOL!
TALK ABOUT A DARK CLOUD HAVING A SILVER LINING!
JIM DAVIS 7-17
© 2006 PAWS, INC. All Rights Reserved. www.garfield.com
Distributed by Universal Press Syndicate

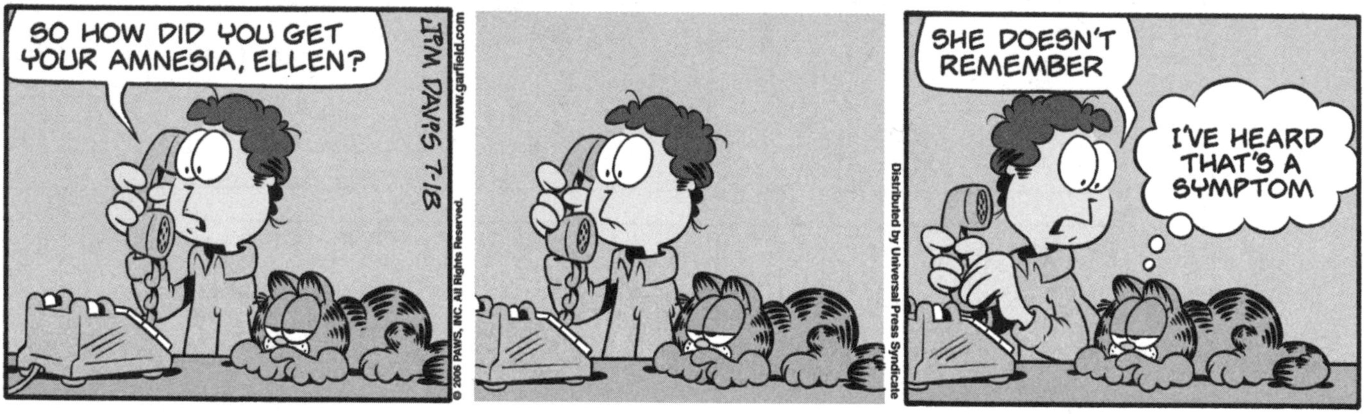
SO HOW DID YOU GET YOUR AMNESIA, ELLEN?
JIM DAVIS 7-18
SHE DOESN'T REMEMBER
I'VE HEARD THAT'S A SYMPTOM
© 2006 PAWS, INC. All Rights Reserved. www.garfield.com
Distributed by Universal Press Syndicate

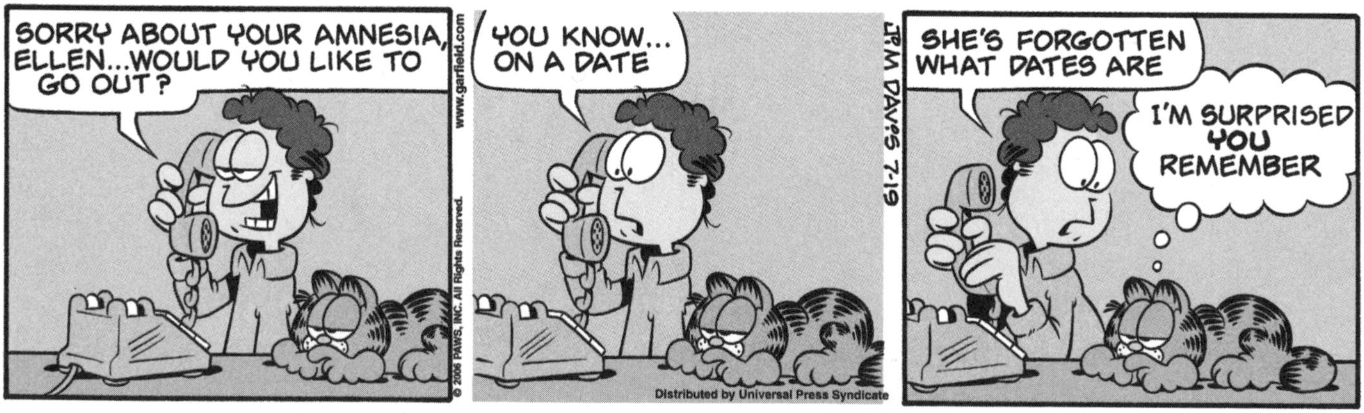
SORRY ABOUT YOUR AMNESIA, ELLEN...WOULD YOU LIKE TO GO OUT?
YOU KNOW... ON A DATE
SHE'S FORGOTTEN WHAT DATES ARE
I'M SURPRISED **YOU** REMEMBER
JIM DAVIS 7-19
© 2006 PAWS, INC. All Rights Reserved. www.garfield.com
Distributed by Universal Press Syndicate

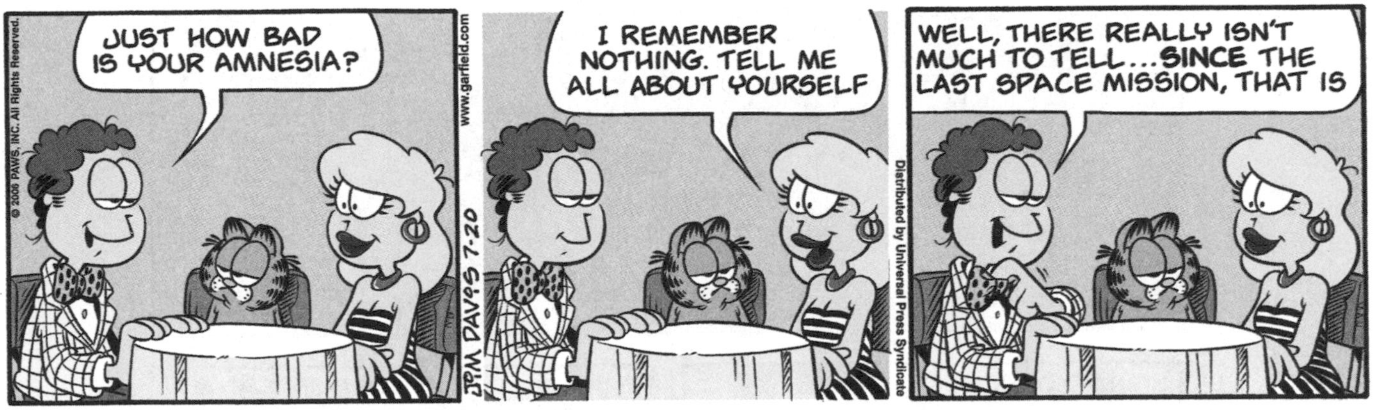
JUST HOW BAD IS YOUR AMNESIA?
I REMEMBER NOTHING. TELL ME ALL ABOUT YOURSELF
WELL, THERE REALLY ISN'T MUCH TO TELL... **SINCE** THE LAST SPACE MISSION, THAT IS
JIM DAVIS 7-20
© 2006 PAWS, INC. All Rights Reserved.
www.garfield.com
Distributed by Universal Press Syndicate

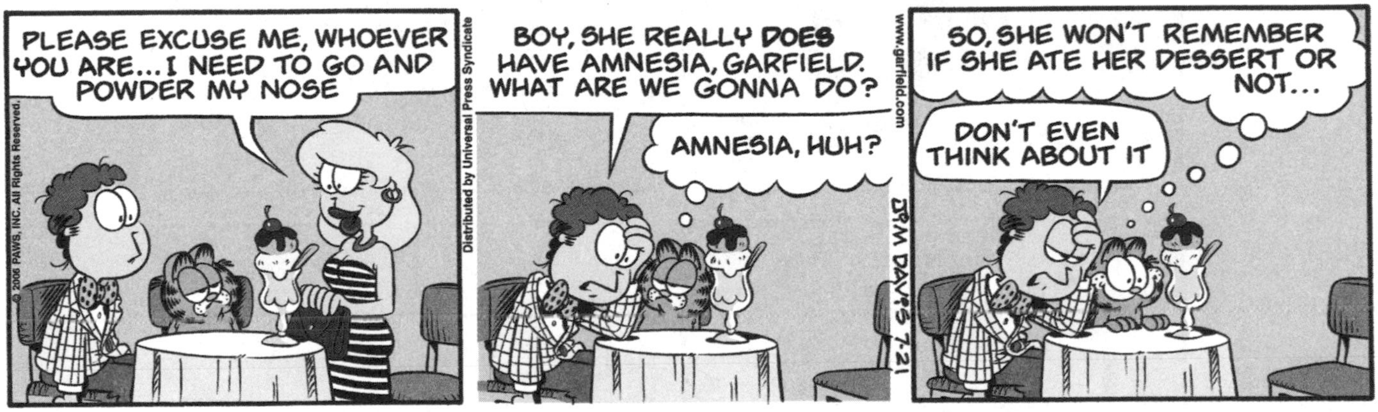
PLEASE EXCUSE ME, WHOEVER YOU ARE... I NEED TO GO AND POWDER MY NOSE
BOY, SHE REALLY **DOES** HAVE AMNESIA, GARFIELD. WHAT ARE WE GONNA DO?
AMNESIA, HUH?
SO, SHE WON'T REMEMBER IF SHE ATE HER DESSERT OR NOT...
DON'T EVEN THINK ABOUT IT
JIM DAVIS 7-21
© 2006 PAWS, INC. All Rights Reserved.
Distributed by Universal Press Syndicate
www.garfield.com

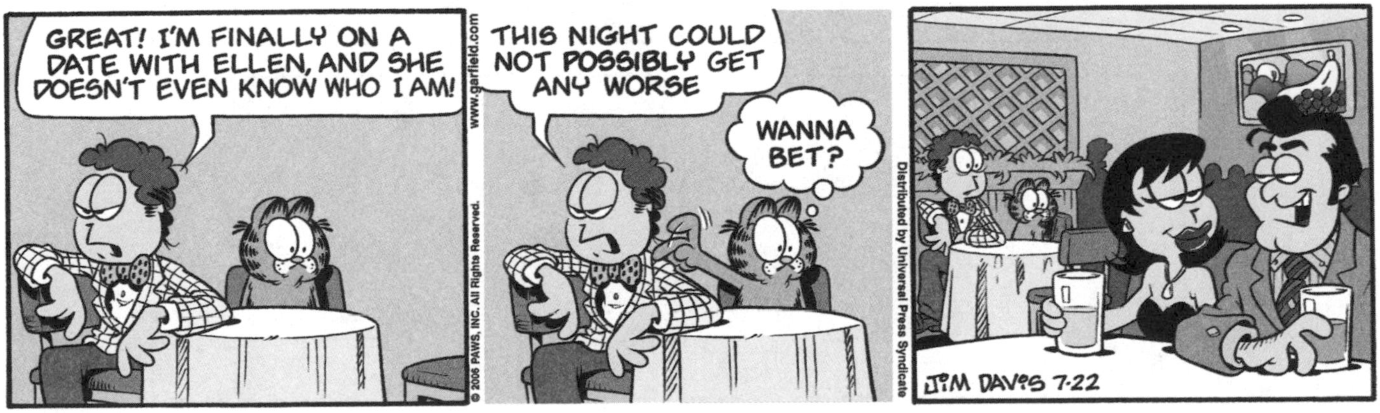
GREAT! I'M FINALLY ON A DATE WITH ELLEN, AND SHE DOESN'T EVEN KNOW WHO I AM!
THIS NIGHT COULD NOT **POSSIBLY** GET ANY WORSE
WANNA BET?
JIM DAVIS 7-22
www.garfield.com
© 2006 PAWS, INC. All Rights Reserved.
Distributed by Universal Press Syndicate

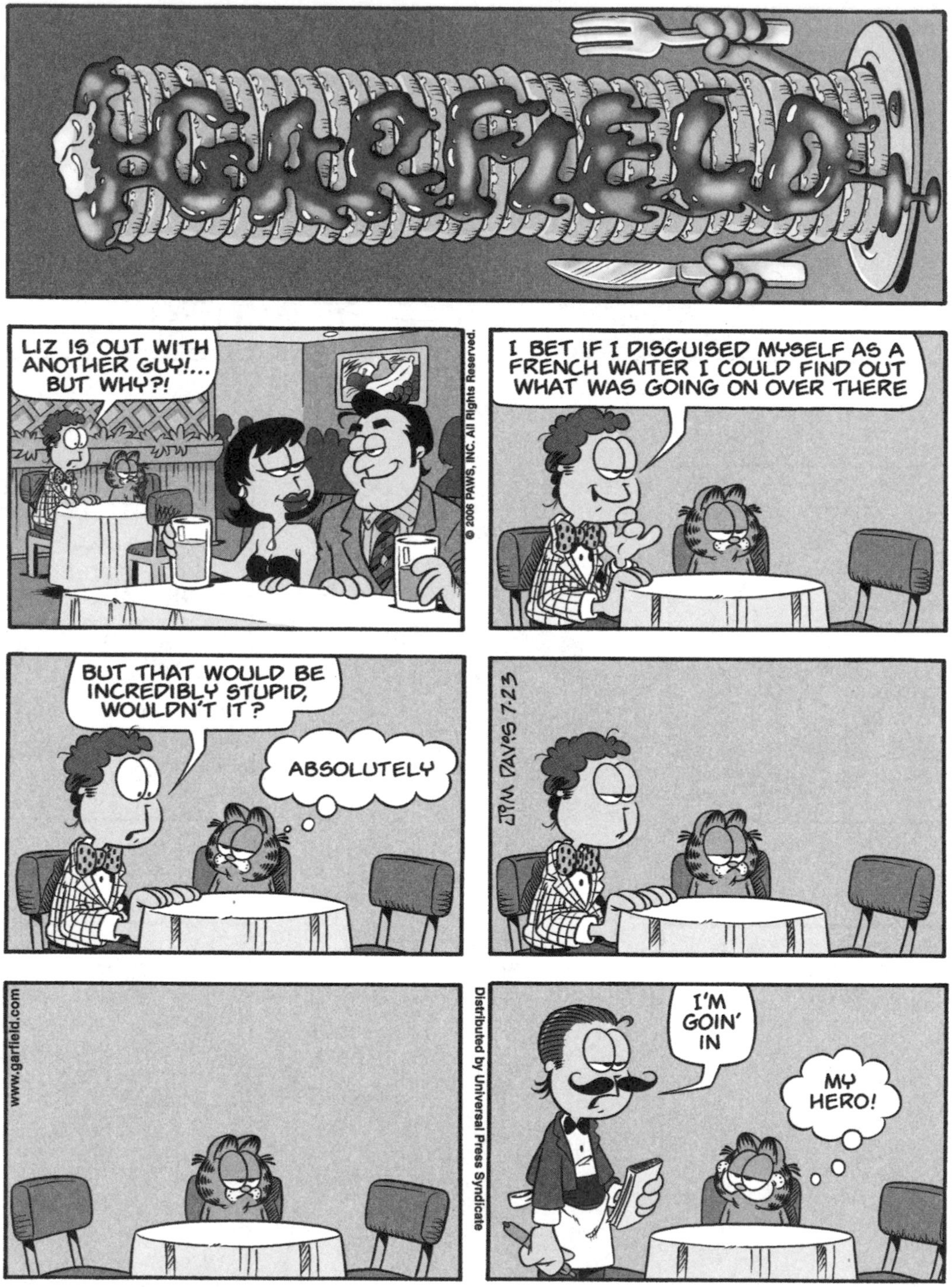
GARFIELD
LIZ IS OUT WITH ANOTHER GUY!... BUT WHY?!
© 2006 PAWS, INC. All Rights Reserved.
I BET IF I DISGUISED MYSELF AS A FRENCH WAITER I COULD FIND OUT WHAT WAS GOING ON OVER THERE
BUT THAT WOULD BE INCREDIBLY STUPID, WOULDN'T IT?
ABSOLUTELY
JIM DAVIS 7-23
www.garfield.com
Distributed by Universal Press Syndicate
I'M GOIN' IN
MY HERO!

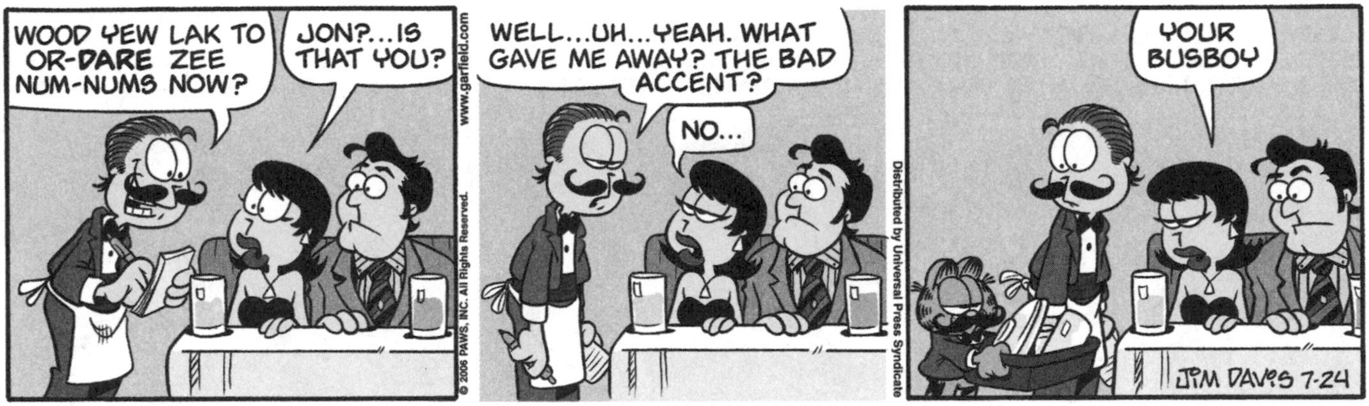
WOOD YEW LAK TO OR-DARE ZEE NUM-NUMS NOW?
JON?…IS THAT YOU?
© 2006 PAWS, INC. All Rights Reserved. www.garfield.com
WELL…UH…YEAH. WHAT GAVE ME AWAY? THE BAD ACCENT?
NO…
Distributed by Universal Press Syndicate
YOUR BUSBOY
JIM DAVIS 7-24

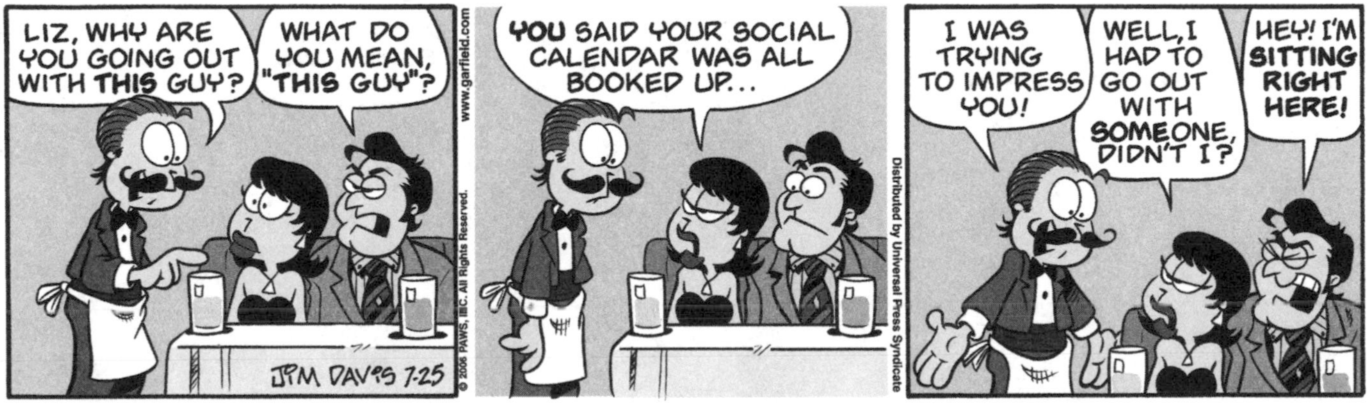
LIZ, WHY ARE YOU GOING OUT WITH THIS GUY?
WHAT DO YOU MEAN, "THIS GUY"?
JIM DAVIS 7-25
© 2006 PAWS, INC. All Rights Reserved. www.garfield.com
YOU SAID YOUR SOCIAL CALENDAR WAS ALL BOOKED UP…
Distributed by Universal Press Syndicate
I WAS TRYING TO IMPRESS YOU!
WELL, I HAD TO GO OUT WITH SOMEONE, DIDN'T I?
HEY! I'M SITTING RIGHT HERE!

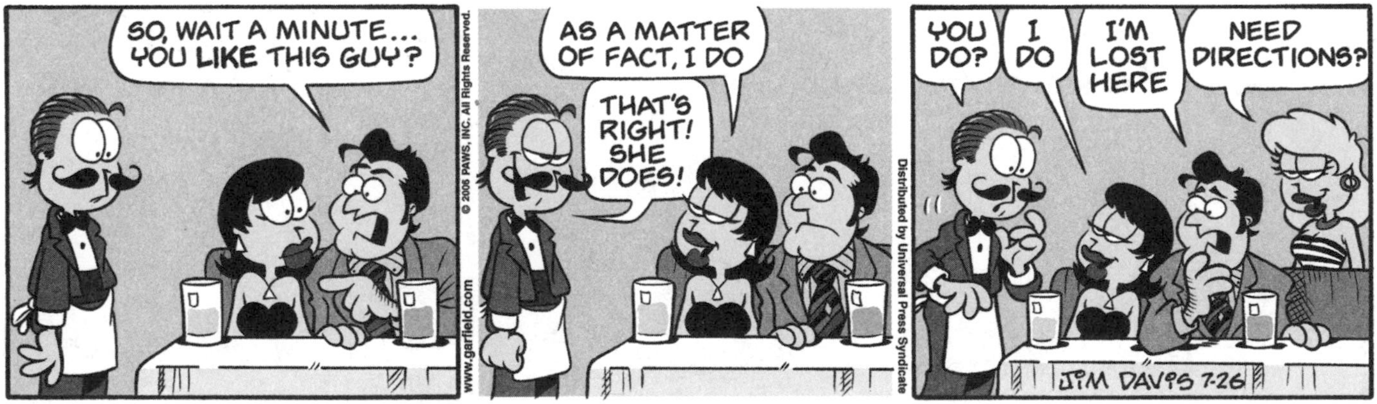
SO, WAIT A MINUTE… YOU LIKE THIS GUY?
© 2006 PAWS, INC. All Rights Reserved. www.garfield.com
AS A MATTER OF FACT, I DO
THAT'S RIGHT! SHE DOES!
Distributed by Universal Press Syndicate
YOU DO?
I DO
I'M LOST HERE
NEED DIRECTIONS?
JIM DAVIS 7-26

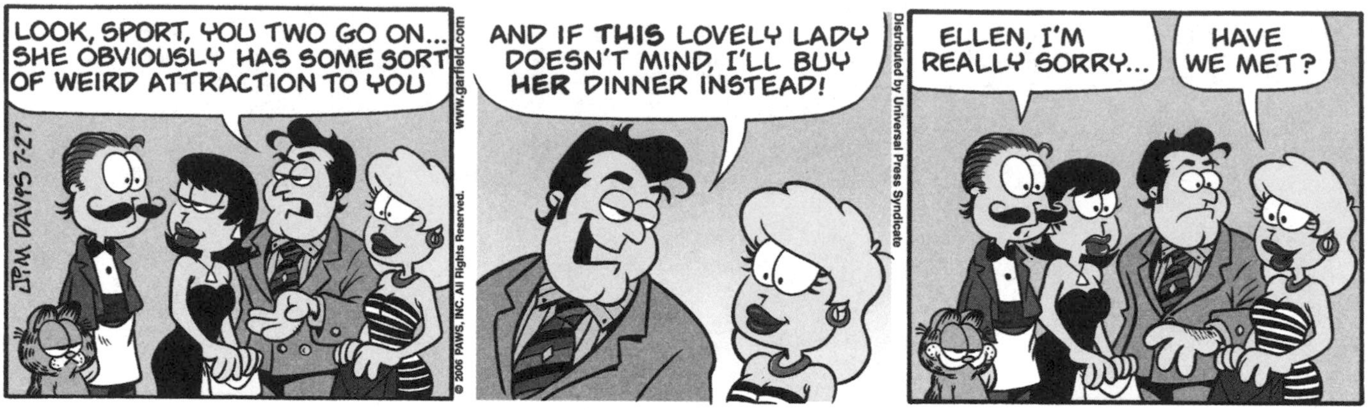
LOOK, SPORT, YOU TWO GO ON... SHE OBVIOUSLY HAS SOME SORT OF WEIRD ATTRACTION TO YOU
JIM DAVIS 7-27
© 2006 PAWS, INC. All Rights Reserved. www.garfield.com
AND IF THIS LOVELY LADY DOESN'T MIND, I'LL BUY HER DINNER INSTEAD!
Distributed by Universal Press Syndicate
ELLEN, I'M REALLY SORRY...
HAVE WE MET?

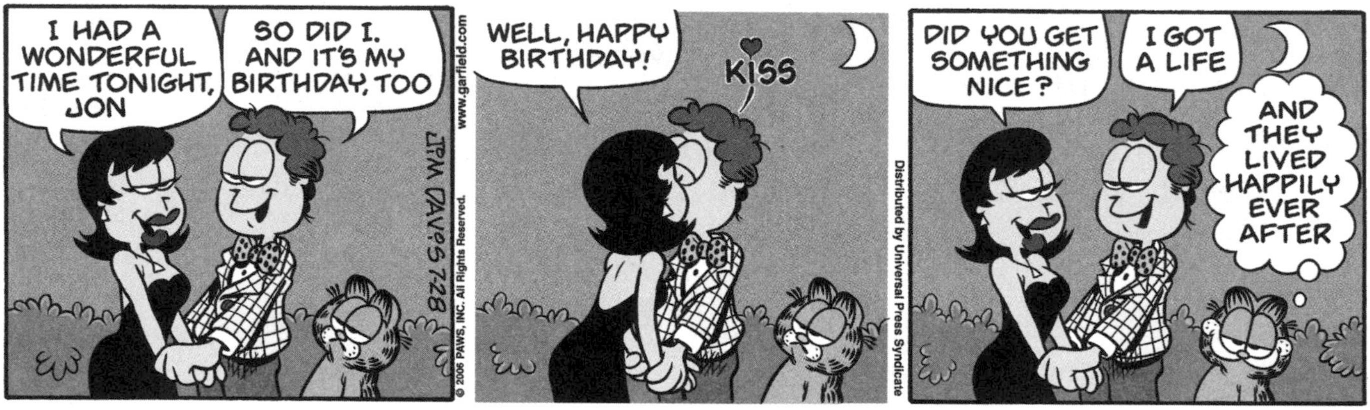
I HAD A WONDERFUL TIME TONIGHT, JON
SO DID I. AND IT'S MY BIRTHDAY, TOO
JIM DAVIS 7-28
© 2006 PAWS, INC. All Rights Reserved. www.garfield.com
WELL, HAPPY BIRTHDAY!
KISS
Distributed by Universal Press Syndicate
DID YOU GET SOMETHING NICE?
I GOT A LIFE
AND THEY LIVED HAPPILY EVER AFTER

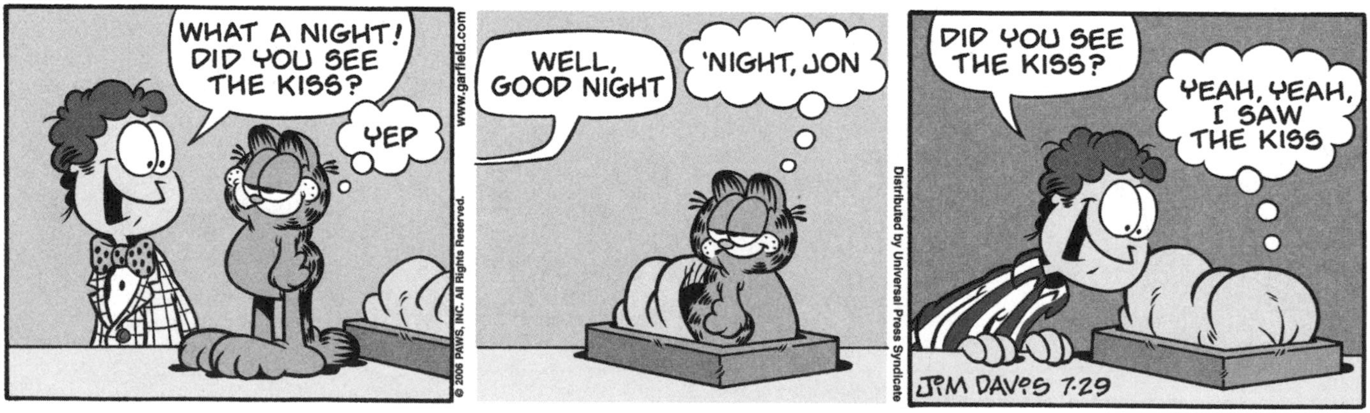
WHAT A NIGHT! DID YOU SEE THE KISS?
YEP
© 2006 PAWS, INC. All Rights Reserved. www.garfield.com
WELL, GOOD NIGHT
'NIGHT, JON
Distributed by Universal Press Syndicate
DID YOU SEE THE KISS?
YEAH, YEAH, I SAW THE KISS
JIM DAVIS 7-29

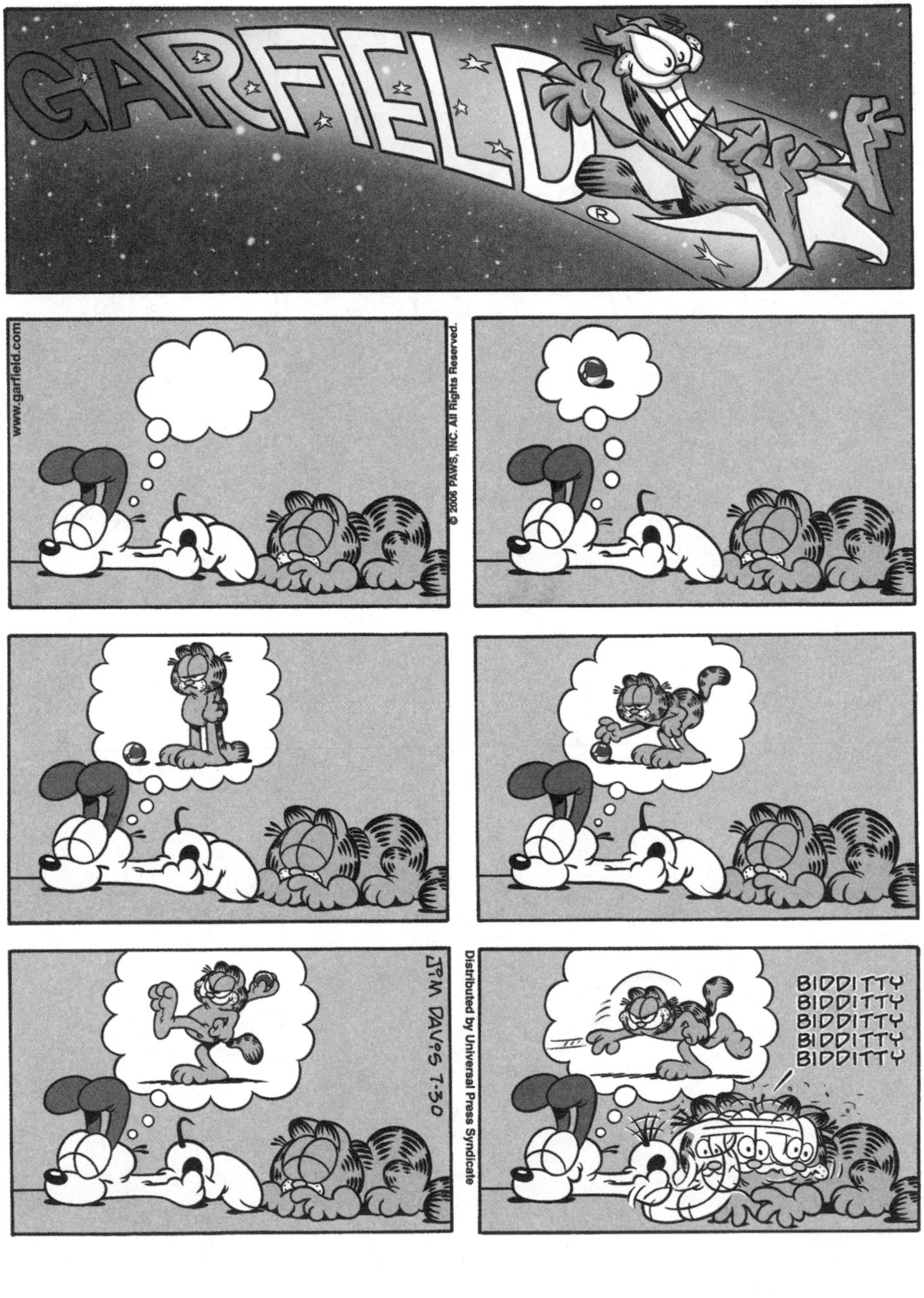
GARFIELD
www.garfield.com
© 2006 PAWS, INC. All Rights Reserved.
JIM DAVIS 7-30
Distributed by Universal Press Syndicate
BIDDITTY
BIDDITTY
BIDDITTY
BIDDITTY
BIDDITTY

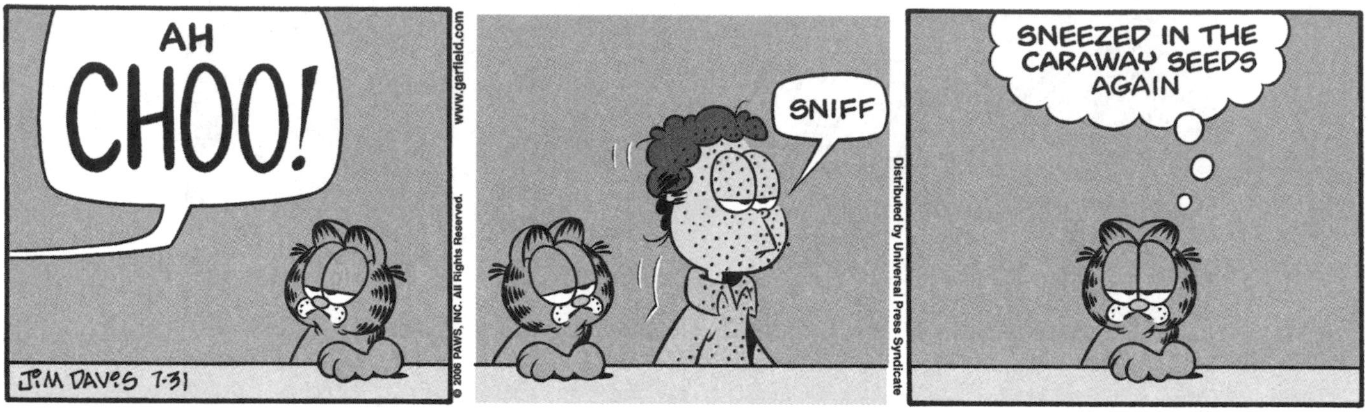
AH CHOO!
JIM DAVIS 7-31
© 2006 PAWS, INC. All Rights Reserved. www.garfield.com
SNIFF
Distributed by Universal Press Syndicate
SNEEZED IN THE CARAWAY SEEDS AGAIN

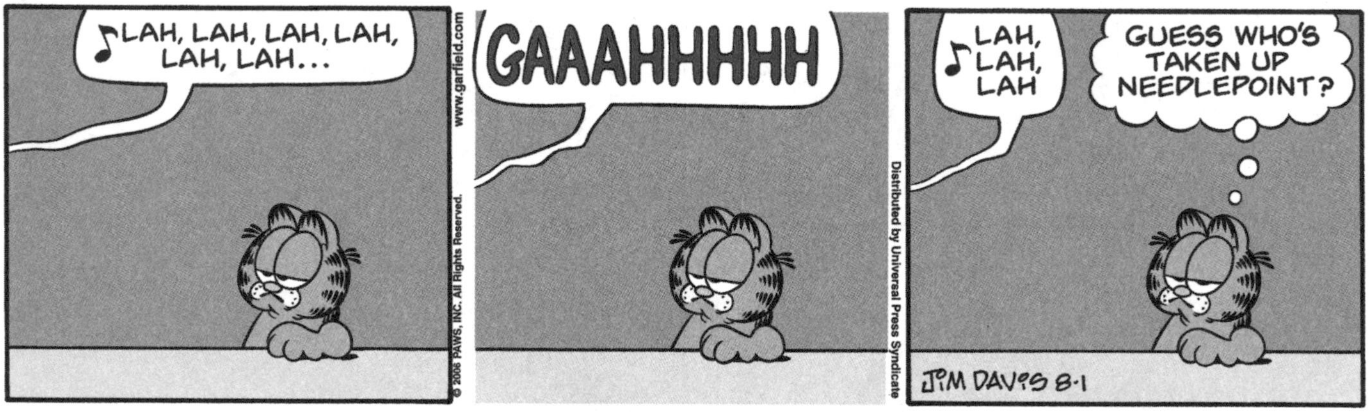
♪LAH, LAH, LAH, LAH, LAH, LAH...
© 2006 PAWS, INC. All Rights Reserved. www.garfield.com
GAAAHHHHH
Distributed by Universal Press Syndicate
♪LAH, LAH, LAH
GUESS WHO'S TAKEN UP NEEDLEPOINT?
JIM DAVIS 8-1

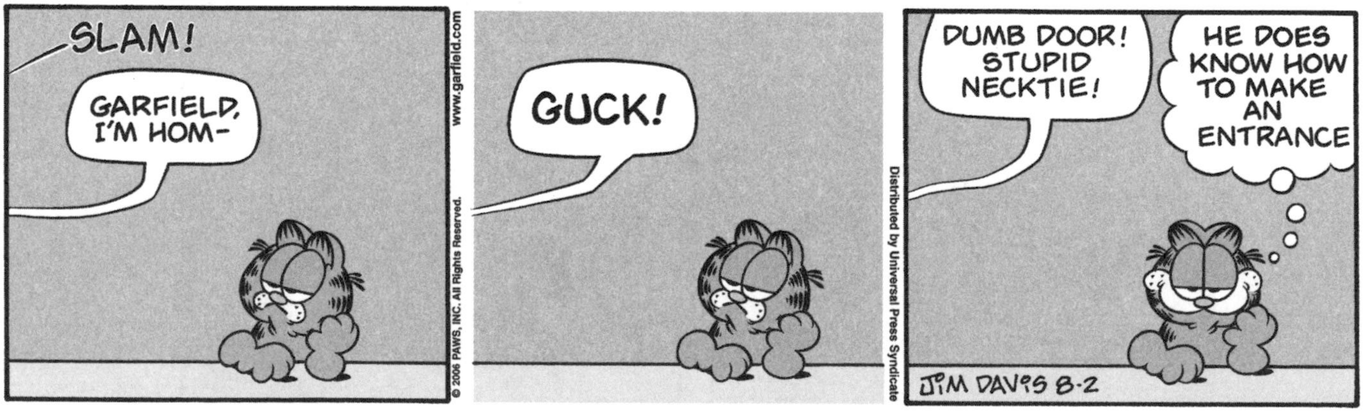
SLAM!
GARFIELD, I'M HOM-
© 2006 PAWS, INC. All Rights Reserved. www.garfield.com
GUCK!
Distributed by Universal Press Syndicate
DUMB DOOR! STUPID NECKTIE!
HE DOES KNOW HOW TO MAKE AN ENTRANCE
JIM DAVIS 8-2

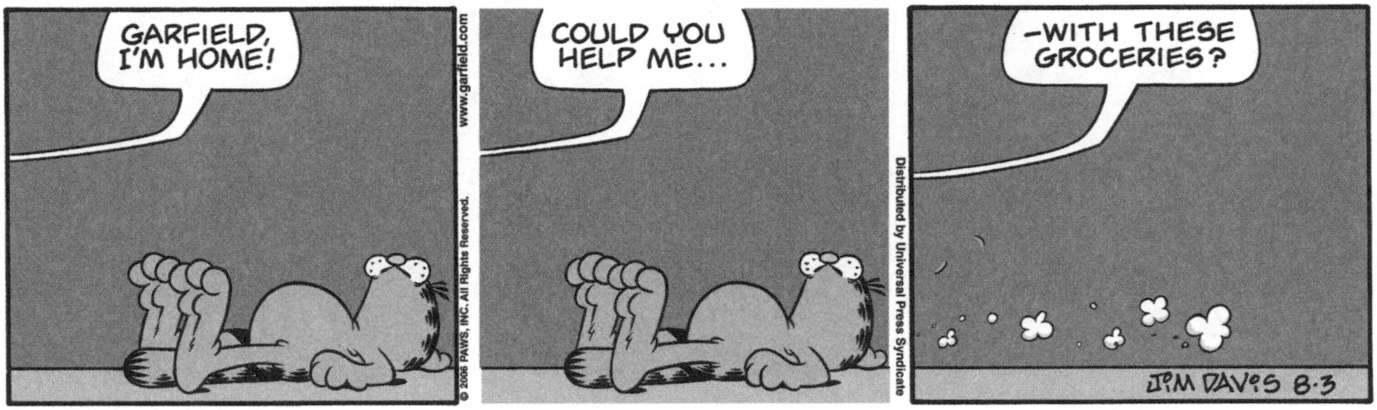
GARFIELD, I'M HOME!
COULD YOU HELP ME...
-WITH THESE GROCERIES?
JIM DAVIS 8-3
© 2006 PAWS, INC. All Rights Reserved. www.garfield.com
Distributed by Universal Press Syndicate

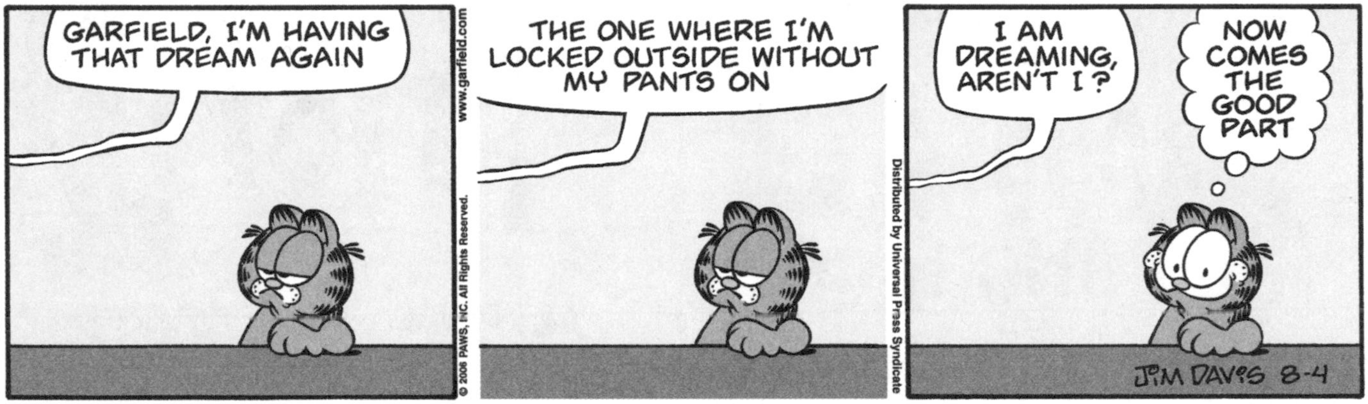
GARFIELD, I'M HAVING THAT DREAM AGAIN
THE ONE WHERE I'M LOCKED OUTSIDE WITHOUT MY PANTS ON
I AM DREAMING, AREN'T I?
NOW COMES THE GOOD PART
JIM DAVIS 8-4
© 2006 PAWS, INC. All Rights Reserved. www.garfield.com
Distributed by Universal Press Syndicate

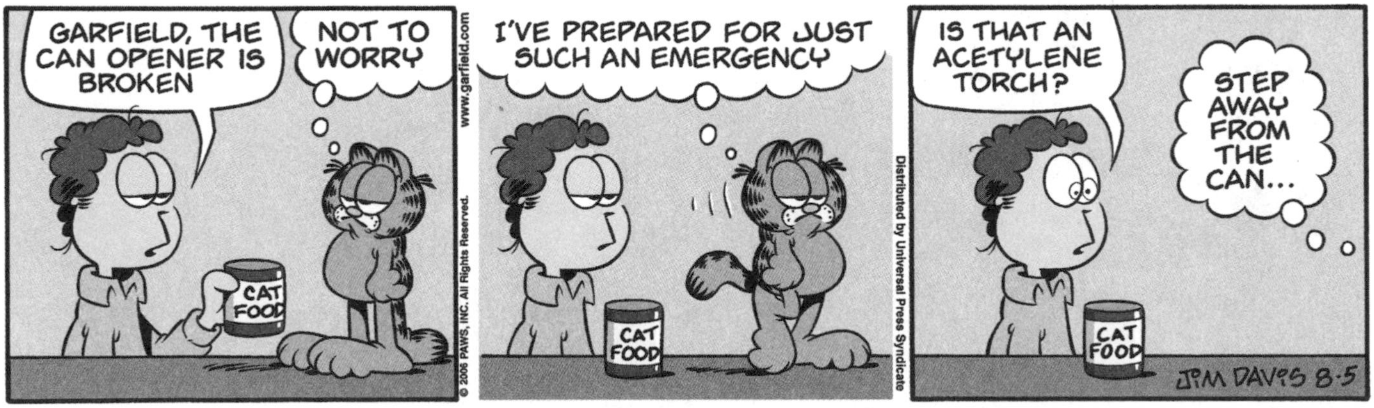
GARFIELD, THE CAN OPENER IS BROKEN
NOT TO WORRY
CAT FOOD
I'VE PREPARED FOR JUST SUCH AN EMERGENCY
CAT FOOD
IS THAT AN ACETYLENE TORCH?
STEP AWAY FROM THE CAN...
CAT FOOD
JIM DAVIS 8-5
© 2006 PAWS, INC. All Rights Reserved. www.garfield.com
Distributed by Universal Press Syndicate

ATTITUDE PART 2

A second helping of sass from the crabby tabby!

Can't **YOU** read **BODY** LANGUAGE?

I think **NOT!**

YES I AM IGNORING YOU

Approach. Bow and scrape. State your business.

Hungry for more? Feast your eyes on all the fun at www.garfield.com

STRIPS, SPECIALS, OR BESTSELLING BOOKS...
GARFIELD'S ON EVERYONE'S MENU.

Don't miss even one episode in the Tubby Tabby's hilarious series!